Reversal of Fortune

Reversal of Fortune

Inside the von Bülow Case

Alan M. Dershowitz

Random House   New York

Library of Congress Cataloging-in-Publication Data
Dershowitz, Alan M.
Reversal of fortune.

Includes index.
1. Von Bülow, Claus, 1926–   —Trials, litigation,
etc.   2. Trials (Murder)—Rhode Island—Newport.
I. Title.
KF224.V66D47   1985   345.73'02523   85–25722
ISBN 0–394–53903–6   347.3052523

Manufactured in the United States of America
24689753
First Edition

This book is lovingly dedicated to my father, Harry Dershowitz, who died two days before we won the von Bülow appeal, and who taught me to obey the biblical precept "Justice, justice shalt thou follow."

Acknowledgments

This book is both an individual and a collaborative work. It is individual in the sense that I wrote every word of it myself, alone on Martha's Vineyard, and am thus responsible for any errors or misjudgments. It is collaborative in the sense that it tells the story of a legal victory that could not have been accomplished without the efforts of many others. The reversal of Claus von Bülow's first conviction and his acquittal at the second trial required a highly coordinated team effort. In the body of the book I describe that effort. But in this acknowledgment section I want to be specific about the roles played by the various participants.

Preliminary drafts of the "search and seizure" sections of the appellate brief were prepared by Jeanne Baker and Susan Estrich (both of whom also worked on the new-trial motion); the "Kuh notes" section, by David Fine; other sections, by John "Terry" MacFadyen, Stephanie Cleverdon and Mark Fabiani. The original research on the medical arguments was done by Joann Crispi and Andrew Citron, who stayed on and brilliantly assisted Tom Puccio in winning an acquittal at the second trial. Joann and Andy were the human computers that fed the relevant facts to the courtroom lawyers throughout the appeal, the new-trial motion and the second trial. Tom Puccio, of course, conducted the second trial in virtuoso style and with great success.

Among the students—many now distinguished young lawyers—who provided research and investigative assistance are the following: Mark Fabiani, Cliff Sloan, Elliot Spitzer, Cindy Aaron, Jim Cramer, Frank Huntington, Barbara Shaeffer, Jeff Leeds, Todd Cronin, Dru Carey, Kate Matson, Mike Levitin, Dan Williams and Rose Zoltek.

Many of the thoughts reflected throughout this book are impossible to attribute to specific persons, since they were the product of brainstorming sessions involving a dozen or more individuals, at which ideas emerged from every corner and changed rapidly before taking final shape. These sessions were exhilarating, as were the class discussions of the intractable ethical and tactical dilemmas. Thanks to all the students who participated in these sessions and classes.

My friends—great lawyers whose judgment I value—who read and critiqued drafts of this book include Sandy Frankel, Jack Litman, Mark Weiss, Bob Keefe, Roanne Sragow and Susan Estrich.

My sons, Elon and Jamin, assisted me in several ways, with both their brains and their brawn, and my brother, Nathan, provided me the excellent counsel and judgment I have come to rely on from him. His wife, Marilyn, and their children, Adam and Rana, read the manuscript and provided me with cogent comments. My mother added her usual insights and coaching. Carolyn Cohen was always at my side, providing me with inspiration, criticism, suggestions and support. Special thanks to Elon for suggesting the title, and to Steve Trachtenberg for his creative kibitzing.

My former assistant Maureen Doherty and current assistant Jane Ewing provided invaluable logistical support in their own very different ways. Maura Kelley word-processed the manuscript with speed, precision and intelligence, working under demanding deadlines but always with a smile. Rob Cowley and Peter Osnos provided valuable editorial suggestions, as did Laurie Stearns and Lisa Kaufman. Other acknowledgments are contained in the body of the book and in the dedication. Because this is a first-person account—as well as for stylistic symmetry—the pronoun "I" is frequently employed in place of "we" or "the team." But it was the team that won this case, and "they" deserve much of the credit.

Finally, a note of appreciation to the subject of this book, Claus von Bülow, who had enough faith to encourage me to write an honest book about his case without asking me to show it to him in advance of publication. As Claus wrote me: "I am confident it will be an honest book, and will paint me, as Cromwell urged his portrait painter, 'warts and all.'" Because he has not seen this book, none of its contents should be attributed to him. Claus's story will be told in his forthcoming book.

Contents

16.	The True-or-False Defense	201
17.	The Last Word	219
18.	The Jury Decides	229

Part IV: THE AFTERMATH: RESIDUES AND REVENGE

19.	Jury versus Jury	241
20.	Suitable for Framing	247
21.	Money Talks, but Who Listens?	253
22.	The Ongoing Story	260

Epilogue	265
Chronology	269
A Note on Sources	271
Index	273

Dramatis Personae

Claus von Bülow, born in Copenhagen, Denmark, on August 11, 1926. Married Martha von Auersperg on June 6, 1966. His only child, Cosima von Bülow, was born in April 1967.

Martha ("Sunny") von Bülow, née Crawford, born in a Pullman car on September 1, 1931. Married Prince Alfred ("Alfie") von Auersperg on July 20, 1957. The two children of this marriage are Princess Annie Laurie Kneissl and Prince Alexander von Auersperg. Married Claus von Bülow on June 6, 1966. Their only child is Cosima.

Prince Alexander von Auersperg, born to Prince Alfred and Princess Martha von Auersperg in 1959. Graduated from Brown University in 1983. Now works for an investment firm in New York City. Recently inherited approximately $45 million from his maternal grandmother, Annie Laurie (Crawford) Aitken.

Princess Annie Laurie ("Ala") Kneissl, née von Auersperg, born to Prince Alfred and Princess Martha von Auersperg in 1958. Married Franz Kneissl on May 31, 1980. Now lives in New York City. Recently inherited approximately $45 million from her maternal grandmother.

Cosima von Bülow, born to Claus and Martha von Bülow in 1967. Now attends Brown University. Recently was disinherited by her maternal grandmother of approximately $30 million for siding with her father.

Maria Schrallhammer, maid to Martha von Bülow since 1957. Born near Munich, Germany. Worked for Ala Kneissl after Sunny's second coma. Retired and returned to Germany after the second trial.

Alexandra Isles, soap-opera actress and mistress of Claus von Bülow between 1979 and 1981.

Andrea Reynolds, constant companion of Claus von Bülow during the appeal and the second trial. Deeply involved in litigation and press strategy.

The Lawyers

Richard Kuh, former District Attorney of Manhattan, now in private practice. Retained by the von Auersperg and Aitken families to conduct a discreet private investigation into circumstances surrounding Sunny's comas.

Stephen Famiglietti, chief prosecuting attorney at the first trial. Now in private practice.

Herald Price Fahringer, chief defense attorney at the first trial.

John Sheehan, experienced and successful Rhode Island trial lawyer, recommended to Claus von Bülow by Senator Claiborne Pell; was co-counsel at both trials.

Alan Dershowitz, chief counsel for the appeal and the new-trial motion, and strategist and consultant for the second trial.

Susan Estrich, Jeanne Baker, Christopher Edley, David Fine, attorneys who worked with Dershowitz.

Joann Crispi and Andrew Citron, graduates of Harvard Law School who worked first with Dershowitz, then with Claus von Bülow, and ultimately with Thomas Puccio on the second trial.

John "Terry" MacFadyen, Rhode Island lawyer and former public defender, retained by Dershowitz as local counsel and associate for the appeal and the new-trial motion.

Thomas Puccio, Claus von Bülow's chief trial lawyer for the second trial. Former Abscam prosecutor, now in private practice in New York.

Roanne Sragow, former assistant District Attorney of Middlesex County, Massachusetts, retained to serve as conduit for all financial dealings with David Marriott.

Marc DeSisto and Henry Gemma, prosecutors at the second trial.

The Sideshow Witnesses

David Marriott, former printer, who swore he had delivered drugs to Clarendon Court.

Father Philip Magaldi, respected parish priest in North Providence, who corroborated Marriott's account.

Truman Capote, noted author and longtime friend of Martha von Bülow, who provided an affidavit for the new-trial motion but died before the second trial.

Joanne Carson, second wife of Johnny Carson and longtime friend of Truman Capote, who corroborated Capote's account.

C. Z. Guest, New York and Newport socialite, who corroborated Capote's affidavit.

The Doctors

Dr. Richard Stock, New York doctor to the wealthy. Martha von Bülow's physician for twenty-nine years.

Dr. Janis Gailitis, a Newport, Rhode Island, doctor who treated Martha during both comas.

Dr. George Cahill, Harvard professor and "expert's-expert" on blood sugar, former director of the Joslin Research Laboratories, who testified for the state at both trials.

Dr. Robert Bradley, Dr. Cahill's colleague at the Joslin Institute, who testified at the second trial that he was 100 percent certain that the first coma had been caused by insulin and 99 percent certain about the second coma.

Dr. Arthur Rubenstein, professor and chairman of the Department of Medicine at the University of Chicago Medical School, who provided an affidavit for the new-trial motion and testified for the defense at the second trial.

Dr. Leo Dal Cortivo, chief toxicologist, Office of Suffolk County (New York) Medical Examiner, who provided an affidavit for the new-trial motion and testified for the defense at the second trial.

Dr. Harold Lebovitz, professor of medicine and head of endocrinology and diabetes at Downstate Medical Center in New York, who provided an affidavit for the new-trial motion and testified for the defense at the second trial.

Setting the Stage

"This case has everything," declared the prosecutor. "It has money, sex, drugs; it has Newport, New York and Europe; it has nobility; it has maids, butlers, a gardener. Clarendon Court [the mansion where the critical events took place] has a big gate. Most people can't see inside. This case is where the little man has a chance to glimpse inside and see how the rich *live*."

One commentator called the von Bülow case "an epic drama" made for the stage. The production—boasting a "cast of thousands" —would have "made Cecil B. De Mille proud, with its plots and subplots, major and minor characters, days of nail-biting tension and periods of comic relief."

No wonder some called it the case of the decade. But media hype-ers bestow such appellations on notorious trials just about every other year. A journalist once described the Patricia Hearst case the "Another Trial of the Century—the Fourth or Fifth in [F. Lee Bailey's] Sixteen-Year Legal Career." The American trial has always been an entertainment—a cross between soap opera, spectator sport and morality play.

To qualify as a case of the decade, a trial has to meet certain criteria: The players must be sufficiently important, wealthy, fascinating or mysterious to capture the popular imagination. The alleged crime should be insidiously clever, motivated by a combination of lust and lucre. It is best if the defendant is convicted at a first trial full of surprising twists and that new evidence is subsequently discovered that casts doubt on the original verdict. The guilt or innocence of the accused must be in real doubt, so that the partisans on each side will have something to root for. Even better, there should be a specter of possible frame-up in the air, so that if the defendant is indeed innocent, *someone* is guilty of something. Eventually justice should be done—with some skeptics still maintaining that it has miscarried.

By these criteria, many Americans (and Europeans) felt that the case of Claus von Bülow—the handsome Danish aristocrat who was accused of twice trying to kill his beautiful American heiress wife—certainly made any short list of trials of the decade.

A reporter who had covered every major American trial of general interest during the past twenty-five years said that she had never seen a trial receive as much press coverage as the first von Bülow trial. The second trial received even greater coverage, with more than two hundred media people in attendance. Since television coverage of criminal trials is permitted in Rhode Island, many hours of the two trials and the entire appeal were telecast live—some over national television. The networks devoted substantial time to covering the trials on their evening news programs. It is likely that more people saw portions of the von Bülow proceedings than of any other case in history.

One of the most widely viewed episodes occurred at the very end of the first trial. Claus von Bülow, sitting ramrod-straight in his aristocratic manner, waits for the jury—people he would rarely encounter in the stratified world of Newport—to pass judgment on him. His effort to seem aloof from what is going on about him falters as he strains to hear the foreman's words. His hands remain clasped while he appears to twiddle his thumbs. His face is arched skyward, highlighting his forehead and nose. His thumbs stop moving as the foreman says "guilty." A slight, almost indiscernible facial twitch is captured by the television camera.

I remember watching that scene on the evening news and thinking that the American system of justice had worked. A jury of typical Rhode Islanders, sitting in judgment over a wealthy and powerful aristocrat, had rendered society's decision.

But the American system of justice does not end with the jury's verdict. This is the story of how Claus von Bülow was convicted of a crime that probably never happened and then succeeded in vindicating himself—both in the eyes of the law and in the minds of many, though certainly not all, observers.

Since I was Claus von Bülow's chief appellate lawyer following the first trial and remained on the legal team as strategist during the second trial, this story is in part a first-person account. My job, as an appellate lawyer, begins after the jury has convicted the defendant. I played no role in the first trial, having been retained to

represent Mr. von Bülow immediately after the initial jury rendered
its guilty verdict. But I have had substantial responsibility for everything that happened from that point on. The second trial was
brilliantly litigated by Tom Puccio, using evidence gathered by the
team I put together after the first trial. Because I was responsible
for appealing from the first trial and gathering the new evidence for
the second trial, I was in a unique position to contrast the two legal
proceedings. I also had an extraordinary window into the case, as
well as access to information and people unavailable to the public.
Now that the criminal case is over, much of what was secret before
can be revealed.

The story of this case begins years before that dramatic day in
Newport when Claus von Bülow's life was shattered by the jury's
verdict of guilty. Indeed, one of the great questions pervading this
case was when, in truth, the relevant story did begin. The prosecution contended that it began just three years before the jury
rendered its judgment in Newport, when Claus fell out of love with
his wealthy wife, Sunny, and in love with a television soap-opera
actress named Alexandra Isles.

Claus was born Claus Cecil Borberg, in Copenhagen, Denmark,
in 1926. His father, Svend Borberg, was a playwright and theater
critic. His mother, Jonna, was the daughter of Frits Bülow, a
wealthy and prominent descendant of the illustrious German von
Bülow family. Svend and Jonna were divorced when Claus was
four. Two years later, Svend married the granddaughter of Henrik
Ibsen. Claus was brought up by his mother, who moved to London
at the beginning of World War II. Claus, who joined his mother
after being smuggled out of Nazi-occupied Denmark, entered
Cambridge University at age sixteen and graduated after the war
with a degree in law. At about the same time, his father—who
had remained in Denmark and had been chairman of a group
called the Danish-German Literary Society—was tried as a Nazi
collaborator and sentenced to four years in prison. Although he
was eventually vindicated on appeal, he was imprisoned for more
than a year and died shortly after his release. Claus later commented that "my grandfather and I took one side, and my father,
more foolishly than criminally, took the other." After graduation,
Claus, who by this time had adopted his mother's name, joined
the chambers of the noted British barrister Quintin Hogg (later
Lord Hailsham), apprenticing at the barrister's trade. Later he
went to work for J. Paul Getty and eventually became one of

his chief assistants. He and his mother lived at one of the best addresses in London—Belgrave Square—in a large apartment, which von Bülow said "dined two hundred with ease and slept three with difficulty." Until 1966 he lived the life of an aristocratic bachelor and man-about-the-various-important-towns-in-the-world.

Sunny was born in 1931 in a Pullman railway car between White Sulphur Springs, West Virginia, and New York City. Her father, George Crawford, was seventy-one years old when his wife, Annie Laurie—whom he had married four years earlier, when she was twenty-eight—gave birth to their only child, whom they named Martha. One of her early nicknames was "Choochoo," because of her birthplace, but that was soon replaced by "Sunny." By some accounts this nickname reflected her cheery disposition as a child; by others, it reflected her father's wish for a son. Four years after Sunny's birth, George died, leaving an enormous fortune. At the time of his death, the company he had founded—Columbia Gas and Electric—was valued at nearly three quarters of a billion dollars.

In 1957 Sunny Crawford married Prince Alfred Eduard Friedrich Vincenz Martin Maria von Auersperg, a handsome sports instructor and heir to the Hapsburg misfortune. Sunny had met the moneyless blue blood in one of the European "heiress trap" resorts where nouveau riche Americans searched for royal mates. The couple had two children during their eight-year marriage. The first, Princess Annie Laurie, named after Sunny's mother and nicknamed "Ala," was born in 1958. The second, Prince Alexander, was born in 1959. Their father, Prince Alfie, apparently refused to submit to the domesticity of married life and continued to be the philanderer he had been before he met Sunny.

During a dinner party in London, an unhappily married Sunny met a debonair bachelor named Claus Bülow. Shortly thereafter he began courting her, and in 1966, following a two-year secret sexual liaison and Sunny's divorce from Prince Alfie, they were married. It was at about this time that Claus and Sunny began to use the "von" in their last name. A year later their only child was born. They named her Cosima, after her godmother's daughter. (The original Cosima von Bülow had been an illegitimate child of composer Franz Liszt; she had married conductor Hans von Bülow but became romantically involved with, and ultimately married, Richard Wagner.)

Following the birth of Cosima, Sunny apparently lost interest in sex and became something of a homebody. A journalist writing for *McCall's* who was extremely unfavorable to Claus von Bülow described Sunny's typical day during this period:

> This is how, by most accounts, Sunny von Bülow spent her days: She woke at 11. She spoke to her mother (whose mansion is across the avenue from Clarendon Court) for an hour. She was driven by her chauffeur to an exercise class. She did "a little shopping." She had lunch (her favorite meal was chicken livers and bacon). She returned home, put on her pajamas, napped, watched TV with Claus. ("Such a dear, wholesome girl," one Newport matron says: "she thought it was pure bliss to watch Lawrence Welk with dinner on a TV tray.") And so to bed, with her four Labradors draped around her, her husband next to her. Occasionally, she appeared at parties, wearing beautiful designer gowns; she left early, many people say, immobilized by her shyness. Friendly witnesses say she swam 20 laps a day when she summered in Newport; her maid says she spent hours arranging flowers.

Everybody seemed to agree that Sunny was a lovely, giving and sensitive person. But whatever the reason, Sunny and Claus grew apart over the years.

Claus looked elsewhere for companionship. In 1978 he met Alexandra Isles—a beautiful soap-opera actress with a Danish aristocratic background—and began an affair with her. By mid-1979, Alexandra was insisting that they marry. At Christmastime 1979, Sunny von Bülow suffered her first coma. At Christmastime 1980, she suffered her final coma.

The prosecution's basic theory was as simple as it was corny. Claus was trapped in an unhappy marriage. He did not love his incredibly wealthy wife. But he did love her money and the lifestyle to which she gave him entrée. He also loved Alexandra Isles. But if he divorced Sunny and married Alexandra, he would have to cut back on his life-style and give up Sunny's money. If he remained with Sunny (and her money), he would have to give up Alexandra, who had given him several ultimatums about divorce.

According to the prosecution, Claus chose not to choose. He wanted both Sunny's money and Alexandra's hand. The only way this could be achieved was for Sunny to die a natural death. And so Claus arranged for Sunny to die a "natural death" by surreptitiously injecting her with insulin, a substance that is naturally in the body and that is difficult to distinguish from an externally administered overdose. The diabolical plot remained uncompleted when Sunny von Bülow recovered quickly from the first coma she suffered during the Christmas holiday in 1979. It succeeded in part when Sunny fell into an irreversible coma during the following Christmas season. But it failed completely when Claus von Bülow was indicted for attempted murder, when Alexandra left him and when he was denied access to Sunny's fortune.

Claus von Bülow claimed that the story had begun decades earlier —even before he met his wife—when Sunny started her decline into the netherworld of pills, drink and depression. It was the defense's contention that Sunny had caused her own coma, either deliberately or inadvertently, either by injecting herself or by swallowing either insulin or barbiturates. The uncertainty in Claus von Bülow's defense—an uncertainty attributed to the claim that since he was innocent he *didn't know* how Sunny had become comatose—was cleverly characterized by the prosecution at the first trial as the "multiple-choice" or "grab-bag" defense. The prosecutor contrasted this with his own "true or false" offense: "true or false—Claus von Bülow administered . . . insulin to his wife in an attempt to kill her on two separate occasions." The jury checked the "true" box, convicting von Bülow of both crimes.

My own story of the von Bülow case began several weeks after the jury had rendered its guilty verdict. It was on April Fools' Day —practically a religious holiday in my family, celebrated by each of us trying to outdo the others with silly pranks. At 7:00 A.M. the phone rang. A man with an upper-class British accent identified himself as Claus von Bülow. A few weeks earlier I had watched the Newport, Rhode Island, jury convict Claus von Bülow of twice attempting to murder his wife, but I was only vaguely familiar with the trial. I knew nothing about the defendant, except that he was rich and Danish. So when the man with the British accent told me he was Claus von Bülow, I thought for sure that some relative—who erroneously believed that von Bülow was British rather than Danish —was attempting a silly April Fools' prank. "Cut it out," I said. "Who is this? It's seven o'clock in the morning. I didn't get to sleep until two o'clock."

"Sorry, Professor," the voice responded, "but I *am* Claus von Bülow, and I would like you to consider taking my appeal."

That early-morning call marked the beginning of a three-year legal battle to overturn the attempted murder convictions of Claus von Bülow. I was the general in the appellate phase of the legal battle, leading a group of eighteen lawyers and law students, and I remained as the behind-the-scenes strategist during the retrial we had earned for Claus von Bülow by winning the appeal. In the beginning I assumed that von Bülow was probably guilty—most convicted defendants are! Over time I became convinced that von Bülow was probably innocent. Eventually I became nearly certain. This is quite unusual for me: generally I become more convinced of my clients' guilt as I get to know them—and their cases—better; and I never become certain of their innocence.* How then did Claus von Bülow manage to persuade me? The simple answer is that he never tried to. But several things that he did—steps he took, attitudes he expressed, questions he asked—impressed me as the actions of an innocent man. For example, he asked me to find a first-rate investigative reporter to probe the evidence with no strings attached. He never hesitated when I proposed avenues of investigation that, if he were guilty, could have proven his guilt. In my experience, guilty defendants generally want to control the investigations.

And then the new evidence began to trickle in. I will recount that evidence in the pages to come—evidence that entirely dismantled, brick by brick, the solid edifice constructed by the state at the first trial.

A legal case is somewhat like a long unedited film containing thousands of frames, only a small portion of which ultimately appear on the screen as part of the finished product. The role of the legal system—police, prosecutor, defense lawyer, judge—is to edit the film for trial: to determine what is relevant for the jury to see, and what should end up on the cutting-room floor. How far back in time should the evidence go? How much detail should be included? Who should appear in supporting roles?

Most of our attitudes about crime and justice come from theater and television. Chekhov once remarked about theater: "If in the first act you hang a pistol on the wall, then in the last act, it must be shot off. Otherwise, you do not hang it there." The point is that in the condensed world of the three-act play or forty-eight-minute television drama, there is little room for coincidence or chance. If an actor experiences a chest pain during Act I, you can be sure he will have a heart attack by Act III. If a businessman takes out life

* For a discussion of why I defend guilty clients, see my book *The Best Defense.*

insurance on his partner before the first commercial, you can count of the murder of the partner before the last commercial. In real life, of course, most chest pains turn out to be indigestion and most insurance policies are routine decisions. But in drama there is no time to present such mundane aspects of daily life. One of the most difficult tasks of the criminal justice system is to distinguish between the rules of theatrical relevance and those of legal relevance. The judge must determine which pieces of evidence—guns, insurance policies, wills, chest pains, romantic affairs, et cetera—the jury should learn about. The danger is that a jury, accustomed to seeing justice portrayed theatrically, will forget that in real life there is no playwright selecting events for inclusion based on their subsequent relevance. Guns hung on the walls of real homes are likely to remain there as unused decorations.*

In the great Japanese film *Rashomon* a brutal rape-murder is presented several times—as seen differently through the eyes of each participant. No version is more truthful than any other. They are just different. In law, as distinguished from art, there *is* generally a truth. It may be difficult, indeed impossible, to discern. But discerning the truth is the central, though not the only, object of the legal system.

In the von Bülow case, the truth may never be learned to the satisfaction of all. Sunny von Bülow will never speak. Indeed, even she may not know precisely what occurred. Between her two comas she was conscious and communicative for nearly a year, yet she provided no clue that she had any idea what had caused her first coma. Claus von Bülow says he knows only that he never did his wife any harm. There were no witnesses to any criminal acts.

Consequently, the question in the von Bülow case is not "Who done it?" It is "Was any crime done at all?" There were two comas. But were these comas induced by criminal actions of a third party? Or were they caused by Sunny von Bülow herself? If they were caused by Sunny, either deliberately or accidentally, then no crime was committed.†

---

* The insight reflected by the Chekhov quote was given to me by my son Elon, then a theater major, who was helping me think through my legal argument in a case where my client had participated in taking out an insurance policy on his partner, who was then gunned down gangland-style. With the help of Elon's insight, we won the appeal and my client was recently acquitted at a retrial.

† It is, of course, possible that one coma was self-induced and the other criminally induced. This was never suggested at either trial by either side—for understandable reasons. See the discussion of other theories on pages 250 to 252.

In this book I leave it to the readers to decide what they believe the truth to be. I will not try to tell *the* story of what happened. I don't know for sure what happened, though I have my strong suspicions based on a thorough review of all the evidence and a close association with, and observation of, most of the central characters. So I can only tell the *stories* that each side claims are the truth. My own biases and hunches will surely filter through any veneer of objectivity. Every reader will have to decide which truth seems more compelling. This attitude may seem unduly nihilistic, but it is simply the product of many years of experience with the adversary system of justice.

This book will present the facts, first as the prosecution successfully presented them at the initial trial. Then it will introduce the dramatic new evidence that came to light only after the verdict—new facts that cast an entirely different light both on the prosecution's version and on the dramatis personae of the case. Finally, it will tell the story as it came out during the second trial. It will recount these different stories through the mouths of the important witnesses, none of whom knows the whole story, but each of whom contributes an important part to the mosaic. In the process, it will tell several stories not previously told, from witnesses and documents that, for one reason or another, remained on the cutting-room floor or behind the locks of secret files.

Not surprisingly, two conflicting but compelling accounts of the same story can sound equally convincing. This bit of folk wisdom is captured in an old Jewish joke I tell my students:

The wise rabbi was holding court in a small Eastern European shtetl. A young rabbinical student had been sent to observe the sage at work. The case involved a domestic quarrel. First the wife spoke: "Rabbi, my husband is a terrible man. He stays out all night, drinks away his salary, beats me, and doesn't clean up after himself." The rabbi pondered for a moment and then offered his rabbinical conclusion: "My daughter, I have listened to you and you are right." Then the husband spoke: "Rabbi, my wife is a shrew, she screams all day and night, she won't sleep with me, she can't cook, and she keeps the house a mess." The rabbi again pondered and offered his view. "My son, I have listened to you, and you are right."

The student leaped up and shouted, "But, Rabbi, they can't both be right." The rabbi pondered for a moment and then responded: "My son, you are right."

But the student was not right. In life, as in law, both sides of a domestic dispute *can* be right (and more often wrong) at the same time. This may not always be true, especially where specific facts are in dispute, as they were in the von Bülow case. But even so, the story of the rabbi makes an important point about advocacy: you cannot expect to win unless your story—standing by itself—is convincing. All too often, the advocate fails to convince even before his opponent has presented the other side. That advocate's only hope is that his opponent's side is even weaker and will be even more self-defeating.

At the first von Bülow trial, the prosecution's case was convincing and the defendant's was not. At the second trial, the opposite was true. This book will tell the intriguing—and heretofore untold—story of why there was such a difference in two trials involving the same cast of characters.

It will also tell a story about how our legal system often serves to promote truth. We hear so much these days about the courts freeing guilty defendants on legal technicalities. That does sometimes happen. But courts also reverse convictions in order to provide defendants with the tools necessary to establish their innocence. That is what happened here, and it is a fascinating story about civil liberties at work in the interest of enhancing truth.

Part

I

THE FIRST TRIAL: OF BLUE BLOODS, BLOOD SUGARS AND SUGAR DADDIES

1

The Maid's Story:
Loyalty and Treachery

The first trial of Claus von Bülow told, in essence, the maid's story. Maria Schrallhammer was the star witness, and a masterful witness she was. In a case based almost entirely on circumstantial inferences, Maria came closer to being an eyewitness than anyone else.

According to Stephen Famiglietti, the state's very able prosecutor at the first trial, "it was Maria Schrallhammer" who "really started this investigation." "If you believe her," asked Lieutenant John Reise, the Rhode Island State Police officer who investigated the case and was credited with cracking it, "how could you think that guy was innocent?" And most observers, including, ultimately, several of the jurors, agreed with one writer's assessment that "Maria's testimony did von Bülow the most harm."

Who, then, was this woman variously referred to as the "iron maid," the "maid of the century" and, recalling the loyal maid in Daphne du Maurier's *Rebecca*, "Mrs. Danvers"?

Maria Schrallhammer was first and foremost a "lady's maid," and second a German *Frau*. Born in a small village outside Munich, she trained for a life of servitude to the aristocracy at a local Catholic convent. Before going to work for Sunny von Auersperg she had performed domestic service for the family of Alfried von Krupp, the notorious armaments manufacturer who used slave labor during the Nazi regime and was convicted of war crimes at Nuremberg. When Sunny married Prince Alfred ("Alfie") von Auersperg, the couple sought an appropriate personal maid for Sunny. Baroness von Krupp's maid was suggested and eventually hired.

From that moment on, Maria Schrallhammer devoted her entire existence to Sunny—whom she always referred to as her "lady." Maria's best friend said "she just lived for the family"; they were "her life." But another life awaited her as well. Her plan was to return eventually to Germany—where she maintained her citizenship—and live out her last years in her beloved fatherland after reaching retirement age.

Although Maria was dedicated to Sunny's entire family, she was not a *family* servant. She was Sunny's personal maid: the "lady's maid." Husbands may come and go, children grow up and leave. But Sunny was the constant. Sunny was Maria's unique responsibility in a home full of servants and domestics.

The relationship between Maria and Sunny may be difficult to understand for people not used to such personal attention. But Maria understood her role in life with exceptional clarity. She took care of every detail of her lady's life; she dressed her, listened to her, and watched over her. "I did everything for her," she told the jury. Another servant—noting that Maria was the only person who had access to the most intimate details of Sunny's life—said they were almost like sisters. But Maria denied being like a sister to Sunny. "Did she ever confide in you?" Maria was asked at the first trial. "No, she very seldom." "Did you confide in her?" "Yeah, I would tell her if something bothered me."

This relationship continued throughout Sunny's marriage to Claus von Bülow. It continues in its own strange way even now, while Sunny lies in an irreversible coma. Until recently, Maria visited her lady several times each week and talked to her. Now she prays for her.

No one—not Sunny's husbands, parents, children or friends—was closer to Sunny von Bülow. No one was in a better position to observe her daily habits and activities. No one could be a better witness at a trial involving her life—and possible attempts to end it. It was almost as if a videotape camera had been following Sunny von Bülow nearly everywhere during the last twenty-three years of her active life.

Maria Schrallhammer told her story several times after learning that her lady would never recover from her second coma. The first lawyer she told it to was Richard Kuh, the attorney hired by Sunny's family to investigate the causes of the two comas. On January 8, 1981, eighteen days after Sunny was stricken with her final coma, Maria met with Richard Kuh in his office. Kuh, a private lawyer who was a former District Attorney of New York County, had been recommended by Sunny's banker as the perfect choice for conducting a discreet investigation to determine whether Sunny's comas were caused by criminal means. The first step in that investigation was for Kuh to interview all the crucial witnesses to the events surrounding the comas—without alerting Claus von Bülow to the family's suspicions.

The January 8 Schrallhammer-Kuh interview was obviously important, because it was the first time Maria had told her story to an outsider, a story that had reached its denouement only two weeks earlier. It was also important because the story was told *before* the family had arrived at any firm conclusions about what had occurred and what they should do. Maria was under no pressure, therefore, to try to fit her story into any preconceived theory. All Kuh was interested in was—in the famous words of *Dragnet*'s Joe Friday— "the facts, ma'am, just the facts."

Maria spent nearly an hour with Kuh giving him the crucial facts about which she would testify at both trials. Kuh took detailed notes of exactly what she said. But neither the prosecution nor the defense had access to the notes' contents during the first trial. The reason they remained secret was that Kuh and the prosecutors claimed that they were protected by the confidentiality of various lawyer-client privileges, which prohibit the lawyer from revealing certain secrets that were disclosed to him in confidence as part of the professional relationship. The trial judge at the first trial agreed and did not require Kuh to produce the notes in response to a subpoena from the defense. Thus, the first jury never learned what Maria had told Richard Kuh during that initial meeting. This was to become a central issue throughout the remainder of the case. So even Maria's silence about her first account of the events assumed an important aspect.

Maria later told her story to the Rhode Island police and a grand jury. And then, on February 4, 1982, the entire world heard and saw Schrallhammer as she testified before the jury—and the television cameras—in the first trial of Claus von Bülow at Newport, Rhode Island. What viewers saw was a fifty-nine-year-old woman who looked the part of the loyal German maid. The thin features, sad expression, grey complexion, nervous smile and dark, conservative dress combined to make her appear frail and diffident—at least during her direct examination by prosecutor Famiglietti.

The prosecutor quickly took Maria through the biographical and historical foundation for her eyewitness testimony. Soon she was describing that fateful day of December 27, 1979, when Sunny von Bülow nearly died in her Newport "cottage," Clarendon Court, the fabulous twenty-room mansion that had served as the set for the motion picture *High Society*.

Maria began by telling the jury about Sunny's mood on the evening before her first coma. She was sad, but not depressed, because her oldest child, Annie Laurie, had left with her fiancé Franz Kneissl, heir to a ski equipment company, for a two-week visit to his family in Europe. The family had been drinking homemade eggnog in the spirit of the holidays. Sunny had imbibed a glass or two. At about 8:00 P.M. she retired for the night to the bedroom she shared with her husband, Claus.

The next morning at about 9:30 Maria was coming down from the servants' quarters when she encountered Claus. Maria was on her way to the master bedroom to see if her lady was awake. Claus told her that Sunny had a sore throat and that Maria should not wake her. About five minutes later, Maria approached Sunny's closed bedroom door and heard her moaning: Maria knocked and then entered. Claus had gotten back in bed by this time. Maria approached her lady and reached for her right arm, which was hanging over the side of the bed. It was "ice cold. . . . I put her arm into the bed and I tried to wake her up," but Sunny did not move.

Maria shouted at Sunny and shook her. Still no response. "She was limp. I thought she was unconscious." Since Sunny was usually a light sleeper who would awaken at the slightest sound or touch, Maria became frightened. "Call the doctor," she urged Claus. "Call her mother," she insisted.

"She's sleeping," Claus responded calmly. "We didn't sleep the previous night," he explained. "Let her sleep."

"She's not sleeping," Maria shouted. "She's unconscious. I can't wake her up."

But Claus insisted that she would be perfectly fine in a few hours, and Maria left the bedroom. A half hour later she returned and saw no improvement. Again she tried to awaken her lady. Again, no response. Maria repeated her request that Claus, who was lying in the giant bed reading next to his wife, call a doctor. Claus told Maria that the family had no local doctor, but Maria reminded him that Sunny had been to see a Dr. Gailitis in Newport. "She was drinking" last night, Claus told Maria. "Let her sleep it off."

Maria knew that Sunny had a low tolerance for alcohol. "She was drunk after two drinks," Maria testified. But this seemed like more than her usual reaction to a bit of post-Christmas overindulgence. Maria kept going in and out of the bedroom, checking on her lady and asking Claus to call the doctor or Sunny's mother. Maria explained to the jury that she would not take the initiative herself "because he wouldn't have liked me to call, and I didn't know a doctor anyway in Newport."

After lunch, Maria went back to the bedroom and saw that her lady's situation had not changed. "Either you have to call the doctor now, or I have to do it," she threatened. Finally Claus acceded to her demands and made the call to Dr. Janis Gailitis. But the doctor was out and Claus left a message. He also called Sunny's mother, Annie Laurie Aitken.

When Claus finally reached the doctor he told him that "my wife has an alcoholic problem and last night was one of these evenings, and she's not well today," but that Sunny had been out of bed and that he had even served her a drink of soda. When Maria heard Claus say this, she left the room, greatly upset because "it wasn't true." Maria was also upset because while Claus was talking to the doctor, Sunny's breathing became very heavy and she continued to moan. But Claus said nothing to the doctor about these ominous developments.

At about 6:00 P.M. Maria approached the bedroom. Claus was rushing to phone the doctor. Sunny's breathing was beginning to rattle. As Maria chillingly described it to the jury: "She was in the rattle—and, I thought she would die any second. [S]he hardly could breathe any more, and I thought she would stop any minute not breathing."

Claus called the doctor: "Please come right away," he pleaded. "I will pay you anything." Dr. Gailitis arrived within minutes. "She stopped breathing," the doctor shouted as he began cardio-pulmonary resuscitation and directed Claus to call the fire department. Dr. Gailitis cleared Sunny's throat of vomit and administered mouth-to-mouth resuscitation, thereby saving her life. Sunny was rushed to the Newport Hospital, where she regained consciousness the next day.

Meanwhile, back at the mansion, Maria removed the bottom sheet from Sunny's bed and noticed a puddle of urine. Maria's suspicions grew darker as she concluded that the urine meant that Sunny had not gotten up to go to the bathroom. Why, she wondered, would Claus lie to the doctor?

Despite her suspicions and her questions, Maria never told her lady how Claus had acted while she was unconscious. "I didn't want to go between married people," she explained. "I was only employee."

That, in essence, was the maid's story of the first coma. It is not, of course, the whole story of that coma. Medical experts would spend hundreds of hours trying to figure out the biochemical causes of Sunny's brush with death. But it was Maria Schrallhammer's chilling account of those critical hours—especially the ones during which Claus did not call the doctor—that formed the basis for what came to be known as Claus von Bülow's "unhusbandly" behavior toward his wife on December 27, 1979.

Almost exactly a year would pass between Sunny's two Christmas comas. During that year—1980—Maria assumed the role of supersleuth. As one journalist later put it: "Claus had [a] formidable enemy in his home." And that enemy was a secret and effective one.

Maria had an early ally in Prince Alexander, Sunny's middle child. Together they went to the matriarch of the family, Sunny's mother, Mrs. Aitken, and told her of their concerns that Claus had been at the very least negligent in ignoring his wife's crisis. Maria was beating the drum on this issue, but not so loud that either Sunny or Claus could hear it. But Mrs. Aitken did, and she admonished Claus that he must call a doctor any time her daughter was ill in the slightest degree—even if she "had a hangnail."

In response to this reprimand, Claus decided to mount a defense of his conduct during the day his wife became ill, and he wrote a letter to Dr. Gailitis asking for his opinion as to whether he was to blame. Eventually this letter was characterized by the prosecutor as Claus's "cover-his-ass" letter, and was used against him at the first trial. The letter, which affords a rare glimpse at the man whose voice was never heard by the jury, reads as follows:

22 January 1980

Dear Dr. Gailitis,

My wife is making excellent progress and has really fully recovered her physical strength. We are both most grateful to you. Now I need your professional opinion, preferably in writing.

My mother-in-law feels that I was remiss in not getting medical aid earlier in the day. On hindsight it is naturally a question I asked myself repeatedly in the days following the crisis. The facts, as I have given them to you, can be recapitulated as follows:

(1) I have witnessed a great many "out for the count" over the last 14 years. None of them, at the time or in retrospect, required a doctor. When my wife broke her hip two years ago, I naturally blamed myself that I had not stayed with her when she went to the bathroom. I did not make that mistake this time.

(2) My wife hardly slept the night of Tuesday 25th. Her voice was

very hoarse, and her throat sore the morning of the 26th. She did not sleep at all the night of Wednesday 26th, and I stayed awake with her then, and throughout the day of the 27th. The only times I left her were when I went to get her ginger ales, or portions of tapioca pudding, which she wanted. When she finally fell asleep the morning of the 27th I felt she needed it. Our perfectly healthy teenagers often sleep through lunch, when we allow it. Anyway her breathing was perfectly regular, and she would get up from time to time to go to the bathroom. I tried to reach you around 2:30 P.M., and reached you on the telephone about an hour later when I gave you a resume of the above facts. Shortly after 6 P.M. my wife's breathing suddenly changed to a rattle and I called you immediately. You came very quickly, as did the ambulance, and you saved the day. It was my impression that the actual crisis came very quickly, and quite unexpectedly. Earlier there had been nothing to distinguish this occasion from many previous vigils I had held. Indeed, if there had been no aspiration, there would have been no crisis on this occasion either. If I were to make a guess I would say that the violent flu my wife had some ten days earlier had not completely left her system, and had left a residue in her lungs. Combined with the depressants this nearly proved fatal. Dr. Stock and you are still mystified about the low blood count factor.

Have I stated everything fairly? Was I to blame? By lunchtime on the 27th I had myself gone without sleep for over 50 hours, and my judgment may have been poor. I already have cause to be grateful to you, and I now need your opinion on this question, even if it turns out to be frank and unpalatable.

Sincerely yours, Claus Bülow*

* In correspondence, Claus generally signed his name Bülow, omitting the "von." He also signed his checks without the "von." The story of when and under what circumstances the "von" was "added" has seemed to fascinate the press. Claus told me that Sunny insisted on her second husband having a "von," though it was a less than adequate substitute for the princely title her first husband had carried. Claus was always entitled to the "von" because of his ancestry—according to people who care about such things. His entitlement is confirmed by the German *Adels Kalender* (*Register of the Nobility*), which lists his great-grandfather and grandfather, as well as a letter from Princess Bismarck certifying his qualifications to use the "von." After the initial patent of nobility was bestowed, all members of the Bülow family were entitled to use the "von." Some chose to, others did not. Claus's own close family included Danish cabinet ministers, an ambassador, a Supreme Court Justice, and a general. Though the von Auerspergs dispute Claus's right to use the von, Sunny always referred to herself as Mrs. von Bülow. When Claus called my office, as he did on a daily basis after the first trial, he introduced himself to my secretary as Mr. von Bülow, pronouncing the "von," in the German manner, to sound like "fun." This led my irreverent secretary, Maureen Doherty, to refer to him incongruously as "the fun guy" or "Fonzie," after the TV character. Our super-secret documents were placed in a separate file labeled "the Fonz."

Dr. Gailitis responded a couple of weeks later, precisely as Claus had hoped:

February 8, 1980

Dear Mr. Von Bülow:
    I am glad to hear that Mrs. Von Bülow is improving.
    The events leading to the catastrophic deterioration of Mrs. von Bülow's condition—vomiting, aspiration of gastric contents and cardio-respiratory arrest—were unpredictable.
    There is no doubt in my mind that by recognizing the change in Mrs. Von Bülow's condition and by alarming me you saved her life.
                                    Sincerely,
                                    Janis Gailitis, M.D.

This letter may have satisfied Claus. Maybe even Mrs. Aitkin, who saw it. But Maria's suspicions darkened further. Several weeks after her first coma, Sunny fell ill again. This time it was in her New York apartment—the palatial fourteen-room home on upper Fifth Avenue. When Maria brought her breakfast that morning in February, Sunny couldn't sit up, was unable to see the tray, and had difficulty speaking. Claus called the family doctor this time, but Dr. Richard Stock—who had been caring for Sunny for twenty-nine years—didn't feel the need to come, because Sunny was suffering from an obvious flu. Claus blamed the episode on a greasy hamburger Sunny had eaten the night before. But Maria remained concerned, always recalling Claus's strange behavior several weeks earlier.

A few weeks after this episode, Maria discovered something that would turn her concern about Claus's unhusbandly behavior into a full-blown suspicion that Claus might be involved in criminal conduct directed against her lady.

    It began quite innocently. Maria was cleaning the walk-in closet off Claus von Bülow's room in the Fifth Avenue apartment. (In New York the couple did not share a bedroom, ostensibly because Claus would wake up earlier than Sunny and didn't want to disturb her. There was another reason as well: Claus told me that the couple had gradually stopped having sex with each other after the birth of Cosima thirteen years earlier.) The closet itself was shared by Claus and Sunny. It contained "all her evening dresses, all her evening shoes, and at that time some clothes." It also contained some of Claus's suits, but "most" of the items in that closet belonged to Sunny.

While cleaning the closet, Maria came upon a "traveling case" that Claus used each week to bring items "back and forth to Newport." The suitcase was open, and as Maria moved it, she noticed inside it a smaller closed case made of black vinyl "about six inches long and had a zipper around." Maria stared at the small black bag and decided to open it: "I really didn't know why I did it. It just was happened." Upon unzipping the black bag, Maria observed "Valium, pills, powder and the liquid." She had no idea what the unmarked powder and liquid were. But the Valium bore a prescription label. Maria quickly looked to see whether it had been prescribed for Claus or Sunny. What she read surprised her. It was made out to one "Leslie Baxter"—a name entirely unfamiliar to Maria.

Upon making this discovery, Maria called Sunny's daughter Ala and told her about it. Several days later she brought the black bag over to Ala's apartment, where they inspected the contents, took notes of the labels, and removed "samples out from the paste and the powder."

The vials were returned to the black bag, which was then placed back in Claus's closet. The samples were taken by Ala to the family doctor, Richard Stock, for analysis. During this entire time period Claus was away and never suspected that the contents of his closet were undergoing such close scrutiny.

While Maria continued to "monitor" the black bag, Dr. Stock completed his analysis of the samples. The yellow paste turned out to be Valium and the white powder was secobarbital, a barbiturate. Dr. Stock knew, of course, that Sunny took both of these drugs. He had prescribed considerable amounts for her over the years. But mystery surrounded the *form* they were in. Sunny took them in pill form. So why were they in paste and powder that were not generally available through pharmacies? That question was compounded by the mystery person—Leslie Baxter—whose name was found on the Valium prescription. Was Leslie a man or a woman? A friend of Claus's or of Sunny's. No one had the answers. And no one was prepared to direct the questions at either Claus or Sunny. For the time being, the black bag and its contents were to remain shrouded in suspicion.

But an effort was made to lift some of the mystery surrounding

Sunny's Christmas 1979 coma and her frequent bouts of illness. In April 1980, Sunny again woke up in her New York apartment feeling weak. Her speech was slurred and her hand motions un-coordinated. This time Maria took no chances. She immediately called Sunny's mother, who summoned Dr. Stock. Dr. Stock decided to try to get to the bottom of Sunny's medical problems and ordered her hospitalized for a battery of tests at Columbia Presbyterian Hospital.

After learning that she would be going to the hospital, Sunny called Maria into her room and angrily instructed the maid never to call her mother again without express approval. Maria was convinced, however, that Claus had "made Sunny say that," because he was "very upset" that the doctor had been called.

In any event, Sunny went off to the hospital for her tests. When they were completed, Maria was given the good news that there was nothing seriously wrong with her lady. There was no tumor or anything of that kind, just a small problem "when they took the tests that her sugar went down and down." In fact, what the doctors had found was that Sunny suffered from a relatively common condition known as reactive hypoglycemia.

Like diabetes, reactive hypoglycemia reflects a problem in the the mechanisms that control the relationship between the body's natural insulin and its blood sugar. Unlike diabetes—where consumption of carbohydrates elevates the blood-sugar level—a patient who suffers from reactive hypoglycemia experiences a lowering of blood sugar after eating or drinking carbohydrates. Sunny's case was on the severe side. During a glucose tolerance test in the hospital, her blood sugar went all the way down to 23,* which one expert later said was "as low a number as I have ever seen in . . . reactive hypoglycemia." Her own doctor, Dr. Stock, characterized her condition in the hospital records as "severe reactive hypoglycemia."

But reactive hypoglycemia, even a severe case, is not regarded as life-threatening. Nor is there much that can be done to treat it. The usual response is a common-sense diet. If intake of carbohydrates causes a lowering of the blood sugar, then the patient should avoid large, acute intakes of such carbohydrate-rich substances as sweets, ice cream and liquor.

---

* 23 milligrams per 100 milliliters after ingestion of 100 units of glucose. A normal reading would be in the range of approximately 65 to 90 milligrams percent.

Sunny was told to watch her diet and her staff was advised accordingly. Diet sodas were substituted for drinks containing sugar, and fresh fruit was kept in the house for dessert. Everybody was relieved to learn that Sunny was not really sick, and—as Maria would later testify—nobody really took the diagnosis of reactive hypoglycemia very seriously.

The best proof that Sunny was recovering from whatever it was that had affected her was her behavior at Ala's wedding in Austria during the late spring. The party was a royal affair, with a guest list out of Burke's *Royal Families of the World*. It included a lavish ball in the Archbishop's Palace. As Sunny stood on the receiving line welcoming the royal guests, there was no sign of her illness. All seemed back to normal amidst the splendor of Salzburg.

Maria remained concerned and suspicious, keeping her eye out for the mysterious black bag throughout the summer. But it was not until the Sunday after Thanksgiving, as she was cleaning Claus von Bülow's room in the New York apartment, that she spotted the black vinyl case once again. This time it was in a white canvas sack that Claus had packed for family excursions to Newport, along with several magazines. Again Maria unzipped the black case. This time she found something different—and more ominous. In addition to the vials, she saw a small bottle marked "insulin," along with several needles and a syringe. She had never seen these items before. Maria immediately summoned Sunny's son, Alexander, and excitedly showed him the new bottle and the implements for injecting its contents.

"Insulin, for what insulin?" she asked incredulously. "Because Mrs. von Bülow was not a diabetic. She doesn't need insulin." This phrase "For what insulin" received much popular attention; as Maria later testified, "Everybody knows that I said 'What for insulin.'"

This was not the first time Maria had seen syringes and needles. Many years earlier—in 1969, to be exact, on the isle of Majorca— Maria had seen Claus in possession of such implements: "He used it to give himself vitamin shots." She remembered the needles and syringes clearly because Claus "used to throw them out and the children played with the syringes"—using them as water guns. Although Claus had also injected Sunny with vitamins, Maria had never seen her lady in possession of needles or syringes.

Maria was stupefied by her new discovery, but still did not know what to do. Should she alert her lady? Should she confront Claus?

Again she decided she had no choice but to continue to monitor the situation, discreetly and silently.

A week later another health crisis developed. Sunny had been feeling miserable all day: "She had a very bad headache and sinus trouble." She took an aspirin compound during the day from the plentiful supply she always kept on hand. (Maria testified that she would buy two or three large family-size bottles of aspirin at a time and make sure that a bottle was always "at her bedside.")

At about 10:00 that night Claus von Bülow came knocking on Maria's door. "I'm afraid something has happened," he explained, "but it's not bad. Don't get excited." When Maria entered Sunny's bedroom, she saw her lady lying in bed "full with blood. . . . She had a hole in the back of her head" from which blood was gushing. There were puddles of blood all around: on the pillow, the bed, and the carpet. Claus explained that Sunny had gotten dizzy and fallen, striking her head in the process. Maria tried to talk to her lady, but Sunny's speech was "so slurry" that she couldn't understand her. She was in "a complete daze." This time Maria did not have to urge Claus to call the doctor. He was already dialing 911. The rescue squad arrived and rushed Sunny to the Lenox Hill Hospital, where her head wound was closed and she was treated for a toxic aspirin overdose. She was kept in the hospital for six days.

Maria did not know how to deal with these confusing incidents. She confided in a German friend—with whom she had a written correspondence—that "not everything is rosy here" and recounted her experiences with her lady's illnesses. After telling her friend about that dreadful day last December when she had tried to get Claus to call the doctor, she described her feelings when the doctor finally arrived: "My God, was that a relief. She literally was rescued from death. With an ambulance from the Fire Department she was taken to a hospital. Thank God she recovered slowly. They found out that her blood sugar level was very low. At least a plus for him."

Maria then went on to tell her friend what she had done and what she now feared:

I found that her condition in February was very peculiar. I went secretly to Mrs. Aitken and told her the truth. Bülow and I are at daggers' points. In April Mrs. Bülow spent almost two weeks at the Medical Center for tests. They diagnosed that her blood sugar was unstable. But at the hospital she was feeling rather well. Sometimes

I get sick thinking what is going to happen next. Mrs. trusts her husband blindly and is totally dependent. He of course has a girl friend. The whole life has changed. No more parties, and they don't go out either. She gained a lot of weight and is very unhappy about it.

Maria's fear about what was going to happen next was well founded. As Christmas approached, the family once again planned to travel to Newport. Maria had wanted to join the family on their trip to Newport, but Claus told her not to come because she was tired and might "get the flu." "Why don't you take some time off in New York instead of joining us," he suggested. In any event, the family was not intending to spend Christmas in Newport, since Sunny's mother, Mrs. Aitken, was ill in New York, and the tradition was for the whole family to be together for Christmas dinner. The plan was to spend the pre-Christmas weekend in Clarendon Court and then to return to New York for Christmas.

Maria's final sighting of the black bag occurred as Sunny and Claus were preparing to leave. While taking some of their bags down in the elevator, she noticed it in an open white canvas bag marked "Metropolitan Opera" with magazines in it. As the elevator was going down, Maria quickly opened the black case and looked inside. Again she saw the insulin bottle as well as syringes and needles. This would be Maria's last opportunity to warn Sunny or question Claus about these inexplicable items in the black bag. But worried as she was, Maria said nothing as she bid good-bye to her lady and Claus. It was the last time she would ever see her lady in a state of consciousness.

Maria later learned from Alex that after arriving in Newport, Sunny spent Saturday decorating the Christmas tree she had ordered for Clarendon Court. The family—Sunny, Claus, Alex and Cosima; Ala was in Europe—planned an early dinner that night so that they could catch the early show of the movie *9 to 5*. It is unclear whether Sunny ate the main course. But she insisted on having a large ice-cream sundae with caramel sauce for dessert.*

After the movie, the family returned home. Claus went off to do some work in his study. Sunny, Alex and Cosima went into the library to talk. Before going to the library, Sunny went to her bathroom for a few minutes. (Although they shared a bedroom at

---

* Although this chapter focuses on the maid's story, portions of it are derived from the testimony of other witnesses and additional sources.

Clarendon Court, Sunny and Claus had separate bathrooms.)
When she returned, she was carrying a glass that Alex believed
was filled with ginger ale.

The three settled into the library and talked for half an hour.
Claus wandered in and asked if anyone wanted anything. Sunny
said she would love some left-over chicken soup, and Claus went to
get it. While Claus was in the kitchen, Alex noticed his mother's
voice growing progressively weaker. Another episode was coming
on. Sunny grew so weak that she had difficulty lifting her glass.
When she tried to get up, she staggered. Alex asked his mother
whether she had taken any sleeping pills or barbiturates. She said
no. But Alex repeated the question "three or four times." He seemed
worried about the possibility that his mother might be taking pills,
because Claus had told him that she was.

Alex picked his mother up and carried her toward her bedroom.
Sunny complained that she did not want to be carried, that she
could make it on her own, but Alex knew better. He laid her down
on her bed, but she got up and went to her bathroom. Alex went to
summon "Uncle Claus," as he called his stepfather, from the library,
but Claus was in the midst of a business call to New York. So Alex
returned to his mother's room just as she was attempting to get back
into bed. He helped lift her legs onto the bed and tucked her in.

As Alex was leaving, after Claus arrived at the bedroom, his
mother asked him to open the windows. Although the windchill
factor was well below zero near the ocean, Alex knew that his
mother loved to sleep in a cold room. Sunny said goodnight to her
son for the last time, and Alex went to join some friends at a local
seaside bar.

The next morning at breakfast Alex asked his thirteen-year-old
half-sister Cosima if their mother was up yet. Cosima told him that
their mother was still asleep. When Claus arrived at the breakfast
table after a morning walk to the ocean, he expressed surprise that
Sunny was not up. Although she was a late sleeper, it was now
past 11:00.

Claus went to the master bedroom, returning a few minutes later.
As he approached the breakfast room, he motioned toward Alex
so that Cosima would not see. Alex followed Claus to the bedroom.
When he got there, he immediately saw there was a serious problem.
His mother was lying unconscious on the marble bathroom floor.
Her head was directly underneath the toilet bowl and her legs were
pointing toward the bathtub. Her mouth was bleeding and her lips

were swollen. Her nightgown was bunched up around her waist. The sink water was running.* There was a puddle of urine beneath her.

Claus came over to her and placed a finger near her nose. "She's still breathing," he exclaimed with apparent relief, running to call the emergency number. Alex felt his mother's neck and realized that she was ice-cold. He found a fur throw and placed it around her for warmth.

Six minutes later the ambulance arrived and took Sunny—with Claus riding along—to the Newport Hospital Emergency Room. Her body temperature was 81.6° Fahrenheit; her pulse rate varied between 36 and 40. A few minutes later Sunny experienced cardiac arrest and two doctors were needed to resuscitate her.

At 2:00 in the afternoon Claus called Maria in New York to inform her that something had happened to Sunny again, and that she had been taken to the hospital. A few days later Maria was driven up to Newport by the chauffeur. But by that time Sunny's condition had been diagnosed as too serious to be treated at the local Newport Hospital, which lacked a CAT scan and other sophisticated diagnostic and treatment resources. She had been transferred to Boston and placed under the care of leading specialists in the treatment of deep coma at the Peter Bent Brigham Hospital.† When Maria went to visit her lady, she was told "there was absolutely no hope." As Maria slowly repeated these words to the jury, she brought her hand up to her eyes, her voice trembled and she cried.

On that note of sadness, the maid's story—the story she told at the first trial—ended. Maria Schrallhammer's testimony was devastating to Claus von Bülow's case. Though the defense attorney at the first trial—Herald Price Fahringer—tried to discredit Maria, his cross-examination only strengthened the impact of her testimony. One of the assistant prosecutors told the press that "Fahringer's a good lawyer, but he couldn't make a dent in Maria." She was able to "take" his question "and throw it back in his face and kill him." One commentator put it this way: "Nothing short of von Bülow's confession on the stand could top Schrallhammer's testimony." The most Fahringer could get Maria to acknowledge was that she had failed to give the grand jury a full answer when she had been asked

* Apparently Sunny generally turned on the water faucet whenever she closeted herself in her private bathroom, which she often did.
† The drama in the courtroom was momentarily disrupted by some giggles when Maria described the hospital as the "Peter Pan Woman's Hospital."

whether Sunny had ever told her why she and Claus von Bülow were considering a divorce. But even Maria's explanation of that failure to tell the whole truth must have ingratiated her with the jurors: "I promised Mrs. von Bülow I wouldn't tell anyone . . . I still was hoping Mrs. von Bülow would come out of the coma, and I did not want to betray her."

2

The Son's Story:
The Search for the Black Bag

Although Maria was the star witness at the first trial, there was also a cast of supporting actors. The other leading characters included Claus's stepson, Alex; the family banker, Morris Gurley; Claus's mistress, Alexandra Isles; and several medical experts. The remaining witnesses were bit players who assumed center stage for a brief moment to fill out the details of the drama. The directors were the lawyers for the prosecution and defense who tried to weave the stories together to serve their clients' interests.

Alex's story really begins after his mother's final coma. He did, of course, fill in some of the details of the maid's accounts of the events leading up to the comas. He also provided corroboration for some parts of her story, especially her discovery if insulin in the black bag. But his own story was primarily important for the information it provided about the events that followed the medical determination that his mother's condition was "hopeless."

He was twenty-one years old at the time, a student at Brown University. The press dubbed him "the Student Prince." Strikingly handsome and soft-spoken, he testified in a sad monotone, giving brief answers and appearing respectful of authority. He was the only witness who had been with Sunny just before both comas. But his major importance as a witness was in describing the quiet investigation conducted by the family after the second coma.

This was a confusing and emotional time for Sunny's children, especially Alex and Ala. Claus talked to Ala about the possibility of turning off their mother's respirator and letting her die. There were discussions of their suspicions of Uncle Claus. A few weeks after Sunny's condition was diagnosed as hopeless, Alex, Ala and Claus were sitting in the New York apartment when Ala blurted out that she had heard rumors that Claus had been involved in an affair. Claus immediately acknowledged his involvement with Alexandra Isles, explaining that their mother had been "unable to have sex" since the birth of Cosima. Mrs. von Bülow, according to Claus, freed him to satisfy his sexual needs with other women, so long as he was discreet. Alex and Ala found it difficult to believe that their mother, a beautiful and very feminine woman, had abstained from sex during the previous thirteen years.

Suspicious of their stepfather, afraid for their mother, unwilling to permit public scandal to infiltrate their very private family, the children convened a secret meeting in the extravagant Manhattan apartment of Sunny's mother, Mrs. Annie Laurie Aitken. In addition to Alex and Ala, the others in attendance were Annie Laurie and Russell Aitken—Russell was Sunny's stepfather—and Morris Gurley, the family's banker and confidant.

The question before the group was whether to leave bad enough alone or to risk an investigation. No one wanted a scandal, especially if there was no objective basis for their suspicions. What would a public accusation of Claus von Bülow do to Cosima? But Alex was insistent that something had to be done, especially for Cosima's sake. "Should we let her spend her life with a man who tried to kill her mother?" he asked. Other matters were discussed as well, but they remained a guarded secret until after the first trial.

Gurley suggested that they move slowly. The first step should be to retain an experienced criminal lawyer to conduct a thorough but private investigation. They settled on Richard Kuh, the fifty-nine-year-old former District Attorney of Manhattan. Kuh had a mixed reputation as a prosecutor. As a young assistant D.A., he had pursued comedian Lenny Bruce with a vengeance, for the "obscenity" of his stage performances. Many considered him too aggressive. But he was also very smart, very determined and quite cultured. He had been appointed District Attorney of Manhattan upon the resignation of his boss, Frank Hogan, in 1974. But Kuh had many critics within his own office, and when he ran for election he was defeated decisively by Robert Morgenthau. (In an article for the *Village Voice* I had supported Kuh over Morgenthau.) He then joined a Manhattan law firm, where he handled a variety of cases. Gurley regarded him as the perfect blend of experience, discretion and determination for the difficult task of handling the von Bülow matter. Kuh undertook it with enthusiasm.

Kuh's first job was to meet with and debrief the important witnesses. His first meeting was with Alex and Ala on January 5, 1981, just over two weeks after their mother went into her final coma. The information given to him by the children—like the information given to him by Maria three days later—was never disclosed during the first trial. Although Kuh took detailed notes of what they told him, he regarded this information as privileged and confidential. After the defense subpoenaed the notes, Kuh brought them into court. But he and his clients formally invoked the privilege. The trial judge ruled the materials were privileged.

The jurors at the first trial did learn, however, that as a result of these initial meetings, a decision was made to investigate further. The target of this next investigative step was the black bag that Maria had shown to Ala in February and to Alex during the Thanksgiving weekend.

After the final coma, Maria had searched for the black bag in the places she had previously spotted it in the New York apartment. But it had vanished. Perhaps it was in Clarendon Court, they thought. Alex had searched for it there. Maybe it was in Uncle Claus's closet. He had gone to look. But the closet was locked. That seemed strange, since it was usually unlocked.

The family decided to send Alex to Newport along with a private investigator, hired by attorney Kuh, to get into that closet. They arranged for a locksmith to accompany them to Clarendon Court.

The trio went directly to Claus von Bülow's study. On top of Claus's desk was a note that read "metal box." It was almost as if a clue had been left in a deadly game of treasure hunt. Alex looked through the desk drawer and found a set of keys. They unlocked the closet door, and the searchers started to rummage around. After about an hour the investigator pointed something out to Alex. It was—sure enough—a metal box. Inside it was a black bag. "It looked similar to the bag that we had seen before in New York," Alex recalled.

Excitedly the three opened the black bag. Inside they found vials —some containing pills, some liquid. There were other items as well. But the most significant find—the one that caught their attention—was "three hypodermic needles." Two of them were sealed in their original containers, but one was loose. It appeared to have been used. They had found what they were looking for—the possible "attempted murder weapon." They also found a vial of Dalmane bearing a prescription label in the name of Claus von Bülow. Alexander had found the equivalent of Claus's "fingerprints" in the bag containing the attempted murder weapon.

Before leaving, they gathered together items they had found in several other rooms around the house, including vials found on Sunny's night table and in her bathroom medicine cabinet and in Claus's coat pockets and bathroom. For convenience they placed everything they had gathered together into the black bag, and they took the bag and its contents back to New York.

A few days later the contents of the bag—including the used needle—were given to the family doctor, Richard Stock, who sent them on to a laboratory. When the test results came back, they provided the last important missing piece of the puzzle. The loose needle had, in fact, been used. The residue that was left on it contained a high concentration of insulin, along with traces of Valium and amobarbital. By the time he received these results, Dr. Stock also knew that unusually high levels of insulin had been found in blood taken from Sunny's body immediately after she was admitted to Newport Hospital upon suffering her second coma.

It all seemed to fit together. Dr. Stock was now sure that Claus von Bülow had injected his wife with insulin. "Either you go to the police or I will," the doctor advised Richard Kuh. Kuh obtained permission from Alex and Ala to go public. He took the information first to the New York authorities—who said they had no jurisdiction over a possible crime committed in Rhode Island—and then went to the Rhode Island authorities, giving them what he believed to be the incriminating evidence against Claus von Bülow, while withholding his notes of interviews with witnesses, which he considered privileged.

The family's suspicions had turned to near certainty. They had the "smoking gun" in the insulin-encrusted needle; they had the matching "bullet wound" in the high level of insulin found in Sunny's blood at the time of the second coma; they had Claus's "fingerprints" on the "smoking gun" because the needle was found in his black bag. If there was any doubt about whose black bag it might have been, that doubt seemed to disappear when it was discovered that Leslie Baxter—whose name had appeared on one of the prescriptions found by Maria in the black bag in February—was a prostitute whom Claus had frequented. They even had a pattern of behavior, established by Claus's "unhusbandly" conduct during Sunny's first coma. Everything was beginning to fall neatly into place.

All they needed now was expert medical corroboration that Sunny's comas were caused by insulin injections, and a clearer sense of why Claus would be motivated to try to murder his wife. The family and their lawyer set out to tie up these few loose ends.

3

The Doctors' Story: Blood Sugar and Insulin

The prosecution's scientific case consisted of three different kinds of evidence. The first was eyewitness testimony of doctors who had hands-on contact with Sunny von Bülow. The second was the testimony of technicians who had tested substances for the presence of insulin and other relevant chemicals. And the third was the testimony of medical specialists who had never examined Sunny von Bülow, but who—in response to hypothetical questions—were able to give their expert opinions on the cause of Sunny's comas.

The primary hands-on medical witness was Janis Gailitis, the Newport doctor who had saved Sunny von Bülow after Claus had finally summoned him. A Soviet émigré from Latvia, Gailitis had been practicing in Newport for thirty years. In 1978 and 1979 he had treated Mrs. von Bülow for minor ailments. And then on December 27, 1979, he saw her suffer her first coma at Clarendon Court, as he described it in his heavily accented English:

> I got to the room, I wanted her quick examination, just listen to her lungs and by the time I got my stethoscope out of the bag, she vomited and she stopped breathing.

Prosecutor Famiglietti continued the questioning:

> Q. When you realized she had stopped breathing and she had experienced cardiac arrest, what did you do?
> A. I put my finger in her mouth, back of the throat, cleaned out as much as I could with my hands of vomitus, pulled her tongue forward, pulled the jaw forward, pinched her nose, gave mouth-to-mouth breathing, two breaths, pinched nose.
> Q. What happened next?

A. Well, after these two, I gave the pericardial punch, that is accepted thing, you take your fist and you whack on the chest. After that, I started chest compressions, cardiac resuscitation.

Dr. Gailitis also examined Sunny after her second coma. He was thus in a unique position to compare her two comas and to give an opinion as to their cause or causes. But he had no clear opinion, other than that the combination of barbiturates, hypoglycemia, alcohol and low body temperature would probably not have caused "permanent coma."

Dr. Gailitis readily acknowledged his lack of expertise in the highly specialized subjects of blood sugar, endocrinology and toxicity. He refused to speculate or to volunteer information or opinion other than in direct response to what he was asked by the lawyers. Ultimately he would tell a very different story, one that would make headlines across the country. But at the first trial Dr. Gailitis was a cautious yet valuable witness for the prosecution, despite his lack of expertise on the specialized issues central to the von Bülow case.

The prosecution was not lacking, however, in expertise. As its primary expert, it summoned Dr. George Cahill, professor of medicine at Harvard Medical School, and a dead ringer for actor James Garner. Dr. Cahill—whom the prosecutor referred to as "the expert's expert"—is "the guy that the endocrinologists go to when they're baffled." Widely regarded as the world's leading expert on blood sugar, he could not take the "Boards" in that subspecialty "because he wrote the examination"—as well as many of the leading papers, chapters and articles on the subject. From 1962 to 1978 Dr Cahill was the director of the Joslin Research Laboratories, a world-renowned center that specializes in blood-sugar disorders. As a young doctor, he had been involved in developing the first tests designed to determine the presence of insulin in the human body.

Dr. Cahill's job was to try to explain to the jury, in terms that laypeople could understand, why the laboratory tests established to a medical certainty that the only cause of both of Mrs. von Bülow's comas must have been insulin injected into her body. The laboratory tests, according to the prosecution, showed that when Sunny was admitted to the hospital for her first coma, her blood sugar was down to 41 milligrams percent. She was then given glucose "pushes"—intravenous sugar. But even after receiving these pushes, her blood sugar continued to go down. Indeed, three hours and forty-five minutes after her admission, her blood sugar had gone down from 41 to 20 milligrams percent.

Dr. Cahill was given a hypothetical question based on the circumstances surrounding Mrs. von Bülow's case and asked whether he had "an opinion within a reasonable degree of medical certainty as to the cause of this woman's coma." He said he did, and that his opinion was that the first coma was caused by "exogenous insulin" —that is, insulin from outside the body. An injection of insulin! Dr. Cahill explained that the continued lowering of the patient's blood sugar even after administration of substantial amounts of glucose "can only be due to insulin or an insulin-like factor telling the tissues in her body to consume glucose at a rapid rate." Cahill excluded "all the other nine possible causes, with the exception of exogenous insulin."

He was just as certain about Mrs. von Bülow's second coma. The laboratory evidence concerning the second coma was even more compelling than the evidence concerning the first. Mrs. von Bülow's blood sugar upon admission was again low—29 milligrams percent. But there was also a serum insulin level that the prosecution claimed was taken from the same blood sample that produced the sugar level. That insulin level was extraordinarily high—216 microunits per milliliter, the normal range being under 15. The combination of low blood sugar and high insulin level supported the prosecutor's theory that her low blood sugar was *caused* by high insulin—an amount far higher than her body would produce naturally. Dr. Cahill agreed with the prosecution's theory, concluding that only exogenous insulin could explain the simultaneous low blood-sugar and high insulin levels.

The defense tried to shake the prosecution's case by challenging some of the lab results, cross-examining the prosecution's experts and introducing one medical expert of its own. But it could do little to cast doubt on the elegant simplicity and clarity of Dr. Cahill's presentation. The most the defense could get out of its own expert witness, Dr. Milton Hamolsky of Brown Medical School, was his opinion that although he believed that other factors had probably caused the comas, he could not "exclude" exogenous insulin as the cause of one or both of the comas "with reasonable medical certainty."

When the prosecution's expert—indeed, the "expert's expert"— is virtually certain of the cause, and the defense expert cannot exclude that very cause, it is not surprising that the jury would be inclined to agree with the prosecution's expert. This would be especially so where, as in the von Bülow case, the prosecution's witness was far more of an expert on the relevant subject, was supported by several other experts and treating physicians, and had the lab tests to back up his conclusion. It seemed clear at the close of the medical portion of the case that the jury would conclude that Sunny von Bülow's comas were both caused by injections of insulin.

This still left open the crucial question—a question none of the experts or scientific tests could answer—*who* had injected Sunny with insulin: Did she inject herself? Or did her husband do it? That question would have to be answered by looking at the souls and hearts of the only two possible suspects, rather than at any test tubes or lab results. The focus was now on "motive"—that elusive quality present in so many, yet acted on by so few.

4

The Banker's and the Mistress's Story: Greed, Love and Lust

Prosecutors like to tell jurors that the defendant is sure to be guilty if he had "the motive, the means and the opportunity" to commit the crime. The family and the prosecutor certainly believed that they could prove Claus had the means; that the insulin found in Sunny's body had been injected by Claus using the insulin-encrusted needle found in his black bag. There was some uncertainty about opportunity, at least for the second coma, because Sunny had begun to grow weak after the family had all been together for several hours and before Claus had been alone with her. But they still thought they could get the jury to believe that he might have slipped something into her drink or chicken soup and then injected her when she fell asleep. Now all they had to prove was motive.

To establish a financial motive, the prosecution called Morris Gurley, who had advised Sunny on her financial and testamentary decisions. To establish a love motive, they called a flashy television soap-opera actress named Alexandra Isles, who had been Claus's mistress during the relevant periods of time.

The banker's story was short but persuasive. Gurley testified that after graduating from Harvard Law School, he had joined the Chemical Bank in New York, where he rose to become vice president in charge of personal trust management. In that capacity, he administered about one hundred "very substantial trusts," including Sunny von Bülow's and her mother's. He did for Sunny financially what Maria did personally: paying household staff as well as other bills; collecting the income; making charitable gifts; taking care of the various houses and properties. Gurley knew as much about Sunny's financial life as the maid did about her personal life. He was the perfect witness to tell the jury what Claus von Bülow could have expected in any eventuality—ranging from divorce to coma to death.

What he told the jurors left them with little doubt that Claus von Bülow had a powerful motive to murder his wife. He explained that under her will, Claus would receive approximately $14 million. This would include Clarendon Court, the New York apartment and all of the lavish furnishings. There were other benefits as well, including control over vast charitable gifts and a fixed income from other trusts. All in all, a widowed Claus von Bülow could live in baronial style, overseeing a fabulously wealthy domain.

Gurley also testified that Claus von Bülow knew precisely what he would stand to gain from his wife's death. While Sunny was somewhat involved in her own financial affairs, Claus had taken a keen interest in Sunny's will and trusts, especially during the last few years. Gurley told the jury that Claus had brought very little capital into the marriage and had earned a pittance during his fourteen years with Sunny. No wonder he had once told Alex that he often felt like a kept man—a "gigolo"—in the company of Sunny's Newport friends.

Gurley's testimony made it clear that Claus would not remain nearly as wealthy if he and Sunny were to be divorced. In that eventuality, Claus would retain the income he was receiving from an irrevocable trust that Sunny had set up for him—approximately $120,000 per year. And perhaps he would get some kind of cash settlement from her, as Prince Alfie had. But he would lose Clarendon Court, the New York apartment and the virtually unlimited funds he would have access to in the event of Sunny's death. More than a hundred thousand dollars a year may seem an awful lot to most of us—and certainly to the jurors—but it was not nearly enough to allow Claus von Bülow to continue the lavish life-style to which he had become accustomed as Sunny's husband. It would certainly not satisfy the combined expensive tastes of Claus and the woman he hoped to marry.

The other woman in Claus von Bülow's life came right out of central casting. Indeed, in her professional life she had been cast in the role of the beautiful Victoria Winters in the TV soap opera *Dark Shadows*. But Alexandra Isles was more than a soap-opera actress. She was a woman of breeding and style, precisely the kind of person who would appeal to Claus von Bülow.

Claus and Alexandra's relationship had family origins. Alexandra was Swedish by birth, but her father was a Danish count who knew Claus's parents. Both Claus's and Alexandra's grandfathers had been ministers in the Danish government—Claus's was minister of justice, Alexandra's was foreign minister. When the Nazis invaded Denmark, Alexandra's father, Count Moltke, was among those who helped to smuggle young Claus out of Denmark in the belly of a Mosquito bomber. Claus maintained his friendship with the Moltkes during his years in England and the United States.

Alexandra left Sweden as a baby and grew up in New York. Her early life was not very different from Sunny's: the Chapin School (which Sunny had attended years earlier), a debut in the 1964–65 season, membership in the Colony Club, marriage and a child, followed by a divorce. But Claus's two women were as different as two people who came from similar backgrounds can be. Sunny's passivity was contrasted with Alexandra's high energy level. Sunny's matronliness was in sharp contrast to Alexandra's torrid sexuality. Sunny's naïveté was strikingly different from Alexandra's shrewdness.

It was inevitable that Claus and Alexandra would meet. What is surprising is that they did not actually encounter each other until a chance meeting at New York's exclusive Knickerbocker Club (most decidedly not a basketball fan club) in April 1978. They discussed their common Danish background, and Claus learned that Alexandra's father was Count Moltke. An instantaneous friendship was formed, soon to be followed by a passionate romance.

By March 1979 they were talking about marriage—and, inevitably, divorce. Claus suggested that "it would save face" if Sunny were the one to initiate a divorce. Each time they met thereafter, the question of Claus's divorce arose.

Finally, in April, Alexandra issued an "ultimatum" in the form of a question: "Would six months be suitable?" She "was thinking about October."

During the summer of 1979, Alexandra went off to Ireland to visit her mother. When she returned, "there was tension between us. . . . I thought maybe he didn't mean that he wanted to be with me . . . I doubted his ability to . . . maybe, to make a breach [and get] a divorce."

Over Christmas, Alexandra returned to Ireland. On December 27, the phone rang in her mother's home. It was Claus. His wife was in a coma.

When Alexandra returned to New York, Claus filled her in on

the details of his wife's 1979 coma, from which Sunny had fully recovered. Alexandra came away believing that it might have been a suicide attempt prompted by Sunny's awareness of Claus's love for his mistress. "I thought that perhaps, not—it may not have been an active suicide attempt, but it could have been a passive one." Because of her fear, Alexandra stayed away from Claus for the next few months. She was relieved to learn, in May, that hospital tests had established Sunny's coma came from "natural causes . . . within her own body, and, so, there wasn't the element of suicide anymore."

The romance continued through the summer of 1980, although Alexandra was still looking for some visible demonstration that her status would soon change from mistress to wife. In the late summer, Claus told Alexandra that he had gotten himself an apartment. Alexandra was thrilled. But when she asked "how his wife felt about it," Claus's lack of response made it clear that he was still trying to have it both ways. Yes, he had an apartment, but yes, he was still living with his wife. Alexandra later commented that Claus's new apartment was furnished with nothing but "a roll of toilet paper."

Alexandra was furious. She went to Washington for a job and moved into a place "where I couldn't be reached." But Claus managed to reach her and they met for coffee at the Watergate Hotel. At this "Watergate meeting"—as it was referred to at the trial—Claus proposed marriage again, but Alexandra was still angry and said no. Claus returned to New York.

At the beginning of December he called to inform her of his wife's concussion and aspirin overdose. Their relationship had ceased being intimate at this time, but Alexandra still had warm feelings toward Claus, and she invited him to her son's carol recitation before Christmas. On December 19, 1980—the day Claus and Sunny made their final trip to Newport together—Alexandra dropped off some Christmas presents at the von Bülows' Fifth Avenue building. One of Alexandra's gifts for Claus was wrapped in paper depicting a broken heart with a Band-Aid over it. The jury never learned what was contained in the packages, which were apparently delivered to the apartment after Claus and Sunny left for Newport.

The next time Claus spoke to Alexandra, it was to advise her that his wife was in an irreversible coma.

In January 1981 the couple saw each other more frequently, and in February they went off together, with her eleven-year-old son,

Adam, to Nassau. (Cosima was scheduled to come along, but she developed chicken pox.) The trip was supposed to be a trial period of living together "as a family," an attempt to "build bridges." Two months later they took another trip, this time with Cosima, to Florida.

As the romance was blossoming, so was the investigation into the causes of Sunny's comas. Alexandra knew that Claus was suspected of trying to kill his wife, "but I thought it was a pack of nonsense." After Claus was indicted in July 1981, Alexandra's attorney advised her to stay away from him. Except for a visit together on Christmas eve of 1981, she heeded her lawyer's advice.

During her examination by prosecutor Famiglietti, Alexandra was asked how she felt about the fact "that people were referring to you as his mistress." "I didn't like it," she acknowledged. "Do you still love the defendant?" she was asked. After a pause, she responded sadly, "I don't know." The prosecutor also asked her whether she still thought the attempted murder charges against Claus were "a pack of nonsense." Courtroom observers turned toward the defense attorney, expecting an objection. But none was forthcoming. Alexandra answered: "I don't know."

For a jury to hear the defendant's lover—a woman who still obviously had strong feelings for the man she had hoped to marry—express uncertainty about her belief in his innocence must have been devastating to the defense.

When Alexandra's direct testimony was over, it was the turn of the defense to cross-examine her. But chief defense counsel Herald Price Fahringer made a dramatic announcement:

> Your Honor, after some consideration last night in discussing this matter with Mr. von Bülow, it was his decision that he did not wish to submit Mrs. Isles to any further public examination. Based upon that judgment, your Honor, we are not going to cross-examine her.

It was reported that Claus von Bülow had said that a "gentlemen does not permit cross-examination of his lover." Some observers suspected that a more sinister motive was lurking behind this gentlemanly façade. In an interview after the trial, Alexandra Isles told a reporter that Claus's "chivalry story" was far from the truth. "Why they didn't cross-examine me was obvious," she told the reporter, continuing suggestively, "There could have been some bombs dropped." One of her friends elaborated: "She could have said a great deal more than she did say. Had she said these things, they would have been very bad for Claus. She did not lie, but she was very generous with the stuff she did not reveal . . . Even if he has treated her disgustingly, she doesn't want to be the one who does him in."

Neither the jury nor the public learned what these bombs were—at least not at the first trial. And although it was not Alexandra's testimony that did Claus in at the first trial—that distinction was reserved for the maid—it certainly contributed to his troubles. The jury had now heard and seen the beautiful woman who had given Claus the famous ultimatum: Leave Sunny or lose me! Was she enough for a man to want to kill for, especially if the killing might also earn him more than $14 million? That would be for the jury to decide—a jury composed of men and women who could only fantasize about the glamour and wealth paraded before them.

That in essence was the prosecution's case: The suspicious maid providing eyewitness testimony about Claus's unhusbandly behavior and the black bag. The angry son searching for the black bag and finding an insulin-encrusted needle inside it. The experts testifying that Sunny's comas had both been caused by exogenous insulin. The banker demonstrating how Claus would profit by the death of his wife. And the beautiful mistress exhibiting to the jury why a man might kill rather than lose her. It was the stuff of which Agatha Christie novels were made. Perhaps a bit too pat and predictable, but everything fit together—unless the defense could dismantle this neat construct during its case. But the defense case at the first trial never managed to get off the ground.

5

Joy O'Neill's Story: The Defense Case

In a criminal case, the defense is not obligated to call any witnesses or introduce any evidence. It can simply try to disprove the prosecution's case by cross-examining its witnesses or by relying on the presumption of the defendant's innocence. Many, perhaps even most, defendants put on no case. This is for a simple reason: They have no case to put on. The defendant is guilty as sin (an inept phrase, for many crimes are worse than some sins). The only case most defendants could put on would be a perjurious one. Lawyers do not relish the prospect of calling liars to the stand to swear that they were in church with the defendant while the bank was being robbed. Nor do most defense lawyers want their guilty clients to testify on their own behalf. Liars almost always make awful witnesses, easy to demolish on cross-examination. It's far easier to remember the details of the truth than to "remember" the details of a lie.

Moreover, most defendants do have something they want to hide from the jury. Guilty defendants want to hide the truth about their involvement in the crime. Even innocent defendants often want to hide their prior criminal records, their affairs, their perversions or their dishonesty. In many cases, the best chance a defense lawyer has—and a slim chance it is—is to point out the weaknesses in the prosecution's case. These weaknesses may sometimes mean that the defendant is innocent. More frequently, they may mean that the prosecution has had difficulty putting together a convincing case even though the defendant is guilty.

In Claus von Bülow's situation, there was no prior record and his affair was out in the open. But there were other reasons for keeping him off the witness stand. His lawyers might have concluded that he would make a poor witness because of his haughty and condescending personality. (He liked to excuse this characteristic by pointing out that he could not help being born a melancholy Dane with an austere upbringing and a dour expression.) There may have been other facts that they feared could emerge if he took the stand.

For example, it was rumored that while von Bülow was a British barrister serving in the chambers of Lord Hailsham, another judge in the same chambers presided over the murder prosecution of Kenneth Barlow. That case involved a hapless hospital attendant who had devised what he considered to be the perfect murder. He injected his wife with insulin, which was then considered undetectable in the human body. But Barlow had not kept up with new developments in medical technology. The insulin was detected and Barlow was convicted.*

The trial judge on the von Bülow case had not allowed the prosecution to tell the jury about Claus von Bülow's possible knowledge of the murder-by-insulin case. If Claus had taken the witness stand, the judge might have let the prosecution ask him whether he was familiar with this case. Although familiarity with the case would mean that Claus also knew that insulin *was* detectable, and that the culprit was convicted in a widely publicized trial, the defense might have feared that the danger of the jury's learning about Claus's knowledge of murder by insulin outweighed the advantage.

There were other unfounded rumors surrounding Claus's bachelor days in England, including suggestions of necrophilia, homosexuality, incest and practically every other imaginable—and some quite unimaginable—human vice. In fact some of these rumors had become so persistent that Richard Kuh, the von Auersperg family lawyer, hired an English investigative agency to probe the background of the bachelor barrister. The defense knew that the agency had submitted a detailed report, but they were denied access to its contents. They feared that the secret report and other information that Kuh had refused to disclose to the defense might provide a basis for blindside questions if von Bülow were to be cross-examined. It was as if Richard Kuh were lurking behind the duck blind, ready to take aim at the sitting von Bülow, if he dared to take the stand. Fahringer later commented that "Claus von Bülow did not take

---

* The British court records reveal that barrister Bülow was assigned to a different circuit during the relevant period and could not have had a professional connection with the Barlow case.

the witness stand because we didn't think the prosecution had made a sufficient case against him. But it's no secret that his personality was another problem."

For whatever reason or reasons, the defense decided not to put Claus von Bülow on the witness stand. That still left open the possibility of putting on a strong defense case without the defendant himself. Some defense attorneys believe that if the defendant himself does not take the witness stand, no other defense witness should be put on. They reason that a defense case without the defendant—*Hamlet* without the prince—serves to underline to the jury the fact that the defendant must have something to hide. Other defense attorneys have had success in putting on a strong defense case even without the defendant himself. (The John DeLorean cocaine case was a brilliant example of that technique.)

The von Bülow defense team at the first trial decided to put on a defense case, but in the end the strategy backfired.

Their star witness, a woman named Joy O'Neill, was an exercise instructor who had supervised Sunny's exercise program at the exclusive Manya Kahn Studio. She was not originally listed as a witness for either side, but midway through the trial she had called the prosecutor's office and disclosed what she knew. The prosecutors alerted the defense lawyers to her information and she was called as a defense witness.

Joy O'Neill testified that she had given Sunny private instruction for four years "on the average of five days a week." During these sessions the two had become very close, discussing family, religion, life and death. They had even talked about Sunny's "marital situation." They had been friends and eventually became "like sisters." In 1978, during an exercise class, Joy had complained to Sunny that she—Joy—was gaining weight because she was drinking wine. Sunny offered some advice: "What you probably need is a shot of insulin or vitamin B." By injecting insulin, Sunny explained, you "could eat anything you want and have sweets and everything." The idea was that insulin "eats up" the sugar and metabolizes it. She also suggested injecting liquid Valium to calm Joy down.

That testimony was just what the defense needed. If true, it would be a complete answer to the government's hard evidence against Claus. Yes, there was a high level of insulin in Sunny's blood. Yes, her comas were caused by insulin. Yes, there was insulin on the needle in the black bag. All that might be true. But it was *Sunny*, not Claus, who administered the injections. It neatly accounted for nearly all the government's evidence, while leaving a reasonable doubt about the defendant's guilt. There were still Claus's motives to kill. But many men who stand to gain from their wives' demise do not kill them. They may think about it. They might even welcome a self-administered death. But that does not make them murderers or attempted murderers. Moreover, the very facts that might lead a husband to want to kill his wife—loss of love, infidelity— might lead a wife who was aware of these facts to engage in self-destructive acts. Indeed, one of the prosecution's own medical witnesses had surmised that the insulin injection might have been self-administered. The Joy O'Neill testimony was the perfect defense —*if* it was true.

No one except Joy O'Neill will probably ever know if any of the alleged conversation to which she testified really took place. What the jury did learn, however, was devastating to the defense case. The prosecution was able to prove in rebuttal that according to the records of the Manya Kahn Studio, Joy O'Neill had not given private instruction to Sunny von Bülow five times a week for four years. Rather, she had taught her only a handful of times, and never during 1978, the year when the alleged insulin conversation had taken place. Joy O'Neill's credibility was torn apart before the jury's eyes. No jury would now believe her testimony about what Sunny—her "close friend"—had allegedly told her concerning insulin injections.

The rest of the defense case did not backfire, but neither did it provide much affirmative firepower. An assortment of minor characters—such as the locksmith who had accompanied Alex and the investigator to Clarendon Court; the family chauffeur; Claus's former boss; an art dealer; Dr. Hamolsky, the expert witness; a medical technician who had heard Sunny discuss suicide; and a psychiatrist who had spent about half an hour with Sunny talking about her unhappy life—all contradicted some details of the prosecution's case and lent some credibility to the defense. But none of these witnesses did any real damage to the tight structure of the prosecution's circumstantial case, which was based heavily on hard scientific evidence, eyewitness testimony and compelling motives.

6

The Lawyers' Stories: Irresistible Combinations

The evidence was now over and it was time for the lawyers to tell their stories. According to law, the prosecutor and the defense attorney are not supposed to tell stories of their own. They are merely supposed to summarize and organize the stories told by the witnesses. But realistically, the lawyers are given substantial leeway to draw inferences from the facts. What emerges are stories as well—stories that may have as much impact on the jury as the testimony of any witness.

Under Rhode Island practice, the defense attorney summarizes his case first. Herald Price Fahringer had to be a pretty good storyteller to win this case. Many courtroom observers believed he needed to tell a fairy tale, since he had so little evidence to go on. The old saw is that when a lawyer has the facts on his side, he should pound in the facts; when he has the law on his side, he should pound in the law; and when he has neither the facts nor the law on his side, he should pound on the table. But Fahringer was not a table-pounder. He was a soft-spoken gentleman—tall, greying at the temples and articulate, he bore a striking resemblance in manner to his client Claus von Bülow. Herald Price Fahringer looked like a rich man's lawyer. In fact, his nickname was "Hy Price" Fahringer. He had a string of successful defenses behind him—especially in the pornography area. But he had not defended many cases of this kind before. When Fahringer got up to address the jury, it was almost—but not quite—as if Claus himself were finally deigning to tell the jurors his story.

Fahringer spoke softly and elegantly, thanking the jurors for the attention they had given throughout the long trial and advising them of "the awful solemnity of the occasion." He reminded them of the pledge they had all taken before the trial to presume his client's innocence and to remain unprejudiced by his marital infidelity. "I believed in you when you said you would follow that law. I trust you."

He then proceeded to discuss the evidence. He began—unexpectedly—with the "man himself." "Is Mr. von Bülow the type of man . . . who would, on two separate occasions, assault his wife with an intent to murder her by injecting her with insulin?" It was a surprising opening, because the jurors knew virtually nothing about Claus von Bülow except what they had heard from Maria Schrallhammer. Nor had von Bülow refuted any of the negative characterizations provided by the maid. By not taking the stand to answer the devastating eyewitness accounts of his callous behavior, he had—in effect—admitted that he was not the most caring of husbands, that he was guilty of "unhusbandly conduct." To be sure, the distance between "unhusbandly" and "murderous" conduct required an enormous leap of logic. But a jury does not always employ mathematical logic in arriving at its conclusions, and it was a questionable tactic to begin the defense argument by focusing the jury's attention on two of the most dangerous aspects of the case against von Bülow —the maid's eyewitness account and von Bülow's failure to dispute it.

Fahringer then went on to discuss the first coma. Arguing that Sunny had consumed enough eggnog the night before to cause her to become intoxicated, Fahringer tried to get the jury to understand why Claus would have been reluctant to call a doctor. "You have a situation where it is well known [Sunny] doesn't want the doctor to be called unless it is necessary." He reminded the jury that Claus did eventually call the doctor, who arrived and saved her life.

Proceeding to the second coma, the defense attorney emphasized to the jury that Sunny had eaten a caramel sundae and later had to be carried into her bedroom—before Claus was alone with her.

He concluded by focusing the jury's attention on the numerous reasonable doubts in the case against his client:

> How do you explain all of her other illnesses? How do you explain December 1st when he saved her life, just two or three weeks before the last episode? I think these are all reasonable doubts. I think if you counted up the reasonable doubts in this case, you could find a dozen or more, any one of which would support a verdict of not guilty in this case.

Defense attorney Fahringer's emphasis on the "dozen or more" reasonable doubts gave prosecutor Famiglietti his opening. Famiglietti contrasted Fahringer's "multiple-choice defense" with his own "true-or-false" prosecution:

> It was interesting for me to sit here [and watch how] the defense strategy gradually evolved. . . . As the State's witnesses came in one by one, and . . . proved beyond a reasonable doubt that it could not be eggnog that caused the 1979 coma, and it was not amobarbital that caused the 1980 coma, then the theory of the defense changed, . . . into what I like to call the multiple-choice defense.
>   . . .
> What is the multiple-choice defense? A, the cause of the comas [was] reactive hypoglycemia which was provoked by (1) eggnog, (2) amobarbital, (3) aspirin, (4) low body temperature, (5) an ice cream sundae with caramel sauce, (6) an ice cream sundae with marshmallow fluff, (7) a mysterious, sudden, spontaneous disease that no one has ever even discovered yet.
> Multiple-choice B: If you believe that it was exogenous insulin, then Martha von Bülow was giving it to herself. That's otherwise known as the Joy O'Neill defense. Martha von Bülow was giving it to herself in an effort to lose weight.
> C, if . . . you don't believe that the comas were the result of a deliberate attempt on the part of Martha von Bülow to lose weight, then they were the results of a deliberate attempt on her part to commit suicide. Now, it's unclear, ladies and gentlemen, whether or not the suicide was with insulin or whether the suicide was with the ice cream sundae or the eggnog. That hasn't been made clear.
> D, multiple-choice D, all of the above.

At this point even Famiglietti began to get carried away by his rhetoric:

> E, none of the above. Martha von Bülow was hit in the head with an invisible meteorite from outer space. That's the multiple-choice defense here, ladies and gentlemen. The only thing that the defense has not argued to you could have been involved in her comas was the fact that she had a face-lift in 1978.

But he soon returned from space rocks and face-lifts and got back down to earth:

Now, the State's position in this case is just a little bit . . . more direct. True or false, Claus von Bülow administered exogenous insulin to his wife in an attempt to kill her on two separate occasions; that's the ultimate issue, true or false.

In his attempt to get the jury to check the "true" box, Famiglietti began at the beginning:

Who was it that really started the investigation? . . . Was it Mr. von Auersperg? Was it Mr. Kuh? No, ladies and gentlemen, it was Maria Schrallhammer.

He then went on to bolster the credibility of the loving and caring maid's testimony about Claus's unhusbandly conduct during the first coma, the discovery of the black bag, and Claus's decision to leave Maria in New York at the time of the second coma.

Turning to motive, Famiglietti riveted the jury's attention on the "irresistible combination" of Alexandra Isles's beauty and Sunny von Bülow's wealth. Claus wanted both, and the only way he could get both was by arranging for Sunny to die, leaving much of her money to him, and leaving him free to marry Alexandra.

Another irresistible combination embellished by the prosecutor was the fact that a high level of insulin was found in Sunny's blood, that insulin was seen by Maria in the black bag, and that insulin was found on the needle. Famiglietti asked the jury, rhetorically: "Do you think that's the most incredible coincidence in the history of mankind?" The prosecutor reminded the jury that "the defense has stipulated to the fact that there was insulin on the needle." Why the defense was willing to so stipulate—thereby eliminating the need for the prosecution to prove it—was never explained. The importance of that stipulation cannot be exaggerated, since the prosecution referred to the needle as the "murder weapon." If the needle was the weapon, then the stipulation that it was encrusted with insulin made it into the "smoking gun." And the high level of insulin found in Sunny's blood was the equivalent of finding a bullet in the victim's body that matched the ballistics markings of the smoking gun.

Nor could there be any doubt whose black bag was found with insulin in it. Famiglietti pointed out that a vial of Dalmane found in the same black bag, at the same time, had a prescription label on it made out to Claus von Bülow. It was like finding his fingerprint on the insulin-coated needle.

Famiglietti also hammered home the fact that Claus was the only person in the household who knew how to administer injections or who had ever had access to syringes and needles: "Where is the only evidence in this case as to which of the two people were familiar with a needle and syringe . . . ?" he asked, reminding the jurors that Claus had been seen with syringes in Majorca and that no one had ever seen Mrs. von Bülow with hypodermic paraphernalia. Nor did Sunny have any problems with alcohol or drugs. Indeed, Claus's suggestion to the doctors that Sunny had an alcohol problem was presented by Famiglietti as evidence of his guilt.

The prosecution's closing argument seemed to leave little room for the jury to find reasonable doubt. The state's case appeared airtight. For the jury to acquit, it would have to disbelieve many different witnesses and to discredit much independent evidence. Even if Maria's testimony—the most direct eyewitness account—was discounted, the jury could base a conviction on the expert medical evidence. If the medical evidence was doubted, there were still the scientific laboratory facts that insulin was found on the "murder weapon" and in the victim's blood. Any doubts about this evidence could be resolved in favor of conviction by looking to the "irresistible combination" of motives—lust and lucre.

In light of this overwhelming amount of evidence all pointing circumstantially to Claus von Bülow's guilt, the only surprise to many observers was how long it took the jury to arrive at its verdict. Part of the reason may have been the length of the trial itself. The longest trial in Rhode Island history, it had taken nine weeks. The length of the deliberations also broke the previous Rhode Island record. It took the jurors nearly six days to decide whether Claus von Bülow had twice tried to kill his wife. Just before they rendered their verdict, the jurors asked to have read to them Maria's testimony about Claus's behavior during the first coma. Shortly after rehearing this chilling account, the jury told the judge it had come to a decision. Claus von Bülow was guilty on both counts.

The gasps and expressions of shock from some courtroom observers may have reflected emotional support for Claus von Bülow as much as a rational determination that he was innocent. A journalist who covered the trials reported that at the beginning "most seasoned reporters believed von Bülow would be found innocent." But as the trial progressed, "informed opinion began to swing against him." By the end "almost everyone who actually saw the trial every day [believed] that he [was] guilty." Indeed, I was told by a reporter for a TV network that one of Claus von Bülow's own lawyers had told the reporter that the evidence pointed to his client's guilt. John Sheehan, the local Rhode Island lawyer who assisted Fahringer in the defense, did publicly comment that "they had overwhelming evidence against us." And Fahringer, after observing that "the prosecution pretty much overwhelmed us with experts," remarked that "in a case like Claus von Bülow's, there's no way in the world you're going to be able to get twelve jurors who can sympathize with him." Claus von Bülow accepted the verdict with his usual stoic posture, interrupted only by the split-second twitch seen throughout the country on the evening news.

Sentencing was scheduled for May 7, 1982. Von Bülow faced a maximum sentence of forty years in prison. Any substantial prison term would mean a life sentence for the fifty-six-year-old Dane. *New York* magazine reported that the Mob had passed the word that it would cost Claus von Bülow $1,000 a week for protection in the rough Rhode Island prisons. There were rumors that von Bülow would try to leave the country or kill himself rather than face imprisonment for the rest of his life.

The next critical issue was whether von Bülow would be allowed to remain out on bail—or would be required to begin whatever sentence the judge imposed—while he pursued an appeal from his conviction. That issue was to serve as my stormy introduction to the case.

Part

II

BETWEEN
THE TRIALS:
A HARD
SECOND LOOK

7

Learning the Rhode Island Shuffle

If the first trial told, in essence, the maid's story, then an account of the period between the two trials tells my story: how I became involved in the case; how I assembled the new team whose goals were to turn around public opinion, obtain a reversal of the conviction, and lay the strategic and evidentiary framework for any new trial; and how we achieved those goals. The period following a trial—the appeal phase—is always the lawyer's time. Clients generally play little or no role once the trial has ended.

The bail issue was to be my first involvement in the von Bülow case, but even before I could get down to working on that important issue, I had to jump through some flaming hoops.

My entry into the case was neither smooth nor pleasant. After Claus called me on April Fools' Day, I went from Cambridge, Massachusetts, to New York to confer with him. Although I am a full-time law teacher at Harvard Law School, I do take occasional appeals in criminal or civil liberties cases. Before agreeing to take this case, I insisted that Claus read the galley proofs of *The Best Defense*, a book about several of my earlier cases which was about to be published. The book described my confrontational legal style as well as my impression that the vast majority of convicted defendants were guilty, and I wanted von Bülow to know exactly what he would be getting if he selected me to argue his appeal. The proofs were sent to him by Express Mail and we arranged an appointment.

I knew very little about Claus von Bülow before our first meeting, barely having followed the first trial. But like most criminal lawyers, I had my opinions. At a dinner party with several professors on the Saturday night before the jury verdict, the assembled guests discussed the Newport circus. I ventured the view that two things seemed clear: first, that von Bülow was guilty; and second, that he would get off. The reason for my second conclusion had nothing to do with either the evidence or the brillance of his defense. It was based on my assessment of the response to von Bülow as a person by the Newport townies. The TV coverage had highlighted the "Clausettes" wearing "Free Claus" T-shirts, and the courthouse crowds shouting their support of the celebrity defendant. A movie theater near the courthouse had even taken down the title of its current film and substituted the slogan of von Bülow's supporters: "Free Claus."

By the time I met von Bülow, my second conclusion had been proved wrong—the jury had found him guilty. But I still adhered to my first conclusion: that he was probably guilty.

Claus asked me to meet him at the apartment on Fifth Avenue. As I approached the imposing façade overlooking Central Park, I reflected on the differences in our backgrounds. For my parents from Brooklyn, Fifth Avenue was a tourist attraction, a part of New York City's culture—to be viewed and appreciated, but not touched or partaken of. Though I had passed by many of the elegant mansions along Fifth Avenue on my way to and from the museums, I had never actually been inside one. Throughout my life I had never been impressed by wealth. To the contrary, I was always vaguely condescending, especially toward those who had inherited or married wealth. As a youngster, I never knew any rich people. My neighborhood in Brooklyn was home to workers, shopkeepers and owners of small family-run businesses. There were few professionals and no old money. My father and a partner owned a small store on the Lower East Side of Manhattan, which sold wholesale during the week and retail on Sunday. My father was proud to be his own boss, even if he didn't always make as much as those who worked for others.

I went to Brooklyn College, a city school that charged no tuition and required its students to live at home. My classmates came from backgrounds similar to my own. My first encounter with the nouveaux riches was at a Jewish summer camp in Livingston Manor, New York, where I worked as a counselor. Many of the paying campers came from the Upper West Side of Manhattan and the wealthier suburbs encircling the city. The counselors—most of whom were from poor families in Brooklyn—treated the rich kids contemptuously. We were the better athletes, the stronger fighters—even the more verbal and (we thought) more clever. All they had was money, and money didn't do them much good in summer camp, where the garb was sneakers and shorts and there were few visible accoutrements of wealth. You made it in camp on your street smarts and natural skills, and in those departments we had it all over the rich kids from uptown and suburbia.

My first experience with old money—real wealth—came at Yale Law School. My classmates at that elite institution, which admitted only 150 students a year from all over the world, included descendants of the wealthiest families in America—the du Ponts, the Danforths and the Heinzes. During my three years at Yale I encountered sons (and a very few daughters) of Supreme Court Justices, governors, senators, and captains of industry. But there again, wealth was not much of an advantage in a system that was based on blind grading. After clerking for two years, I entered the law-teaching profession and have been at Harvard for the past two decades. Justice Felix Frankfurter once described Harvard Law School as the "most democratic institution I know anything about. By democratic I mean regard for the intrinsic and nothing else." And it was in that kind of environment that I had decided to spend my professional life.

If law school was the most democratic environment, then Claus von Bülow's world was about the least. Antecedents were everything; the intrinsic worth of the person meant little. There was no blind grading in the world of Newport society. *Who* you were— really who your "people" had been—was the primary basis for evaluation.

The person who initially recommended me to Claus had one foot planted squarely in each of our worlds. I met Gilbert Verbit when we were both on the *Yale Law Journal*. He had also become a law professor—at Boston University Law School, across the Charles River from Harvard. He had family connections with Newport society and summered amidst the splendor of the mansions and exclusive beach clubs of that gilded ghetto. After Claus was convicted, he had asked Verbit for a recommendation of a lawyer who specialized in criminal appeals, and Gil had given him my name. I remember having wondered how von Bülow had come up with me; I doubted that we knew anyone in the world in common. When he told me it had come from Verbit I was pleased, because I have the highest regard for Gil as a scholar and a person.*

---

* Claus had also conferred with retired Justice Abe Fortas just days before his death.

All these jumbled thoughts were racing around in my head as I approached the entrance to 960 Fifth Avenue. The uniformed doorman anticipated my introduction by saying, "Professor Dershowitz, Mr. von Bülow is expecting you," and sending me to the wood-paneled elevator, which took me to the von Bülow floor. As I left the elevator, I felt I was in a different world. The two hallways I passed through to get into the sitting room (which led into the enormous living room) were decorated with museum pieces. Marble, silver and gold were the dominant materials; open space—both depth and height—was the dominant feeling; opulence was the dominant impression. I noticed immediately one striking difference between von Bülow's home and mine: the Fifth Avenue apartment had no aromas of home cooking, no smells, no odors. There was no sense that his home was lived in, loved in, eaten in, slept in. It *was* a museum.

Claus greeted me at the door to the library. He was wearing clothes that were supposed to be informal, but on him they looked a mite stuffy, as if they had been overtailored to appear casual. I was surprised to see how tall Claus was. He stood a half-foot taller than my five-foot-nine-inch frame. (Because of his height and nationality, the press dubbed him "The Great Dane.") "Professor," he said formally, "how nice of you to come." It was almost as if I had accepted a social invitation to tea, rather than a business appointment to discuss his life.

"It's nice to meet you, Mr. von Bülow," I responded with a formality that was as stilted as his was natural.

He ushered me into the sitting room, which was adorned with antique leather-bound books and family portraits. Directing my attention to a group portrait of robed gentlemen, von Bülow told me that his ancestors had been judges and justice ministers of Denmark. After showing me around the "public" rooms, he asked, "Shall we go to lunch first? Then after we've gotten to know each other a bit better over a glass of wine, we can come back here and talk business." I fluffed up the cushion of the chair in which I had momentarily sat, in order to restore it to its untouched look.

We walked a few blocks to the dining room of the Carlyle Hotel, where the maître d' and waiters all knew von Bülow. The conversation during the walk over was awkward, Claus pointing out interesting sights and telling me about the restaurants in the neighborhood. I was already bored with the small talk and anxious to hear about the case and my possible role in it.

As we sat down, the waiter was already pouring a dry red Bordeaux—my favorite. I wondered if it was a coincidence or if Claus had somehow found out about my recently acquired taste in wine. (A couple of years earlier, a glass of Manischewitz would have done just fine.)* The first thing Claus told me about himself was that he was a lawyer too. "I was a barrister in England. Lord Hailsham's chambers. I didn't hold a candle to you, of course, but I wasn't bad in my day." I wondered why he had chosen to open the conversation with that comparison. Perhaps to point out that we had *something* in common.

We ate cold poached salmon and continued to talk about little of consequence. Suddenly as we were finishing, he turned and looked at me. I could see a physical change come upon him. His rigid posture—which seemed to require considerable flexing of muscles in his face, shoulders and midsection—began to sag a bit. He was letting down his guard, just a little.

"I need the best lawyer I can get. I am absolutely innocent and my civil liberties have been egregiously violated."

At his mention of civil liberties, I recalled the cliché about a conservative being a liberal who's been mugged. What immediately occurred to me was that a liberal is often a conservative who's been indicted—or, in this case, convicted. As these thoughts crossed my mind, von Bülow immediately added: "But I also need a friend and supporter. Herald Fahringer and John Sheehan let me down. It may not have been their fault. But they led me to believe that everything was going to turn out fine. I need someone who will always be straight with me."

It would have been easy to let these remarks go by with a bland assurance that I could do all of these things. But Claus von Bülow was asking me to serve him in two very different—and incompatible—capacities. "Mr. von Bülow, I'm sorry, but I can't be both your friend and always straight with you. I can be your lawyer, or one of your lawyers, and I will always be straight with you. But I can't be your friend and supporter. A friend sometimes has to put up an encouraging façade. A lawyer has to be brutally honest."

I had to go out of my way to make this point because I have

---

* For Christmas, Claus sent me a bottle of Sauternes (and a pair of boxing gloves). I know little about dessert wines, but this bottle seemed very nice. I shared it with a dear friend and we really enjoyed it. Several days later my enjoyment turned to guilt when I told another friend the name and vintage —Château d'Yquem 1970— and learned that we had downed a bottle worth several hundred dollars.

seen too many lawyers confuse their roles as professional attorney and personal friend. Sometimes they do it out of genuine concern for the psychological well-being of their client/friend. Other times they do it for financial reasons. Many clients don't want to hear the truth. They want to be told how wonderful they are and how certain it is that they're going to win the case. Unless the lawyer becomes a cheerleader, he risks being replaced by a more upbeat attorney. But clients must be given a realistic view of their situations, so that they can make intelligent choices. And the lawyer—because of his general expertise and specific knowledge of the case—should be in the best position to give an accurate and realistic assessment of the likely outcomes. Oliver Wendell Holmes once defined law as nothing more pretentious than "prophecies of what the courts will do in fact." And the prophets of the law are the lawyers who offer these predictions. But a lawyer who cannot step back from his role as friend and supporter will have difficulty making accurate predictions. Jimmy the Greek does not rely on the cheerleaders for an accurate assessment of a team's chances.

After discussing what I would not do, we turned to what role I could play in the case. "I have several problems about retaining you," Claus explained. "But they're my problems, not yours." I was sure he must be referring to some of the critical comments I had made about judges and defendants in my book. But he assured me that he was not disturbed by anything in the book. "To the contrary," he assured me, "the book is a big plus. I like your directness and honesty."

The first problem, he explained defensively, was that some of his acquaintances were upset at the prospect of "an aggressive Jew" taking over the case. "Mind you, I don't buy any of that for one minute," he assured me. "My boss—the man whom I admire second most in the world after Lord Hailsham—is Mark Millard, a brilliant Russian Jew who is a master at finance and a true gentleman. I don't have an ounce of the anti-Semite in me. But some of these other people have never encountered Jews like you, intellectuals, cultured people. It's their loss, but there you have it." He assured me that he would make the decision and that if I were his choice, others would just have to live with it.

There were also some friends from Newport who were concerned that an outsider like me would not hesitate to "air our dirty laundry in public."

"That's absolutely right," I snapped back. "I wouldn't hesitate to air anything if it was truthful and would help your case. I won't represent your friends or your society. I will only represent you and your interests, and they should know that."

The next problem he told me about was far more delicate and immediate. "I want you to be my lawyer for the appeal, but I can't get rid of Fahringer and Sheehan just yet."

I assured Claus that this wouldn't be a problem, that I was a team player and could work with his trial lawyers. "I've played second fiddle to some of the best, and most egotistical, lawyers in the country. I can work with them."

"But they can't work with you," he retorted. "Herald insists on working alone. He can't work with anyone else unless they are totally under his control."

Claus was clearly dissatisfied with the Sheehan-Fahringer team. He had lost confidence in their ability to back up their enthusiasm with results. Why then was he so concerned about how they might react to my being added to the defense team?

I asked him why he couldn't tell Fahringer and Sheehan that he insisted on having me work with them. "If they don't like it, they can leave. I can handle the sentencing and bail, although I would prefer to work with them—certainly during the transition period."

Claus looked at me as if I were a naive schoolboy. "Professor, you probably know more law in your pinky than Fahringer, Sheehan and I know all together, but you don't understand the politics of Rhode Island justice." He proceeded to give me a lesson in what he called that "cesspool of corruption."

He explained that he had retained John Sheehan on the advice of Senator Claiborne Pell—a Newport neighbor. Sheehan was a highly successful criminal lawyer in Providence who was a tough and effective cross-examiner. He knew his way around the Rhode Island courts and political clubhouses. Von Bülow believed that if he retained Sheehan, there would be no indictment. Sheehan was retained, and there was an indictment. Sheehan recommended that von Bülow hire Herald Price Fahringer as the high-visibility lawyer. They would make a great team. Sheehan could use the Rhode Island old-boys' and old-girls' network, as well as his experience with Rhode Island judges and juries. Fahringer, the elegant and smooth-talking New Yorker, would be the media star and examine the major witnesses. Sheehan had worked with Fahringer on several obscenity cases. Ironically—as it would turn out—they had called me during an obscenity trial they were handling jointly in Boston to ask me to appear as an expert witness on constitutional law for their client. I had declined the role.

Claus explained to me the "Rhode Island Rules of the Game." "Nobody will listen to a word you say," he assured me, "unless you have the right people behind you, and Jack Sheehan is the right person." I reminded him that the Sheehan connection had not succeeded in preventing an indictment or a conviction. "Jack is partly blarney stone," Claus responded, "but I can't take any chances, especially not now." The bail decision, Sheehan had told him, was completely up to the discretion of Judge Thomas Needham, the trial judge. If Judge Needham turned down the request for bail pending appeal, it would then be up to Judge Florence Murray of the Supreme Court. Sheehan was "working it out" with both judges. He was using the "old-boy—or in this case old-girl—statute," as Claus liked to refer to it.

This is not my way of practicing law, but it is fairly widespread in certain parts of the country. I am generally skeptical of lawyers who claim that they can achieve results in this manner. In an article in *Parade* magazine I had written critically of lawyers who promise to "deliver": "Beware the lawyer who promises too much . . . Most lawyers who promise to use their influence are bluffing," I wrote. The tragedy for the legal system is that not all such lawyers are bluffing.

I told von Bülow about my doubts, and he was quick to respond, "Professor, that's exactly why I want you and need you in this case. I can't afford to take any chances—to rely *either* on your intelligence *alone* or Jack's *contacts alone*. I need *both*. I'm asking you," he continued, "to become part of a two-track approach to my legal defense. The outside track will consist of you and your team developing the best legal arguments possible. The inside track will remain Sheehan."

I told Claus that I would not participate—even on an entirely separate track—in a legal defense that was in any way improper or unethical. He assured me that this was the way the game is played in Rhode Island by both sides. "Everybody goes to see the judges. Everybody relies on the inside track. It's the only way to practice law in Rhode Island. Any outsider who tries to win without tipping his hat to the insiders is immediately given the Rhode Island Shuffle." It was the first time I heard that phrase, but certainly not the last.

I told Claus that I would agree to prepare an application for bail pending appeal. We decided that Fahringer and Sheehan would represent von Bülow at the sentencing. Claus said he would have to make the decision as to who would argue the bail application to the court: whether he would take the inside or the outside track on that important issue.

I quickly assembled my support team to work on the bail application. My secret weapon is that I never work alone. I always assemble my team, consisting of some junior colleagues and students. Whenever I put a team together, I always think of one of my favorite old TV programs—*Mission: Impossible*. The head of that team would be asked to perform a difficult task, and he would immediately assemble a team of experts, each of whom was capable of performing a discrete task and working in cooperation with other team members. Generally, he relied on familiar associates in whom he had confidence.

This time I called Jeanne Baker and her partner David Fine. Jeanne and I had worked together numerous times. I asked Susan Estrich and Christopher Edley, both recent Harvard Law School graduates who had returned to the law school as assistant professors, to join us. And I recruited Joann Crispi, also a Harvard Law School graduate and former research assistant of mine who had just finished one year at a New York law firm. Then came the students—a dozen or so of the very best I could find.

My other secret weapon is my younger brother, a New York lawyer whose approach to legal advocacy is somewhat different from mine. I never make an important professional decision without running it by him. His judgment is remarkably perceptive and I nearly always follow it. The few times that I haven't, I have regretted it.

I assigned each of the lawyers one issue. He or she would be responsible for having the students conduct the library research and produce a rough draft of a section of the brief in support of bail. I held several group sessions in my office in which—seminar-style—we reviewed all the angles and options. At these sessions, we were all equals; ideas rose or fell on their own merits or demerits, not their source. When it came to writing the final brief, I would have to make the tough decisions about what to include and how to frame the argument.

We completed the thirty-page bail application in time for the sentencing proceedings, which were scheduled for May 7, 1982. Even before that day, I smelled trouble. Fahringer was extremely resentful about my involvement in the case. "The last thing we need is another cook," he snarled when I called him to try to work out our respective responsibilities. "If you want to prepare a draft, I'll look at it," he said. "But I'm in charge. I'll make the decisions. We can't have two captains."

I assured Fahringer that I could work with him in the best interests of our mutual client. But he was clearly unhappy. He repeatedly delayed sending me the transcripts and records necessary for me to prepare the brief, and he persisted in bad-mouthing me to Claus. Fahringer was engaged in a full-fledged campaign to remain the sole captain of von Bülow's sinking ship.

I wrote to Fahringer telling him that I had been retained to prepare a memorandum outlining the appellate issues to be raised and advising him that "I look forward to working with you in the spirit of cooperation and in the hopes that we can undo the terrible injustice done to Mr. von Bülow." He responded that he was "shocked" to receive my letter suggesting that I would be responsible for preparing the appellate briefs, and asserted that he "will be in charge."

But nothing that happened during this stage prepared me for what was to happen on the day of Claus von Bülow's sentencing and bail application.

At Claus's request, I drove down to Newport with Susan Estrich for the combined sentence and bail proceeding. Claus still had not decided who would actually argue the bail application before Judge Needham, and—especially—who would argue before the higher court if Judge Needham were to turn down the bail application.

We all met together in von Bülow's room at the Sheraton Islander in Newport. Claus was accompanied by his daughter, Cosima, and his friend Andrea Reynolds. Fahringer was there with Sheehan.

Sheehan began the discussion by announcing that I would have to stay back in the hotel room during the legal proceedings. "I have an understanding with Judge Murray," he explained. "She doesn't want you in court, and she's told me that if you stay away, she'll make sure that Claus gets bail. Judge Needham has told me that he is going to deny the application for bail," Sheehan continued, "but that he would give us time to appeal his denial to the single justice of the Rhode Island Supreme Court who hears emergency motions." Sheehan explained that Judge Murray was the emergency judge this week. "I met with her yesterday and she's ready to grant bail until the entire Supreme Court can hear the application. Florence has assured me that the rest of the court will do whatever she says on this one." It seemed bizarre—especially by the Massachusetts standards I was used to. But then Sheehan went even further. He told me that a dean at one of the other Boston-area law schools had told him "why Judge Murray didn't like you. I can't remember what the reason was, but it had something to do with a statement you once made about judges."

The story had a ring of truth to it, since I have, in fact, been critical of some members of the judiciary and it is certainly true that some judges don't like me (a feeling that is sometimes reciprocated). But I knew I had never commented specifically on the Rhode Island judiciary, since I had appeared only once before a Rhode Island judge—Federal Judge Raymond Petine—and he was a superb jurist. I also wondered about the connection to the dean; coincidentally, the dean he referred to happens to be a friend and professional colleague of mine, and he had never mentioned anything about Judge Murray. Indeed, I remembered that he had once invited me to appear at an alumni function at his school with some Rhode Island judges.

This was the time to call Sheehan's bluff, I decided. If he was telling the truth about his back-door access to the Rhode Island judiciary, I had to know that and act accordingly. If he was bluffing, then Claus had to know that. Without missing a beat, I picked up the phone and placed a call to the dean. In front of everybody, I asked him if he had ever told his friend John Sheehan that Judge Murray disliked me.

The dean expressed surprise. "I don't think I know anyone named John Sheehan," he answered hesitantly. I described Sheehan, and the dean said that he vaguely recalled a Rhode Island alumnus who fit the description and who sometimes attended alumni functions. But he was crystal-clear in remembering that he had never discussed either Judge Murray or me with any John Sheehan. "I'm certain Judge Murray holds you in the highest regard," he assured me. Sheehan's face was turning bright red as he heard my side of the phone conversation.

Claus became visibly worried. I wondered whether I had done the right thing. Claus had enough to worry about without any internecine warfare among his lawyers. But it was *his* freedom that was at stake, and he had to decide which track to follow. If Sheehan *was* bluffing, then bail might be denied because we had not presented our best legal arguments. But if he was telling the truth, Claus certainly didn't want to have bail denied because the judge didn't like one of his lawyers.

Claus became frozen with indecision. He simply could not make up his mind. He could see both sides, but he didn't know what to do. My phone call to the dean had confirmed his worst suspicions that much of what he was told by Sheehan was blarney. But was the blarney mixed with some truth? *Was* there a deal with Judges Needham and Murray?

The difficulty of the decision was exacerbated by Claus's utter dread of having bail revoked immediately and thus being taken to prison right from the courtroom, without an opportunity to "set my affairs in order." I inferred that Claus meant more by this phrase than simply paying some bills and bidding a private farewell to friends and family.

"I need time to do the right thing," he kept saying. The implication sent chills down my spine: Was Claus telling me—without putting it in precisely those words—that if he knew he would have to go to prison, he was prepared to take his own life? "In Europe, a gentleman is given the opportunity to end things properly, to leave the proper memories behind for his loved ones. . . . There are worse things than death," he told me somberly. "There is disgrace, and a life in prison is disgrace, even for an absolutely innocent man."

My original draft of the bail application had contained a proposal designed to assure the court that Claus could not flee if he were to lose the appeal. Generally, when a defendant is out on bail while his appeal is being decided, he learns whether he has won or lost from a public announcement. He is not in court when the decision is announced, as he is when the trial verdict is rendered. Thus, if he hears that he has lost, he can go into hiding or try to leave the country. Because von Bülow was a Danish and not an American citizen, if he managed to escape to Denmark, he could not be returned—extradited—back to the United States against his will.

In order to encourage the court to grant him bail pending appeal, I had drafted a section of the application proposing that before the Supreme Court announced the results of the appeal, it could simply announce that it had decided the case and require the physical presence of the defendant in court when it "opened the envelope." This would assure that if von Bülow lost the appeal, he could be taken directly to jail without any opportunity to flee.

When I showed this proposal to Claus, he became agitated. "Does this mean I would not have a chance to go home and put my things in order? That won't do at all. I must have at least a few days to put things right."

I knew that Claus was not contemplating an escape. With a now well-known face atop a six-foot-three-inch frame, it would be impossible to sneak out of the country. "Can you imagine me in one of these funny nose and mustache masks?" he once quipped. The image of him trying to pass for Groucho Marx was enough to convince anyone that Claus von Bülow would not become *The Fugitive*.

The realization that Claus might have wanted time to consider suicide had a profound impact on me. It raised the stakes, but it also made me angry. Doesn't he have faith in me? I wondered. But why, I thought, should he have faith in any lawyers, considering the situation he is facing? For me, this was no longer a case of life imprisonment. It was now a capital case. I believed that Claus von Bülow might be facing death if he lost the appeal.

A man facing death certainly has a right to make his own decisions about which lawyer should argue for his freedom.

Claus asked me to give him my candid advice. I told him that in light of what I knew, he could not count on the Sheehan connection.

"Do you want to argue for bail?" he asked.

"I am willing to," I said, "but I don't insist on it."

"Sheehan *insists* that they must argue it," Claus explained, "and that you cannot under any circumstances be in the courtroom. What should I do?"

"I can't make that decision for you," I responded. "You're a big boy and you have far more at stake here than any of the lawyers. Whatever is done must be done in your interest alone, without any consideration for the lawyers' egos or feelings."

"But if I alienate Sheehan, I'm a goner," he said despondently, thus disclosing that deep down he really did believe that Sheehan was capable of delivering.

"I'm going to go with Fahringer and Sheehan," he decided. "But only if Sheehan has called it right about getting time to appeal a denial by Judge Needham to Judge Murray." He looked directly at me and gave me my instructions: "You stay back in the hotel room —you can watch it all on television. But if Judge Needham orders me to jail, I want you to take over immediately and rush up to the

Supreme Court to argue for a stay, or whatever it takes to get me out."

"Are you going to tell Sheehan and Fahringer about this plan?" I asked.

"No, I can't do that. They would quit and leave me in the lurch. It's enough that I've told you. Let's just hope that it doesn't come to where I need you as my parachute." It would not be the last time he would compare me to that instrument of desperation.

I wasn't satisfied. The spectacle of two sets of lawyers racing to the Supreme Court, each claiming to represent the imprisoned von Bülow, was not one that I looked forward to, especially since only one set included a Rhode Island attorney. I told Claus that he would have to give me written authorization to represent him before the Rhode Island Supreme Court in the event he was in jail. He quickly typed out and handed me a note authorizing me to argue all appeals from a denial of bail. I put it in my pocket, hoping I would never have to use it.

Everyone else drove to the courthouse, leaving me behind. I felt strange being excluded from the courtroom. Hundreds of defendants beg me to go to court on their behalf. But in this case, the defendant had politely asked me to stay back in the hotel. It was the most palpable reminder that I was in Rhode Island. I was feeling the Rhode Island Shuffle with a vengeance.

I turned on the TV and watched as Judge Needham imposed a sentence of ten years' imprisonment on Count I and twenty years' on Count II.

It was now time for him to decide the bail application. As I fiddled with the note Claus had given me, Judge Needham surprised everybody by granting bail—of $1 million. Claus von Bülow would remain a free man until his appeal was decided.

I wondered whether the entire story about Judge Murray was simply a charade to keep me out of the courtroom so that I would not deflect any media attention from Sheehan and Fahringer. Was it also their last desperate effort to keep me from remaining in the case for the appeal—to persuade Claus to opt for the "inside track"? I would never learn for sure whether Sheehan had actually met with any judge, alone or with the prosecutor, but I would remain suspicious of Sheehan and concerned about the Rhode Island Shuffle throughout the remainder of the case.

When Claus returned to the hotel room, he was in a somber mood. He was relieved that he would not be going to prison in the immediate future. But he was—quite naturally—upset at the prospects that faced him in the long run. He thanked me profusely for being "so reasonable about the unreasonable demands of the others." In an attempt to appear sympathetic to the thirty-year sentence, I remarked, almost automatically, how unfair the long sentence was. He looked down sharply and rebuked me: "A thirty-year sentence is entirely fair for a man who twice tried to murder his wife. Anything less would be monstrous." As I wondered what he was trying to tell me, he quickly added in an assertive voice: "But for me any sentence would be unfair, because I never tried to harm my wife."

The Sheehan-Fahringer show at the sentencing–bail hearing finally convinced von Bülow to dismiss Fahringer as his chief counsel and to ask me to take over the case. I was willing to work with Fahringer, but Fahringer was not prepared to work with me. And Claus wanted me as his appellate lawyer. Eventually Claus von Bülow was forced to write to Fahringer rejecting his "ultimatum" and insisting that he—Claus—"would have the final say.
. . . This was what I was taught was the correct client-attorney relationship many years ago in England. You may be surprised to know that many American attorneys of repute still practice with that principle." Claus berated Fahringer's attitude that he, and only he, was "the Captain of the Ship," a principle he had applied "like a martinet, allowing no debate." Von Bülow concluded by referring to the principle of "maritime law that the crew was clapped into irons for disagreeing with the Captain of the Ship," but insisted that this principle "should not apply to the client-attorney relationship, and I have no intention of letting the same rule apply to my appeal as I had to live with during my trial."

In September 1982 Fahringer terminated his relationship to the case and I took over as chief counsel. (Fahringer went on to argue the appeal of Jean Harris, the woman who killed the "Scarsdale doctor"; her conviction was affirmed.) Claus was still reluctant to make a clean break with Sheehan. "We need local Rhode Island counsel," he reminded me, "to take care of the ministerial details. Why don't we keep Jack on for that. And also to give us insights into the kinds of arguments the Supreme Court judges might want to hear."

I told Claus that I would prefer to retain my own local counsel from Rhode Island, someone who practiced law my way, someone who I could work with comfortably, someone who would not give me the Rhode Island Shuffle. I had no one particular in mind, but I knew there must be someone in Rhode Island who fit the bill. Claus authorized me to add another Rhode Island lawyer to the team, but still would not sever his connection with Sheehan. Sheehan remained on during the appeal as Claus's personal adviser on Rhode Island matters, and eventually redeemed himself with one brilliant ploy that saved a crucial day.

I started calling around and inquiring about good young appellate lawyers. Virtually everyone I spoke to included John "Terry" MacFadyen on their list. MacFadyen had just left the post of chief appellate lawyer for the Rhode Island Public Defenders. In that capacity, he had argued dozens of criminal appeals for indigent defendants before the Rhode Island Supreme Court. Prior to working for the P.D.'s office, he had been a law clerk to a justice of that court. Everyone I spoke to emphasized MacFadyen's honesty, integrity and brilliance, both as a legal theoretician and as a courtroom advocate. "He isn't a typical Rhode Island criminal lawyer" was a common refrain. "He's not like most of the others. He really cares about issues and he's smart as hell," one lawyer told me. The fact that MacFadyen's experience had come from representing the poor provided a nice contrast with his new role as local counsel for one of Rhode Island's wealthiest criminal defendants. I hired MacFadyen to be my Rhode Island associate.

8

The Old Story Retold

In theory, a criminal appeal is not supposed to tell any new stories; it must be based entirely on the paper record of the trial—the transcript and other documents that record the stories told at trial. An appeal is a review of what the trial judge did. It is not, again in theory, a mechanism for persuading the Supreme Court that the defendant is innocent or that the jurors came to the wrong conclusion. Only the trial judge is on trial in an appeal. As Judge Needham himself had commented after imposing his sentence: "The Trial of Claus von Bülow is over. The Trial of the Trial Justice is about to begin." If there wasn't enough evidence to convict the defendant, then the trial judge should never have allowed the jury to consider the case; he should have—based on legal principles—directed a verdict of not guilty. If some of the evidence was improper, irrelevant or prejudicial, then the trial judge should have kept it from the jury. If the trial judge made any legal errors that denied the defendant a fair trial, then the defendant is entitled to a new trial—this time without prejudicial legal errors.

Every issue raised on appeal *must* be a legal one. Strange as it may sound, the defendant's possible innocence—based on old or new evidence—is not supposed to be the concern of the appellate court, which is supposed to decide whether there was *enough evidence* for the jury to conclude beyond a reasonable doubt that the defendant was guilty. But that is very different from deciding whether the defendant was, in fact, guilty. "Enough evidence" may include extremely weak—even unbelievable—testimony. Even if the appellate judges personally believe the defendant to be innocent, they are supposed to affirm the conviction as long as there was sufficient evidence for the jury to convict.

But appellate judges are just people in robes who sit behind oak

benches in marble chambers. Many of them care deeply about mis-
carriages of justice. They care whether the flesh-and-blood defendants whose paper records come before them are guilty or
innocent. They assume, like most people who work in the criminal
justice system, that the vast majority of defendants whose cases
come before them are, in fact, guilty. Indeed, convicted defendants
whose cases are argued on appeal are not even *presumed* innocent,
as are defendants prior to trial. After they have been convicted,
defendants on appeal are presumed guilty. And this presumption
is much harder to overcome than the pretrial presumption of
innocence—because it is even more firmly grounded in reality. The
criminal justice system is like an isosceles triangle: at the base is
the large number of arrests; near the middle is the smaller number
of trials; above that are the convictions. As you climb from the
broad base to the tiny pinnacle, the system filters out the vast
majority of innocents. By the time you get to appeals, you are
near the narrow top, and there are few innocents left.

In most appellate cases, the lawyer has little choice but to focus
on the dry legal issues. The last thing the lawyer wants the
appellate court to think about is the guilt or innocence of the
client, for the vast majority are not only guilty but—even more
important from an advocate's point of view—*demonstrably* guilty.
Their guilt jumps out of the record at every page. For example, in
a case where the police improperly break into a hotel room and
find the defendant in possession of cocaine, scales and large
amounts of cash, the only issue to raise is the propriety of the search
and the applicability of the so-called "exclusionary rule," which
forbids the prosecution from introducing into evidence any material it obtained in violation of the Constitution. The primary
reason why the exclusionary rule is so unpopular with the public is
that it is almost always invoked by guilty defendants caught with
the goods. An appellate court's freeing a defendant found in possession of contraband—or found guilty of something even worse—
because the constable bungled is not easy for the public to accept.
(This also explains why it was the *appointed* Supreme Court, rather
than the *elected* Congress, that established the exclusionary rule
on a national basis.)

In the rare appeal for a defendant who may really be innocent,
the lawyer is presented with a dilemma. If the lawyer argues only
the dry legal points, the judges will probably assume that the

defendant is guilty. Worse, they will probably assume that even the lawyer thinks he is guilty. But if the appeal focuses on the factual innocence of the defendant, the lawyer is sure to alienate at least certain judges who are sticklers for considering only the legal issues. This dilemma was to recur throughout the von Bülow appeal.

I am a firm believer in interjecting claims of innocence into any appeal where appropriate. The trick is to try to find legal issues in the case that implicitly make the claim of innocence for the defendant.

I had some ideas for the appeal, but I didn't yet have a cohesive theory. By this time, I thought that Claus might well be innocent. He certainly had always insisted that he was, and he never did or said anything inconsistent with his innocence. But the trial record was dismally barren of any convincing reason for disbelieving the twelve jurors who had found von Bülow guilty beyond a reasonable doubt, or trial judge Needham, who had gone out of his way—both publicly and privately—to declare his firm belief in the defendant's guilt. Needham had publicly declared that von Bülow "belongs in jail" and that he had little respect for him. He claimed to be basing his views on confidential information.

There was one legal issue that was obvious to everyone. Even the trial judge had commented that it would eventually be decided by the higher courts. That issue was the propriety of the search conducted by Alexander von Auersperg and the private investigator. They had opened a locked closet belonging to Claus von Bülow and had searched through his clothing, drawers and other personal effects. What they found—the black bag with the insulin-encrusted needle was the most important piece of physical evidence in the case. The needle had been hailed by the prosecutor as the "murder weapon." The search and seizure had been conducted without a warrant or probable cause. But it had been conducted by private citizens. And private citizens are not directly bound by the Bill of Rights, which imposes limits only on government agents.

Judge Needham had ruled that Claus von Bülow's rights of privacy had been violated by the search; that the search had been conducted "for the specific purpose of obtaining information which could be used in a criminal prosecution"; and that *had* the search been conducted by the police, "there is no question" that it would have been unconstitutional. But he ruled that since the search had been conducted by private citizens, rather than by government agents, the Constitution did not apply.

Prosecutor Famiglietti himself acknowledged in a newspaper interview that

> Had the children gone to the police instead of to Kuh, I doubt it would have gone any further. They would've needed a search warrant to look for the black bag, and at that point in time I don't think they would have gotten one. So it was fortunate that the case developed this way.

The constitutional issue posed by this private search whose fruits were then turned over to the police and public prosecutors was an important one. A wealthy family's hiring its own private police—who are not bound by the Bill of Rights—raised a profound civil liberties issue which had long interested me. The increasing utilization of private security guards and vigilante organizations had already forced several courts to confront this problem with differing results. The issue could go either way in the Rhode Island Supreme Court. Claus told me that John Sheehan was urging him to base his appeal on this issue, assuring him that the Rhode Island Supreme Court would not tolerate this kind of private end run around the Constitution.

I certainly wanted to include this line of argument, but I was concerned about focusing too heavily on it. "It's a guilty man's argument," I told Claus. "The kind of argument that creates a stench of guilt throughout the entire brief. An innocent defendant," I emphasized, "wants evidence *in*, not evidence *out*. How are we going to persuade anyone of your claim of innocence if we base our appeal on an extension of the exclusionary rule to private citizens?"

I was also leery of asking any court to expand the unpopular exclusionary rule at a time when the United States Supreme Court and many state courts were doing everything in their power to cut back on it. "There are at least six Justices of the Supreme Court in Washington who would love to overrule a state court that applied the Fourth Amendment to private parties," I told Claus, naming the Justices as I stuck out each finger.

"We need an innocent-man issue," I insisted as the team began to review the case. The media had already concluded that the guilty Claus was sure to lose his appeal. *New York* magazine, in an article about my involvement in the case, had quoted "one of the country's leading criminal lawyers" predicting that I would lose the appeal: "He'll add something useful and do a brilliant analysis of the record. He isn't going to make it. Of some guys you can say 'That's a patient he isn't going to save. He can only make him more comfortable.' "

Esquire magazine had commented that the von Bülow appeal "looked like another ritualistic exercise in civil libertarian dogma" that "would churn through the courts simply because there was money available and a set of arguments that *could* be made, rather than because [I] had any real sense that justice had in some way gone astray."

And one commentator snidely observed that von Bülow's "recruitment of Harvard Law Professor Alan Dershowitz shortly after his conviction would tend to reinforce" the view that Claus von Bülow "was no longer protesting his innocence, merely the methods used to catch him. . . . Dershowitz enjoys a wide reputation as a last resort for convicted criminals, being especially keen at finding legal loopholes that render his clients' convictions unconstitutional."

We needed an issue that would be seen as more than a mere loophole through which a guilty client could escape. We needed one that would raise the specter of an injustice that had caused an innocent defendant to be wrongly convicted. We needed a compelling innocence issue that could help overcome the heavy odds against our winning the appeal. Suddenly the perfect issue popped into my mind.

I remembered that the first interviews of the crucial witnesses had been conducted not by the police, but rather by Richard Kuh, the lawyer hired by the family to conduct a private investigation— the same lawyer whose client had willingly turned over the black bag to the police. "Where are Kuh's notes of those original interviews?" I asked Claus.

"I have no idea," he responded. "I suppose he still has them, but maybe he destroyed them. They were ruled by the judge to be privileged," he reminded me.

"Has anybody ever seen them—the prosecutors, the police?"

"I don't think so, at least not officially," he said with a note of skepticism.

Claus's new woman friend, Andrea Reynolds, who was quickly becoming an inseparable part of his daily life, was even more cynical: "One thing you can be sure of: if there are any notations that could help us, they're gone by now—or changed."

I told them that I doubted that: "Kuh may be a tough lawyer, but he wouldn't change any notes, or throw anything away that he was ordered to keep."

I checked back in the transcript and discovered—to my joy—that Kuh had sworn under oath that he had preserved every scrap of his notes and that he would throw nothing out until the appeal was over.

I wanted those notes. I knew from experience how witnesses' trial memories worked—exactly the opposite from the way one might expect. In a legal case, the memories of witnesses—particularly those with a stake in the outcome—tend to get better as time passes. Often their initial recollection of an event is hazy, because it's not part of any coherent pattern of events or theory. While the theory begins to emerge, the memory begins to fit into it, losing some of the haze. As the trial approaches and the witnesses are coached and rehearsed, they tend to "remember" the event with even more clarity and less ambiguity. And eventually, what began as a hazy recollection becomes frozen into crystalline clarity. In the end, what is remembered is not even the event. It is the *memory* of repeating and clarifying the event through a process of enhanced certainty.

Sometimes, of course, the process is not so inadvertent. Some witnesses' memories improve over time because their stakes in a particular result increase. Whether consciously or unconsciously, these witnesses mold their stories to fit the result they seek. Lewis Carroll once mocked false memories by having one of his characters "remember things even before they happened."

I have seen these insidious processes of memory enhancement operate time and time again. The masters of cross-examination understand them, and use their understanding to create doubt about trial memories. That is why access to the notes of early witness interviews is so important as a tool of advocacy. I had a strong hunch—it was really stronger than a hunch—that the Kuh notes would demonstrate this process at work in the von Bülow case.

The question was how to get those notes. Fahringer had never explicitly sought the notes for use at the trial itself as an aid in cross-examining the trial witnesses. The trial court had refused to order their production in response to Fahringer's pretrial subpoena. That refusal could be argued as an issue on the appeal. But the issue had been neither clearly raised at the trial nor well preserved for appellate review. Moreover, this issue had a problem similar to the one that plagued the search and seizure of the black bag. The Kuh notes had been taken by a private party, not by a government agent. The court might hold that private parties are not bound by the same obligation of disclosure as the government. If so, the prosecution would get the best—and the defendant the worst—of both worlds: the unfavorable black bag found by the private prosecutor would be admissible, while the potentially favorable notes would be excluded. It did not seem just. But it might be the law.

Furthermore, even if we won an appeal on this point, all the Supreme Court might order would be for Kuh to turn the notes over to the court for its inspection. If they didn't contain any "smoking guns"—any obvious inconsistencies that might warrant a new trial—the courts would not reverse the conviction on that ground. I wanted the notes *before* the appeal so that I could use their contents to help us win a new trial. I wanted to make the decisions as to whether they might be helpful at a new trial, rather than leaving it to a "neutral" court or an advocate for the other side.

With that in mind, I first tried to get the notes in a gentlemanly manner—by writing the following letter to Richard Kuh:

Dear Dick,
   I hope this note finds you well.
      . . .
   It is our position that counsel for Claus von Bülow and for Rhode Island should be permitted to inspect your files . . . in order to determine whether any materials might be relevant to the appeal or to a motion for a new trial . . . I believe that such cooperation would . . . serve the interest of truth and full disclosure, which you and your clients have said they are seeking.
      . . .
   Dick, I know that we represent conflicting points of view on this litigation, but I know you well enough to believe that your ultimate interest is that the truth should emerge. I sincerely believe that a tragic miscarriage of justice has occurred in this case. You and your clients may well believe—with equal sincerity—that Mr. von Bülow

is guilty. Only two people in the whole world really know the truth. Tragically, one lies in a coma. The other strongly maintains his innocence. I implore you to consider the possibility that you and your clients may be wrong, and to cooperate in the continuing search for truth. If the files contain nothing helpful to Mr. von Bülow's assertion of innocence, little will have been lost to your clients. But if there are materials that might—when viewed by me as his counsel—be helpful in the search for truth, you will certainly agree that I should have access to them.

I welcome further discussion of this or any other issue. And, I remain respectfully,

Alan M. Dershowitz
Attorney for Claus von Bülow

Kuh's gentlemanly response—which gives no hint of our future acrimony over this case—arrived by return mail:

Dear Alan:

How nice it is to hear from you! But how unfortunate that it takes the von Bülow tragedy to bring us together. After too much time had gone by, I became reacquainted with Herald Fahringer . . . now, about a year later, that cycle repeats when I find another friend at the side of the same now proven scoundrel.

So be it. . . .

Alan, your superlative academic credentials are such that you, of all persons, know that privileges and other exclusionary concepts may on occasion keep highly relevant information from the eyes of those not privy to the privilege. So, on occasion, the search for truth may in fact be frustrated by the proper assertion of a privilege. Happily, that it *not* here the case. *I am satisfied that there is not a scrap of paper in my files that might even arguably be viewed as exculpatory.* [Emphasis added.]

This lawyerly assurance would later prove to be unconvincing. The letter continued in its flattering tone:

The fact that Mr. von Bülow chose not to testify at trial, and to make no statement on his own behalf on sentencing, but to give his own version to one Barbara Walters—who did not seek to question it—and to a growing queue of lawyers who apparently have been well paid to represent him and to espouse his positions, does not dictate that his current versions, however suavely presented, are those that should soundly be credited.

On a more pleasant note—and one upon which we *can* agree—my congratulations, Alan, on your recent most readable book. I have so deeply enjoyed it that I have, so far, sent two copies to friends. One day, if we should meet on the von Bülow matter, or more happily for some unrelated small talk, I shall ask you to inscribe my copy.

Meanwhile my warm personal regards.

Sincerely,

Richard H. Kuh

The next time we were to meet was in a bitter courtroom battle. He did not ask me to inscribe his copy of my book.

I really didn't expect Kuh to turn over his work product just because I asked for it. But I thought I had to go through the motions of writing to him. I also thought that if there was absolutely nothing in there—if the note were entirely consistent with the witnesses' trial testimony—then maybe he would turn them over in order to avoid the risk of a possible new trial based on the withholding of meaningless notes. That would save everybody hours of fruitless work.

After receiving Kuh's letter, we filed a motion before the Supreme Court asking it to order Kuh to turn over the notes. We asked the court to consider this issue in advance of the appeal because the notes might contain information relevant to the other issues on the appeal.

Again, I had little expectation that the Rhode Island Supreme Court would consider the case in such piecemeal fashion, but I wanted it to understand —as early in the process as possible—that we were serious about our claims of innocence. We were even willing to have the court look at evidence that *we* hadn't seen. Our motion was the opposite of a suppression motion under the exclusionary rule. It was an *un*suppression motion seeking an *in*clusionary ruling.

The court declined to consider the issue of the Kuh notes separately from the rest of the appeal, but we were satisfied that we had begun to set the stage for an appeal based entirely on a theory of innocence. We would use the issue of the Kuh notes as an organizing theme—a framework—for our appeal of Claus von Bülow's conviction. One reason for our persistence about the Kuh notes is that at the same time we were preparing for the appeal, we were receiving leads, from some unusual sources, that strengthened our suspicions that the Kuh notes might contain information useful to our defense.

9

High Society

The first lead came when author Truman Capote read about the verdict. Capote was a cherubic man, then in his late fifties. Among the most gifted American writers of the twentieth century, he spent much of his life socializing with the so-called "beautiful people" of high society and media fame.

I first met Capote on a warm Sunday in May 1982. I had called him after reading a brief interview he had given to *People* magazine about his long friendship with Sunny Crawford (as he first knew Sunny von Bülow before her marriages). During our telephone conversation, Capote told me that he was shocked that the real story of Sunny's life had never come out during the trial. I asked how *he* knew the real story, and he told me that he had known Sunny for thirty years, though he had never met her current husband, Claus. We agreed to meet in New York to discuss his evidence.

Truman Capote's story of Sunny von Bülow's life provided a striking contrast to the trial testimony. He told it in his lilting, high-pitched whine, but the detail he provided made me soon forget the unpleasant quality of the voice. We recorded his story precisely as he told it. The writer's story—never disclosed at either trial—presented a side of Sunny about which no one else had ever told us. This is what he said.

Capote was first introduced to Sunny Crawford by a prominent socialite named C. Z. Guest, whose husband Winston was a cousin of Churchill's and a noted horseman and polo player. Sunny was a shy young woman when she met Truman Capote at the Guest estate in Old Westbury, Long Island. The estate, called Templeton, was an enormous expanse of white marble where the wealthy congregated. Truman and Sunny went for a walk and then made a date for lunch at the Colony restaurant several weeks later. Capote remembered that they sat around the corner from the bar "underneath the television set that never worked."

At that time Capote was working on his book *Breakfast at Tiffany's.* Anemic and exhausted, he had sought help from a famous Park Avenue "Dr. Feelgood" named Max Jacobson, who later was accused of overprescribing mood drugs. Jacobson was injecting him with vitamin B_{12} every other day.

At his lunch with Sunny, the discussion turned to their respective weight problems and then to medicines and drugs. When Truman complained that his every-other-day visits to the doctor were disrupting his writing, Sunny asked why he didn't inject himself. "It's the simplest thing in the world," she said. "Once you do it, there's nothing to it at all." Truman hesitated, but Sunny persisted: "I'll teach you to do it."

They left the Colony and walked along Fifty-seventh Street until they came to a drugstore just above a theater called the Sutton. They bought distilled water, because Sunny preferred to inject with that liquid. At Truman's apartment, Sunny took a small black bag out of her purse. "It was a black alligator thing about eight or nine inches long and about two inches wide and it had a zipper running around it." Sunny opened it up, and inside it "she had these disposable hypodermic needles."* She took out one of the needles and "she rolled up her—this little jacket she was wearing, she had on a little blouse—she rolled up her sleeve and she said, 'I usually give this to myself in the hip . . .' but with a little laugh she said, 'I think I'll just teach you in the arm.' "

Sunny injected herself in her left arm. Handing a hypodermic to Truman, she tried to show him how to do it. "I just simply couldn't do it," Capote continued, "and we kept on and on with this until, I swear, my arm was getting quite bloody and I was nervous. . . ." Eventually they gave up on Truman's injecting himself. "I could easily be injected by somebody, but I just couldn't seem to work it out—it made me too nervous."

Truman told Sunny that he would just have to continue to get the injections from Dr. Jacobson. At the mention of Jacobson's name, Sunny said "Oh, I know all about Max Jacobson . . . I went there with Peggy Bedford Bancroft." Peggy, who had first married

---

* At one point, I asked Capote whether disposable hypodermic needles were in use at that time. He explained he was speaking colloquially, not technically, and that he was referring simply to syringes that could easily be carried in a small purse.

Thomas Bancroft and later became the Princess d'Arenberg and then Duchess d'Uzès, was a friend of Sunny's and an heir to the Standard Oil fortune.*

Truman and Sunny continued to meet for lunch over the years—perhaps thirty times in all. Their favorite restaurants were La Petite Marmite, Quo Vadis and Antolotti's. The conversation generally turned to doctors, injections and weight problems. Truman liked Sunny because she reminded him of his mother. In fact, Truman brought Sunny to meet his mother, and they got on very well. (Eventually Capote's mother became alcoholic, spent much of her time alone in bed and committed suicide.) Sunny and Truman injected drugs together on several occasions. "She had a handbag and inside the handbag every time I've ever seen her—it was not always the same handbag, but she had inside of it a little purse that had disposable injection things in it and other things—pills."

Capote saw her use these drugs: "I certainly saw them and she was using them on me and using them on herself. She took this ampule of Dr. Jacobson's out of this tray and she gave it to herself." She said it was a combination of amphetamines and vitamins. "I've been giving myself amphetamines off and on for a long time," she boasted.

Truman and Sunny met for the last time in the early winter of 1979—only weeks before her first coma. Capote had just come from his dentist when he ran into Sunny on Madison Avenue. She was wearing a light fur coat and carrying Christmas gifts. They walked up Madison Avenue "laughing and talking about things, remembering things." They decided to stop for a drink at the Bemelmans Bar in the Carlyle Hotel. It was about 3:30 in the afternoon. They ordered a drink she always used to like—a Manhattan made with Southern Comfort. They talked about his books and her marriage to Claus von Bülow. Truman asked what Claus did, and she said that he had worked for J. Paul Getty, but that he was also quite a good writer. She told Truman about a pamphlet he had written on Newport.

Truman regaled Sunny with stories about his newest book, *Music for Chameleons*, and how he had started to snort cocaine while he was writing it. She said that she had tried cocaine a few times, but that she didn't like it at all. Then she told Truman that she had been

* Sunny's family insists that she was never a patient of Dr. Jacobson and that the entire affidavit is false. Following Capote's demise, Richard Kuh characterized him as a "dead perjurer."

taking something for a while that "was the most relaxing, pleasurable experience you could have—mixing Demerol and amphetamines together as an injection." She also explained to Truman how she used to grind up Quaaludes into a powder and mix them with amphetamines and distilled water. She let him in on another little secret about an "absolutely terrific" drug called Lotusate—a rather long lavender pill—which was very hard to get.

Sunny also told Truman about a wonderful book she had discovered called *Recreational Drugs*, which described every possible combination of drugs. Capote later tried to buy a copy of the book, but he couldn't find one because it was published by an obscure California firm. He called Sunny and told her of his difficulties. She sent over her copy by personal messenger.

That was the last contact Capote ever had with Sunny von Bülow. A few weeks later she was afflicted with her first coma; a year later she was forever silenced by her second.

Truman Capote did not hear about Sunny's first coma. Nor, in fact, did many of her friends. It was regarded by the family as a private medical problem, to be treated discreetly. Capote did hear about her second coma: "It never crossed my mind that she hadn't done it to herself." Capote believed that Sunny's drug problems were widely known within the circles in which she traveled. He was confident that they would be fully disclosed at any trial relating to her coma. He was busy at work on a book and away in Europe, and did not believe that he had any useful information that was not also known by many others. It was only after he heard about Claus von Bülow's conviction that he decided, after conferring with friends, to come forward. Although he had never met Mr. von Bülow, "it never occurred to me for one minute that Mr. von Bülow had done it."

I met with Truman Capote several more times to discuss his story. Each time, I pressed him for details and precise dates. He seemed to have an excellent memory, especially about social events. He would remember who was at which cotillion, who had been snubbed, and who had made a fool of himself.

Our meetings took place over lunch at restaurants like La Côte Basque, places I had never been in before. Capote seemed at home in these lavish celebrity haunts. Everyone knew him, and waiters knew what he would want to eat. He talked endlessly about people I had never heard of—counts, countesses, duchesses—especially women. "I love beautiful women," he told me. "And they love me."

Even more important, he emphasized, "they trust me—or at least they used to before some of my recent publications. But even the ones who *say* they don't trust me anymore tell me everything. I'm like a sister to them." I could understand what he meant.

Following one lunch, he invited me to his apartment to look for the drug book Sunny had sent him. After a fascinating search through his library, we found it. As he started to reach for it, I stopped him. "Don't touch it," I said. "We should check it for prints." I placed it in a plastic bag and took it with me. (We later learned that no fingerprints could be lifted off its pages.)

I asked Capote whether he would be prepared to submit an affidavit and testify if necessary. He was very diffident, especially about testifying. "Do you think I would make a good witness?" he asked me.

"No, I don't," I responded, "but you may be the *only* witness who has actually seen Sunny inject herself." I explained how important his testimony was, telling him that the trial prosecutor had informed the jury in his closing argument that Claus was the only person in the household who had ever used a syringe, that "no one had ever seen Mrs. von Bülow with hypodermic paraphernalia."

"How can anybody believe that?" he shouted. "Everyone knew that Sunny was an expert at injections. How could the prosecutors say something like that?"

Capote authorized me to prepare a transcript of our taped conversation. "I'll read it and if it is accurate, I'll sign an affidavit swearing that it is the truth." He was hesitant to appear as a witness but said, "I'll do it if I have to."

Truman Capote's account was immediately corroborated by C. Z. Guest, the socialite who had originally introduced him to Sunny. She confirmed the meeting at her estate and the continuing friendship. She also put to rest any possibility that Capote had made up the drug story only after reading about the case in the papers: she swore that Truman had told her on various occasions after their first meeting "that Sunny, to his surprise, was an expert on self-injection of some kind of drug and feel-good shots and that apparently the two of them had been doing this together." She remembered particularly once after Capote and Sunny had met in New York that "Truman mentioned that Sunny still had this problem and was injecting herself." These conversations, Mrs. Guest said, ranged over a period of years, and many "took place long before there was any indication of an accusation against Claus von Bülow."

Later on—after Capote's death at age fifty-nine—the woman in whose house he had died provided additional corroboration of his story. The woman was Joanne Carson, Johnny Carson's wife between 1963 and 1970. Joanne Carson—not to be confused with Joanna Carson, Johnny Carson's third wife—is an accomplished nutritionist who hosts a nationally syndicated TV show. She and Capote had been close friends since 1967, when they met at the home of publisher Bennett Cerf. "He became my closest friend and confidant," she said. They spoke every day and lived in the same building at United Nations Plaza in New York City.

I asked her to recount a conversation she'd had with Capote before Thanksgiving in 1969. What she told me—and I had transcribed—has never been revealed before. This is what she disclosed:

> Well, I had lunch with Truman that day, and I had not been feeling good for some time, and a friend of mine, Jacqueline Susann, had recommended a doctor that could give me vitamin shots that would make me feel very good, and I had mentioned that I had an appointment with doctors on Park Avenue, and Truman was very aghast and told me that this was a Dr. Feelgood, that what he was giving in the injections was more than vitamins because it was very addictive and that a friend of his, Sunny Crawford, had gone to this doctor for vitamin injections again for the same reason of tiredness, and she . . . had gotten hooked . . .

Mrs. Carson told me that Capote had described "this little zippered lizard or some kind of skin bag that she carried her little syringe and her little bottles in." He told her that Sunny "would shoot herself in the hip." Mrs. Carson commented that "the thought of that made me rather upset because I hate needles, and I lost my appetite." She said, "That helps a lot, not only have you ruined my lunch, but now I don't have a doctor to go to."

I asked Joanne Carson how she could be so certain that the Sunny Crawford he referred to in 1969 was the same Sunny von Bülow who became comatose. Joanne told me that she was positive because after Natalie Wood died, Truman had again lectured her about the dangers of an overdose:

> "See the danger. You remember I told you years ago by getting hooked with that doctor, see the danger of taking drugs like that. [You] can overdose very easily like Sunny did, and she's probably going to die, too, just like Natalie."

He thought that Sunny had injected herself with something in an attempt to kill herself. He said, "Both of my dear little friends tried to kill themselves," because he thought at that time, it was the day that the news of Natalie Wood came out, that she had also committed suicide.

Joanne also told me that while she was studying for her Ph.D. in biochemistry and physiology, Truman had asked her if she could find out "what were in these vitamins supposedly, concoctions his friend Sunny had been injecting herself with."

I asked Joanne whether she and Truman had discussed his decision to come forward with his information about Sunny. She said,

I said to him . . . "Truman, if there's anything you know about this, you should get in touch with somebody and let them know about it," and he said, "Oh, I really don't want to get involved in something like this," and I said, "But a man's freedom is at stake. If you've got information," I said, "I don't know the procedure of this, but you've got to get ahold of somebody and at least tell them what you know."

Although neither she nor Truman had ever met Claus von Bülow, Truman had become very interested in righting the wrong done to him. On the night before his death at Joanne Carson's Hollywood home, Truman and Joanne had talked about the case and about Truman's willingness to subject himself to what he knew would be embarrassing cross-examination about his personal life and habits.

Capote's account could not have been fabricated after the fact unless both Mrs. Guest and Mrs. Carson were lying. Moreover, it contained so much detail, and such particulars—many of which, including Sunny's friendship with Capote and Guest, could be independently corroborated—that it sounded credible. I was also impressed by what was *not* in the story. There was no mention of insulin. If Capote had simply come forward and made up a story to help Claus von Bülow, he certainly would have included seeing Sunny with insulin, or at least hearing her talk about it. Truman Capote was no Joy O'Neill. Nor was Capote's account particularly self-serving. He did not emerge as any kind of hero, but rather as a weak-willed participant in Sunny's self-destructive habits.

My mother, who sat through one of my sessions with Capote, gave me her average-woman-on-the-street appraisal: "I can't stand the way he talks. He sounds like some of my canasta partners. But why would he lie about something like this? I don't like him. But I do believe him."

All in all it sounded true, not only to me and my mother, but also to the other lawyers who read and checked his account. If it was true, then Clarendon Court had indeed become a real-life set for a modern-day version of *High Society*.

There was, however, one large gap. Capote himself noticed it. Where was Sunny getting all these drugs? She was certainly not the type to buy them on the street. And no doctor—not even a Dr. Feelgood—would prescribe the quantity and variety of drugs she seemed to be using.

At about the same time Capote was providing his information, another witness was beginning to answer that question. His name was David Marriott. He and Capote had never met, nor were they aware of each other's accounts when they first disclosed them. But their stories fit together so perfectly that the combined account read like a movie script.

10

The Prince, the Pusher
and the Parish Priest

David Marriott is a tall, sandy-haired, attractive young man now in his late twenties. Born in a suburb north of Boston called Malden, he graduated from Malden High School in 1976 and then worked at various printing shops in the area. He lived with his mother in a house estimated to be worth about $100,000 in nearby Wakefield. Though not well educated, Marriott looks, and occasionally dresses, the part of a preppy, wearing designer jeans and Top-siders. On other occasions he dresses like a pimp, sporting a fur coat and ostentatious jewelry. Whatever he wears, he always includes dark glasses, which make it appear that he is hiding something. His neighbors describe him as having been a friendly kid who mowed the lawn and always had a pleasant word. They wonder, however, about his penchant for being driven around in rented limousines. He claimed that since his father uses limousines in conjunction with his mortuary work, the family has friends in the business.

The Marriott incident—which eventually made headlines—illustrates how difficult it is for a lawyer to decide whether to rely on promising evidentiary leads from questionable sources.

According to Claus, several days after the jury had rendered its guilty verdict, Marriott called Claus at his Fifth Avenue apartment and—without giving his name—asked him if he would be interested in information about Alexander von Auersperg's having received drugs and injection paraphernalia. Claus said he would be. The caller said he would phone again. When he did, they arranged to meet—with Herald Fahringer, who was then Claus's lawyer—in Newport at the Sheraton Islander on April 2, 1982. Marriott came with his mother, who was left outside while he told von Bülow and Fahringer the outline of his story about delivering drugs to Alexander von Auersperg.

A few days after this meeting, Marriott phoned von Bülow once again, this time to say that he had just received a threatening phone call. "I don't want to have anything more to do with you or your case," he told Claus, hanging up the phone.

After that, he just disappeared from sight and there was no further contact for months. Claus told me the story a few weeks after I took over the appeal. I told Claus that I thought the information would be important if true, but that we would have to be awfully sure about its validity before using it. "One Joy O'Neill is too much," I cautioned. I also didn't want to sully anyone's reputation without substantial corroboration of the accusations contained in the story.

We hired a private investigator to give us a complete line on Marriott. Eventually, after exhausting every lead we could pursue without actually talking to Marriott himself, I called him. I took the precaution—as I often do when calling potential witnesses—of having someone listen to my side of the conversation. Marriott seemed reluctant to talk over the phone, but he did tell me that he had some information about drugs being brought to Alex. I asked if I could meet with him. "As long as you come alone and without any recording equipment," he stipulated. I agreed, with some reluctance. I had no desire to meet alone with a drug dealer. But those were his conditions and I had little choice but to accept.

I had our private investigator, who always carried a weapon, drive me to Marriott's house in Wakefield. He would wait in the car, and if I wasn't out in an hour, or if he saw anything dangerous, he would come after me.

I knocked at the door of Marriott's house at 7:00 P.M. on January 17, 1983. Mrs. Marriott, David's mother, introduced herself. She was a middle-aged woman with glasses and light hair, and she seemed a bit frightened. We stood there looking awkwardly at each other until David made his entry. He took me to a family room, down a few steps from the entrance. It was plushly carpeted and crammed full of objects which were neither art nor furniture (*tchotchkes*, my grandmother used to call them; knickknacks would be the closest English translation). We sat across from each other on facing couches. "You got some ID?" David asked. I took out my wallet and also a couple of articles that described my role in the von Bülow case.

He expressed reluctance to talk at first, and explained why: "I don't want to get in any trouble with the law, because what I could give you might be incriminating against me." I told him that was an important consideration and asked him whether he had spoken to a lawyer. "Yeah, there's somebody on the North Shore I talked to. He's a politician and a lawyer. He said it would be all right to talk to you, but only for the purpose of giving you some leads. I'm not going to testify or anything like that." His second reason made him visibly nervous: "I could get my throat slit or my head blown off," he said, gesturing appropriately. "What I have involves some people pretty high in the drug business." He didn't wait for any response to this last point; suddenly he just started telling me his story. I took notes as he talked.

Marriott began very quietly and spoke in short, fast sentences, pausing after each to see if I seemed satisfied. He began by telling me of his friendship with an interior decorator named Gilbert Jackson. Jackson was a "flaming queen" who often dressed in flashy feminine clothing—jewelry, furs, et cetera—and was a well-known character in certain gay establishments. Jackson and Marriott would drive to Newport on occasion for fun and games.

One night in the summer of 1977, Marriott said, they met a kid named Alex outside a café near the waterfront. Gilbert knew Alex, and this meeting had obviously been prearranged. Gilbert introduced David to Alex and then gave Alex a package, saying that it was "a present." At this meeting, no second names were exchanged.

A few weeks later the three met again. They had dinner together at a Newport restaurant on Thames Street, after which Jackson gave Alex another "present." This time Jackson told David a bit about Alex. He was a rich kid at school somewhere, but he spent part of his summers at Newport. He lived in a beautiful house that had been decorated by one of Jackson's interior-decorator friends. Jackson mentioned Alex's last name: it was something like "Owrsberg."

David would sometimes drive to Newport alone for a night on the town. On several such occasions, Gilbert asked him to bring presents to Alex, which he did.

I asked David if he knew what the presents were. David smiled and said that since Alex was an attractive young man, he had been sure they were just affectionate gifts.

David told me that he brought these gifts to Alex about a half dozen times over the course of two summers. David started to become concerned when he noticed how suspiciously Alex acted on several occasions. Once he ducked behind some cars in a parking lot when he saw a car pass on Bellevue Avenue that he thought might belong to someone who knew him.

During the summer of 1978, Gilbert asked David to bring a package to Alex. David called Alex to arrange a meeting.

At this point I interrupted the conversation and asked Marriott where he had gotten Alex's phone number. He told me that Jackson had given it to him. "Do you still have it?" I inquired.

"I might," he said and walked upstairs. A few minutes later he returned with two worn phone files: one was a plastic box with a sliding alphabetical index; the other was a yellowish soft-cover booklet. He looked up Alex's entries and read me three numbers, which I copied down.

Marriott resumed his story. Alex asked him to bring the package to his home, Clarendon Court, but to use the side entrance on a small road. When David arrived, the butler told him that Alex was out. David returned to his car, parked on the side road and waited. His suspicions aroused, he decided to look inside the package. It was tied together with string. David untied the knots and opened the package. He was gripped by fear as he saw what he had been carrying. The package contained hypodermic syringes, needles, a plastic bag with white powder, a vial of Demerol and several pills and capsules.

He quickly closed the package and tried his best to retie it in its original manner. Walking quickly back to Clarendon Court, he nervously rang the bell. This time a woman came to the door. She was pretty, in a matronly sort of way, with blond hair. David began to panic, trying to conceal the package he was carrying, but the woman noticed it and said that Alex was expecting a package and had left word for her to take it. Relieved to have it out of his hands but confused at the strange turn of events, David timidly gave her the package and made an awkward retreat back to his car.

About six or seven weeks after this episode, Gilbert Jackson asked David to deliver another package to Alex. David didn't know what to do, so he took the package and called Alex to arrange a meeting. He drove to Newport shivering with nervousness. This time there was no denying what was in the package or what David was doing. Alex was waiting for him near a supermarket. David asked Alex to get into his car and demanded, "Open the package."

"Not here," Alex replied.

"Look I know what's in it. I found out what was in the last package."

Alex started to get angry. "What are you trying to pull? Do you really mean that you haven't realized what you've been doing? What are you up to? Are you trying to pressure me?"

David insisted that he had no such purpose; he just wanted to find out the whole story and to see for himself what was in the package.

The two of them crouched down in the car as Alex opened it. David saw so many different kinds of drugs and paraphernalia that he commented there was an "awful lot for one person." He asked Alex whether he was dealing some of it. Alex responded: "Oh, I give some to my mom to keep her off my back."

I asked David whether he had ever been given any money or envelopes by Alex after dropping off the packages, and he told me he had not. The finances, he assured me, were always taken care of directly by Jackson.

David was still troubled by how he should deal with Jackson. He tried to stay away from him. He dreaded answering the phone for fear that he would be sent on yet another errand. He didn't want to become a full-time drug courier.

Then David started experiencing sharp pains in his right lower abdomen. He went to his doctor, who diagnosed it as acute appendicitis. He was rushed to the hospital and his appendix was removed. While recuperating, he couldn't get his mind off Gilbert and Alex. What would he be asked to do next? How long before he would be caught? Could he really get out now before he dug himself deeper and deeper into the drug dealer's world?

Even more quickly than the problem had arisen, it suddenly disappeared in a barrage of bloody blows to Gilbert Jackson's head. While David was in the hospital, Jackson was brutally murdered by two men from Lynn, Massachusetts. His body was found bound, gagged and beaten. His apartment had been ransacked.

But Jackson's death did not put an end to all of David's—or Alex's—concerns. Within days of the murder, Marriott continued, Alex started to call Marriott's home. His mother answered and Alex asked her if she knew anything about Jackson's death. Then Alex called Marriott in the hospital and they talked about the murder. Alex was frantic. "Will they investigate everyone he knew?" Alex asked. "Do you think there will be any trouble?" David had no idea, but he too was worried.

Eventually, the police arrested the two Massachusetts suspects somewhere in Kentucky. Both pleaded guilty and received long sentences.

David said he never saw Alex again. Nor did he think much about him until early 1982, when the name and picture of Alexander von Auersperg began to appear regularly in newspapers and on television in connection with the von Bülow case. David became frightened and confused once again. He realized that he was a witness to events that could be important to the trial, but he also realized that he was himself culpably involved in at least some of the crimes. There was also his own personal background— his friendship with Gilbert Jackson, his personal life-style, his somewhat questionable past. He did not want all this to come out. And he certainly didn't want to end up in jail for having carried some drugs several years earlier. So he just kept his mouth shut and tried not to pay too much attention to the widely publicized events down in Newport. But eventually—for reasons he refused to discuss —he decided to call von Bülow.

That was the gist of the story David Marriott told me. I listened with equal doses of interest and skepticism. The reason for my interest was obvious. If Marriott's story was true, it undercut an important part of the prosecution's theory. Capote's information was, of course, far more central, since, if true, it would directly establish that Sunny was an expert in self-injection. Together the two new stories constituted a coherent explanation for Sunny's comas. At the trial the prosecutor had repeatedly emphasized the "fact" that the only person in the von Bülow household who had any familiarity with syringes, needles and injections was Claus. The prosecution also argued that there was "no evidence whatsoever that Alexander was familiar with the use of a needle and syringe."

But here was a witness who claimed that he had personally delivered syringes, needles and injectable drugs to the von Bülow household, just a year before Sunny's first coma. Moreover, Marriott's new evidence—which was completely independent, yet corroborative of Truman Capote's eyewitness account—answered the question raised by Capote's evidence: Where might a fancy Newport lady get the drugs and paraphernalia she habitually used?

The reason for my skepticism probably reveals more about me than it does about what I knew about Marriott at the time. I am by nature—and by training as an attorney who primarily represents guilty defendants who lie—a skeptic.

Marriott's story contained certain hallmarks of credibility. It included specific details that would be difficult to invent. It was consistent with the account given by a man who was a stranger to him.

But it almost seemed too good to be true. It was exactly what we wanted to hear. Well, not exactly! As with the Capote account, it would have been more dramatic—and also more suspect—if Marriott had seen insulin among the drugs he delivered. But then again, insulin is an over-the-counter drug. Only the syringes require a prescription.

Because the story was so perfect, it had to be subjected to the most testing cross-examination before I could even consider using it. Putting on my mock prosecutor's hat, I used every trick in the book—not excluding some dirty ones I would never dream of trying in a real courtroom—in an effort to blow holes in his story.

I tried to trick him: "David, who do you think you're kidding? Alex and his mother were in Europe during the summer of 1977. The incidents you described in Newport couldn't have happened." Marriott stuck to his story, becoming even more specific about the times during the summer that the various events had taken place.

I told him he'd be accused of being a drug dealer, a homosexual prostitute, a thief and a liar.

I made him repeat the story a dozen times—each time in a different order.

He stuck to his guns, becoming more precise with each challenge.

I checked the phone numbers that Marriott had retrieved from his files. Sure enough, they were numbers where Alex could have been reached. One of them was Clarendon Court and another was the apartment at Fifth Avenue.

I was becoming less and less skeptical of the core of the story, but that still wouldn't be enough. I had to be convinced that Marriott was telling the truth before I would consider using him. But it wasn't enough for *me* to be convinced. I was neither judge nor jury. I was an advocate for one side.

It was imperative that objective outsiders—judges and jurors— be convinced that David hadn't made up his story. And that was where David's weakness as a witness was most pronounced. A jury just wouldn't like David Marriott. His close friendship with a notorious drag queen and drug dealer would certainly raise questions about his own sexual preferences and his own contact with drugs.

His claim of not knowing what was in the packages he delivered to Alex would be greeted with skepticism, at best. And his lack of a stable employment record would engender doubts about his general behavior. Finally, his motive to come forward, at so great a risk to himself, simply to help a wealthy man in trouble, would raise the suspicion of a payoff.

Prosecutors frequently use—and pay—witnesses with even more sordid backgrounds than Marriott's, sometimes even out-and-out crooks, perjurers and killers. They justify the use of these sleazy witnesses by the old saw: "When you're trying to prosecute the Devil, you have to go to hell for the witnesses." We could try the same approach, arguing that when you're trying to prove drug transactions you have to use witnesses who are close to the world of drugs. But somehow this kind of argument works less well for the defense than for the prosecution. In this case, I suspected it wouldn't work at all.

I tentatively decided that despite the importance of Marriott's information, I would not use him as a witness—unless we could corroborate his story. Moreover, Marriott had not agreed to become a witness. At this point, all he was willing to do was provide leads, information and some investigative assistance.

I had no dealings with Marriott over the next several months because I was busy working on the appellate brief, but he spoke and met with Claus von Bülow and Andrea Reynolds on several occasions to discuss his leads. Claus told me that during one such meeting, Marriott mentioned that he had told a monsignor his story about delivering drugs at the time that it had happened. Claus pressed him for the name of the priest, but Marriott wouldn't disclose it.

Corroboration by a priest would be crucial for several reasons: If David had indeed told the story to a priest *two years before* Sunny von Bülow's first coma, then David could not have made it up after reading about the trial. And even if the judge or jury didn't like David and wouldn't want to believe *him*, they would certainly believe a priest. Indeed, the example of the perfect witness often given in legal literature is "the parish priest."

When Claus told me about Marriott's mention of the monsignor, I called Marriott and asked him for the name of the priest, but he adamantly refused. "I don't want to involve the father," he kept saying.

"But he involved you," I insisted. "You know what they'll do to you on the witness stand without the father's corroboration. They'll destroy you. Make you out to be a liar looking for a payoff."

"But I'll tell them the truth. I'll even tell them that I told it to a priest," David insisted.

"That's the worst part," I assured him. "If you tell the jury there was a priest involved and then you refuse to tell them who the priest is, they'll be sure you're making the whole thing up. They'll crucify you even worse for involving a priest in your lies."

When David persisted in his refusal to name the priest, I began to wonder about the whole account. Why didn't he want to involve the priest? Was there more to the story than had come out? I put these questions to David, but still he persisted in his refusal, becoming vaguer and vaguer about the reasons he didn't want to involve the priest.

Finally, I said to David: "Look, you're off the hook. We'll use the information you gave us for leads to other witnesses, but I'm not putting you under oath or using you as a witness."

David was furious at me. "If you don't believe me, why don't you put me through a lie-detector test?" he asked challengingly. I have only mixed faith in the polygraph for select situations, and I rarely use one in my cases. But Marriott had thrown out a challenge, and after conferring with Claus, we accepted.

Joann Crispi arranged for a highly regarded polygrapher to administer the test in the early summer of 1983. But before Marriott would submit to it, he insisted that Claus sign an agreement promising that his name would not be disclosed without Marriott's permission. We approved, and the agreement was executed.

As we expected, the results of the polygraph were inconclusive. Marriott was withholding so many parts of the story, as we well knew, and in light of this withholding of information, the examiner told us that "the examination does not support the answers" but that "should DJM elect to fill in the willfully withheld relevant facts and features, a reexamination would seem to be in order."

I again told Marriott that we would not be using him as a witness, though we would appreciate any leads he could provide us, especially the name of the priest or anyone else who might corroborate his claims about Alexander.

Without the priest's testimony, there were still several options available for the use of Marriott's information. We could try to find someone else of unquestionable character—or at least of substantially better character than David—who might be able to corroborate his story. But we had no clue as to whether any such witness existed: there was nothing in David's account to implicate anyone other than Alexander von Auersperg and the dead Gilbert Jackson in the alleged transactions. Marriott had dropped some hints about other people who could corroborate aspects of the story, but these hints were so vague that no one except him could follow them up.

We turned our attention to Jackson, investigating everyone who was known to have been close to him. My son Jamin, who had worked in a newsroom, checked all the news accounts of his murder. We obtained copies of police reports and consulted police officers and lawyers who were involved in its investigation and prosecution. Everything we found fit into Marriott's story, but nothing—and nobody—directly corroborated the specific drug deliveries that interested us. That was, of course, not surprising; drug sellers do not generally leave paper trails of their transactions. David had told us that after the Jackson murder Alex had expressed fear that the police might find something linking him to Jackson. We wondered whether the police had, in fact, found that something; or—if not—whether we could.

But the murder had occurred five years earlier and the trail was cold. Indeed, it had never been very hot, because the suspects in the murder had arranged a plea bargain shortly after their apprehension. The effect of this plea bargain was to abort a full-fledged investigation.

At one point during our attempts to corroborate Marriott's story, I received a strange phone call. The caller, who refused to identify himself, said that he had information that might be useful to me in the von Bülow case. This was not the first telephone offer of assistance I had received. The calls had included mediums who could talk to Sunny and find out the real story, an acupuncturist who could bring her out of the coma, women who volunteered to serve Claus von Bülow's sentence for him, and assorted "witnesses" who had "seen" Sunny—sometimes in person, sometimes in a dream—injecting herself with insulin. One witness even claimed she herself was Sunny von Bülow and the woman in the coma was an impostor who had stolen her Claus. It was she, the caller, not Claus, who had attempted to kill the impostor—and for good reason. But now she was sorry and wanted to turn herself in and get her Claus back.

Generally, a few questions quickly put the lie to the caller's claims, but occasionally we went to some lengths to check them out. Several of the calls, including one from an anonymous Newport neighbor, provided useful leads.

This latest caller surprised me by saying, "I hear you're interested in Gilbert Jackson." I had no idea how he could know that, for our interest in Jackson had remained discreet. "Do you know what a keg of dynamite you're playing with?" he asked in a sinister tone.

I demanded to know how he had found out about my interest in Jackson. My first suspicion was that he had been put up to the call by David Marriott in an effort to bolster his credibility. The caller did nothing to allay my suspicions. "I have my sources of information, just like you have yours," he said. "Now let's get off that issue and let me caution you, because I respect you as a lawyer, that Jackson was only a small fish, a front for a much bigger, and much tougher, organization. And he wasn't the only one killed."

I asked him what he was talking about and he said he would tell me, but only in person. He gave me an address and told me to meet him in the third-floor office that afternoon. I asked if I could bring my student research assistants along to take notes. (I made this request as much out of fear as out of the need for note-takers.) He said that it would be okay as long as we were unarmed and not wearing tape recorders.

The student assistants who were working with me on the von Bülow case at the time were both "preppy" intellectuals from somewhat sheltered backgrounds. Imagine their surprise—and mine—when we arrived at the address and went upstairs to find ourselves in a gay male bathhouse that catered to wealthy stockbrokers, accountants and other professionals in search of a midday break.

We were all nervous as we passed through the bathhouse area with its locker-room smell and darkened interior. One of my student assistants whispered: "If my mother and father knew what kind of education their tuition was buying, they'd transfer me to business school." The other researcher responded: "But if they saw the number of business school graduates that are clients here, they'd send you to divinity school."

We finally found the third-floor office and knocked. A man in his middle thirties invited us in. "I'm the guy who called you," he volunteered. "The information I've got for you is really gonna knock your socks off."

"But how did you know we were interested in Jackson?" I asked again.

This time he told me. "I work with cops, and you were snooping around the Jackson police files. There aren't many secrets between me and my police friends."

I asked him if the bathhouse was some kind of front for his police activity. "No," he assured me. "I make a million bucks a year off of this place. Lots of rich guys come here. You saw the location— close enough to the financial district so they can run over for a quickie, but not so close that everybody will see them. This isn't exactly the Harvard Club," he quipped, "though sometimes there's enough Crimson and Blue in here to hold a Harvard-Yale football game."

He told me that he wasn't a formal undercover agent, but that he had a working relationship with several police departments: "They need certain information about the sort of people I come in contact with. I get it for them. They return the favor. You know how it is. I scratch your back, you scratch mine," he said with a rehearsed giggle that suggested he had used that expression—particularly appropriate for the setting—before.

"Why are you willing to help me?" I asked, not wanting to get any further into the back-scratching metaphor.

"Lots of reasons. Maybe if I help you, you'll feel indebted to help me if I ever need you."

I quickly cut him off. "Look, you have to understand, that's not the way I play the game. I don't want to feel indebted to you. If you have any information you want to give me, fine, but don't expect anything in return."

"I figured you'd say that," he said casually. "You're a professor and everything. But I'm still gonna help you. Let's say it may help me too."

"How could what you're going to tell me help you?" I wondered out loud.

"You'll figure it out soon enough," he said smilingly. "Don't ask me to paint you a picture—at least not yet."

With that cryptic comment, the bathhouse operator began to tell me what he knew of Gilbert Jackson. The story involved a rambling account of a wealthy oil investment counselor who had been accused of molesting young boys. It included allegations of multiple murders, extortion, drugs and cover-up. It all sounded bizarre and incredible. Gilbert Jackson played only a small role in the story, but his alleged involvement was entirely consistent with what Marriott had told me.

When I checked the bathhouse operator's story, I found that most of it was corroborated by press accounts and police reports. I also discovered that the operator was himself a suspect, or at least an alleged witness, in one of the murders, since the victim is believed to have spent his last night at the bathhouse. There was no question that at least parts of the story were true. There was also no question that he had a personal stake in providing his version of the bizarre story so as to deflect the finger of suspicion away from him.

The bathhouse operator gave me one lead that I was unable to follow up. It involved a Massachusetts man then on death row in Florida. By the time I learned enough to try to contact him, he was literally on his way to the electric chair.

The bathhouse story—and what we were able to derive from it—gave me increased confidence in the truth of David Marriott's account. It corroborated the claim that Gilbert Jackson was involved in dealing drugs.

But it still wasn't enough. In the first place, a gay bathhouse operator does not have the credibility of a priest—to say the least. In the second place, even if a judge or jury believed everything the bathhouse operator said, it would still not corroborate the essential thrust of Marriott's story—that he had delivered injection paraphernalia and drugs to Alexander von Auersperg. For that we still needed the priest, and there was no reason to expect that we could find him.

Suddenly we got the break we were hoping for, and it proved far better—at least initially—than we had even dared to expect. One day Claus called me and said, "We've found out who the priest is. Marriott finally gave us his name. We've spoken to the priest ourselves, and he's willing to talk to you. His name is Philip Magaldi. He's the pastor of St. Anthony's Church in North Providence."

Before calling the priest, we decided to check him out through some acquaintances in the Catholic hierarchy. Von Bülow and his Rhode Island lawyers did some checking as well. We didn't say why we wanted to know, but asked about Father Philip Magaldi. "He's an absolute saint," we were told. "One of the most respected and beloved parish priests in New England." He served a large parish and had an enormous personal following, was reported to be in line for a promotion within the Catholic hierarchy and was even rumored to be a candidate for bishop sometime in the future. "Not only is he a wonderful counselor and priest," one source said, "but he's quite worldly. He knows many of Rhode Island's leading politicians, and he uses his contacts to help his parish." We learned specifically that Father Magaldi had been a friend of Rhode Island Attorney General Dennis Roberts for years.

Roberts was more than just the highest-ranking legal official in Rhode Island, he was directly responsible for the von Bülow prosecution. I wondered what effect the relationship between the priest and the Attorney General might have on the case if the priest did corroborate David's story. Moreover, rumor had it that Roberts would be challenged for the attorney generalship by a unique Republican opponent: a former Catholic nun.

I had learned enough about Father Magaldi to be bursting at the seams to speak to him. I called. The voice on the other end of the phone was gentle but down-to-earth. The priest introduced himself as "Philip Magaldi" and said that he had heard about me and was expecting my call. I thanked him for his willingness to talk with me. He assured me that he deserved no thanks because he was just doing his duty.

I asked him if he knew David Marriott. He said he had been introduced to him several years earlier by a Massachusetts relative, who had told the priest that a friend named David Marriott badly needed some spiritual and moral guidance.

The counseling relationship began quite informally. At first the priest spoke to David over the telephone. Then they met for dinner a few times. David seemed to distrust everyone, even the priest. But eventually Magaldi won David's confidence and David spoke more freely.

There were never any confessions in the formal religious sense. The conversations were either over the phone or face to face, usually at dinner. Nor were there regularly scheduled meetings. David called whenever he needed a quick counseling fix—about every six to eight weeks.

I asked Father Magaldi whether he had ever met Alexander von Auersperg.

"I believe so," the priest answered.

"Could you tell me the circumstances?" I pressed.

"It was during the summer of 1977. I remember it clearly be-

cause they came so late at night and because of the awful thing that
the young man had shouted."

"What was that?" I asked.

"Something about a black couple wanting to get married. But he
didn't say 'black.' "

"Father, I'm sorry to have to ask you to say the word, but it's
important that you tell me exactly what he said."

"I understand," the priest said softly. He paused, seeming to seek
some divine permission, and then spoke as if he were attempting
to imitate someone else's voice: " 'It's two niggers who want to
marry. Tell him it's two niggers who want to marry.' "

"How did the young man come to shout about the black couple?"
I asked the priest.

"Oh, that was in response to my somewhat angry question why
someone was waking us up so late at night. It was said in a kind of
wise-guy or clever manner. Obviously it wasn't true. There was no
one there but the two of them."

I asked the priest to describe the scene he witnessed. "It was
something out of a movie. There was the big limousine, white, I
think. I got angry and whispered—a kind of loud stage whisper—
'Shh . . . get in here, so you won't wake up the neighbors.' "

"Both David and the young man came in. I invited them into the
kitchen and waited to be introduced. David introduced the young
man as 'my friend Alexander von Auersperg from Newport.' "

"Had you ever met or seen this young man before? Had you ever
met Alexander von Auersperg?" I asked the priest.

"No, I hadn't. At least I don't recall having met him."

"So you can't actually be sure," I pressed, "that the young man
you met was actually Alexander von Auersperg?"

"Yes, I can and I am," he answered. "When the trial began
several years later, I remember reading an account of the court
sessions and seeing the young man on television. I recognized him
as the one who had been in the kitchen with David. And who had
made the obnoxious remark about blacks.

"I wasn't absolutely positive the first time," the priest said slowly.
"The person on TV was older, sadder, dressed more conservatively.
The whole setting made him seem different. But the more I looked,
the more certain I became. Then when I started reading about the
syringes and needles they found in the black bag, I knew I had to
call David, because of what David had told me after the meeting in
the kitchen."

I asked Father Magaldi about his call to Marriott.

"After I saw this von Auersperg kid on television and read about him in the papers, I called David and urged him to tell someone about what he knew. We both discussed it with one of my former altar boys who became a lawyer."

"What's his name?" I asked.

"John Tarantino, he's still in the parish. I spoke to him first and then David insisted on talking to him also. It was after that David called von Bülow and they arranged the meeting in Newport at the hotel."

"Okay," I said, "let's get to the summer of 1978."

"I don't remember if David called first or just came by. But eventually he came by. He was shaking with fear: 'I'm a nervous wreck. You've got to tell me what to do,' he said. David was always a bit nervous around me, but this time it was worse than ever. He was in a real panic.

"He started by telling me that he had driven from Boston to Newport earlier that night to visit friends. He told me that his friend Gilbert Jackson had asked him to bring a package to their common friend Alexander. At this point David started on a detour, telling me all about Gilbert Jackson's interior-decorating business and how he thought the package probably contained draperies or hooks of some kind. Then he started to tell me about Alexander, how rich he was and what kind of a house he lived in. Then he stopped short and said, 'Alexander's the kid from last year, remember "the niggers who want to get married?" ' I groaned a sigh of recognition. 'Yeah, that kid,' David said. 'Boy, am I sorry I ever got mixed up with him.' "

Father Magaldi continued to recount the story David had told him. It was the same story David had told me weeks earlier: His arrival at Clarendon Court. The butler telling him to wait. His decision to open the package. His discovery of needles, syringes, powders, pills and liquid. His eventual delivery of the package to a woman.

Father Magaldi told me that as soon as David finished his account, he—the priest—"flew off the handle. I didn't respond in a very priestly way. I called David names: 'stupid,' 'nuts,' maybe even worse. I remember being ashamed of myself afterwards. You don't get anywhere calling people names, especially when they're in agony like David was.

"But I had to get my message across. I had to convince David to drop these people. To stay away from them. David had enough of his own problems without getting involved in crimes and drugs. I warned him to stay out of Newport, and never to see this Alexander or Gilbert Jackson again.

"After my outburst I tried to gather my thoughts and asked David whether he had ever delivered any other packages. He told me that he had, but he swore that up until that night he had no idea they contained drugs. He thought they had drapery material. I remember responding very sarcastically, 'What did you think you were delivering—gold-plated drapery hooks?' David didn't laugh. He swore again he just didn't know."

I pressed Father Magaldi about how much of the elaborate story he believed. The priest started talking to me like a lawyer.

"Look," he said, "let's divide the story into its component parts. First, there is what I saw directly. David Marriott together with a young man whom I recognize to be Alexander von Auersperg. David also tells me—at a time when he has no motive to lie—that it is Alexander von Auersperg. I certainly believe that much."

"Then we come to the drug deliveries. Why would David lie to me in 1978 about delivering drugs to the von Bülow house? He certainly didn't do it to please me or to have me respect him. Why would he incur my anger if the basic story wasn't true? So I believe that, although I can't possibly be as sure of that as I am of the meeting with Alexander von Auersperg.

"Finally, we come to David's denial that he knew he was delivering drugs. Here," the priest said sounding a bit like a poor imitation of Sherlock Holmes lecturing Dr. Watson, "we do have a motive to lie. And although I would never accuse anyone of lying without proof, I do have to say I would not be surprised to learn that David suspected that he was carrying drugs. My own personal theory is that he probably believed he was carrying marijuana or cocaine or maybe some pills, but that he was very surprised when he found syringes and needles. That made him worry that he might be involved in something more serious—heroin maybe!"

I pressed the father again: "If you disbelieve some of his story, doesn't that make you doubt the rest?"

"Professor," he answered with a tone of impatience, "don't you understand what I'm saying? I'm not relying on David's inherent honesty. I'm relying on two things. First, what I saw myself. And second, that even if David is a pathological liar, he had absolutely no reason to lie about delivering drugs to Alexander and his mother. In fact, he would have had every reason to lie and *not* tell me about an event that made me so angry at him."

I listened carefully to the priest's logic, which was reminiscent of the logic used by judges and legal commentators in allowing certain kinds of "hearsay" testimony to be used in court. The law is that if someone like David tells someone else like Father Magaldi a bad thing about himself—for example, that he has been dealing drugs— the person who heard the statement (Father Magaldi) can testify about it even though it is hearsay. The reason for this exception to the usual rule against using hearsay is the general observation that the bad things people say about themselves are generally true be- cause there is rarely a motive to put oneself down; whereas the good things people say about themselves are often false because there is a motive of self-aggrandizement.

Having heard Father Magaldi's corroboration of Marriott's story, I asked the crucial question: "Father, I assume that you're prepared to put all that into an affidavit and, if necessary, testify to it before a judge or jury?" I waited anxiously while the priest, after a long pause, began his answer.

"I would strongly prefer not to have to testify or become part of the case. I feel very uncomfortable revealing what someone told me, even though he has given me permission to reveal it. Some people might misunderstand and become more reluctant to confide in a priest."

"But without your testimony," I insisted, "David is worthless. You're the key to getting Mr. von Bülow a new trial. We really need you, Father. I wouldn't ask you if we could do without your testi- mony."

Again the priest pondered. "You're the lawyer and I'm putting myself in your hands," he said with resignation. "If you honestly believe you need me, then you have me. But please use your best judgment." Father Magaldi then went on to question me about the order of proceedings. "Doesn't the appeal come first? And if you win that, isn't it possible that you won't need me or David?" he asked hopefully.

"Sure, it's possible," I responded, "but not very likely. I think we have a strong appeal, but you just can't count on it. And even if we were to win, there could still be a new trial."

The priest seemed unaware that there could be a new trial if we won the appeal: "Wouldn't that be double jeopardy?" he asked, proud of his knowledge of legal principles.

"I only wish it were. But it depends on the grounds—the reasons —why we might win. If we win because the court believes there wasn't enough evidence to convict Mr. von Bülow, that would be the end of the matter. There couldn't be a new trial. But if we were to win on some legal ground, such as illegal search and seizure, then they could try him again, but this time without the illegally obtained evidence. And of course we could lose the appeal."

I told the Father that only about 5 percent of all appeals in criminal cases are victorious—on any ground. This surprised the priest, who said that he always read about convictions being reversed on appeal. "Yeah," I assured him, "those are the ones they write about in the newspapers, but every day in every court there are dozens of convictions affirmed by the courts of appeals that you never read about. That's the reality. Being an appeals lawyer is a very frustrating profession—especially if you like to win."

Father Magaldi agreed to provide an affidavit to a lawyer he knew in Rhode Island, detailing what he had seen and heard, but I promised him that I wouldn't disclose it or use it without first checking with him.

"Now I really hope you win the appeal," he said with a laugh. "My continued tranquility may depend on it."

There is really no certain way for a lawyer to decide whether witnesses are telling the truth. There are plenty of old wives' tales— *boobe-mysehs*, my grandmother would call them—about sweating palms, evasive looks and nervous tics. But the liar par excellence rarely displays such obvious manifestations, and honest witnesses, if they are nervous, often do. A lawyer has to go with his or her best judgment, based on experience and insight, but with no guarantee that the judgment will always be correct.

The rules of the profession require the criminal defense lawyer to resolve reasonable doubts or close questions "in favor of his client." To me, the credibility of the Magaldi story did not seem like a close question.

Based on my assessment of the truth of Father Magaldi's story, and therefore necessarily of the Marriott story, I was prepared to submit their affidavits as part of a new-trial motion, if they were willing to sign them. Since affidavits are legal documents that must follow a particular form, they are almost always drafted by lawyers, based on the facts provided by the affiant—the one swearing the truth. Claus eventually arranged to have the affidavits prepared by Rhode Island attorneys who were more familiar with local forms and rules.

I later learned that on August 6, 1983, Father Magaldi and David Marriott met with the Attorney General of Rhode Island, Dennis Roberts, and told him of their story and of their intention to sign affidavits. Marriott asked the Attorney General if he could be prosecuted for drug violations on the basis of his sworn admission that he carried drugs into Rhode Island. Although he tried to discourage Magaldi and Marriott from signing any affidavits for the defense, Roberts did apparently assure Marriott that he would not be prosecuted for his role in any delivery of drugs to the von Bülow house.

Father Magaldi and Marriott then went to the Rhole Island home of Earl and Mary Levenstein—family friends of the von Bülows who were hosting Claus and Andrea Reynolds for part of the summer—and signed the affidavits that were prepared by the Rhode Island lawyers.

I didn't know about any of this until after my return from my summer vacation, when I received copies of the affidavits. I read them to check whether they reflected the essence of the stories told to me by Magaldi and Marriott. They did. The affidavits were then ready for us to use. But a great deal would happen between then and the time when we would have to decide whether, and in what context, to use them.

Ten days after Marriott signed his affidavit, I received a panicky call from the Melrose-Wakefield Emergency Room in Melrose, Massachusetts. The caller was David Marriott. He told me he had been driving down a dark road not far from his home in a borrowed Cadillac when a Lincoln Continental with two men in it started following him. He tried to evade them, but they drove alongside his car, trapping him. He continued: "I'm bouncing all along the guardrail," using it as "a protection from being pushed off the road and into a ditch." Suddenly he saw that the guardrail was ending and he became frightened about ending up in a ditch. At this point, "this man with a stocking mask over his face stood up out of the sunroof of this Lincoln Continental and threw this rock that was three-quarters the size of my head through the glass, and I lost control of the car."

The rock hit Marriott on his shoulder. "I let go of the wheel, and the car, after the guardrail, went off into the trees." The Continental stopped and another rock was thrown at the immobile Cadillac. But this one missed Marriott and hit the trunk.

The police arrived shortly thereafter, and Marriott was taken by ambulance to the hospital.

Marriott told me that this had not been his first encounter with violence. On several recent occasions he had received threatening phone calls. I asked him to tell me what the caller said: " 'Listen, you mother-fucker. You open your mouth and we'll have you blown away . . . You'll never hit the courtroom steps, because you won't ever know what hit you. Don't talk to the old man, he'll get you in a lot of trouble.' "

David's voice was shaking as he described these events. "I never had one problem before I met Claus," he shouted, "Now I'm scared to go home, to go out, to answer the phone." Marriott demanded that I try to get him "some sort of protection. I'm not leaving this hospital alone."

Eventually, the private investigator who had accompanied me to Marriott's home was reached, and he accompanied Marriott home and stood watch through the night.

But this was not the end of the threats. Father Magaldi received a threatening message that had been transcribed by a telephone operator at the Boston Park Plaza Hotel, where he was staying. When I heard about this, I immediately dispatched one of my student researchers to the hotel to retrieve a transcribed copy. It was a warning to "tell your friend David Marriott to keep his mouth shut or sooner or later we'll kill him."

Marriott began to call me on a daily basis. "I'm not risking my life for no Claus von Bülow. He's sitting pretty in his fancy apartment on Fifth Avenue and someone's out there trying to kill me."

Marriott told me that unless he got some official protection, he would simply disappear and have nothing further to do with the case. I told him that only the government can provide official security and that prosecutors often do that for their witnesses, but that a defense attorney can only ask—as a private citizen—for some assistance. He pleaded with me to ask.

I called the United States Attorney's office in Boston and told them about the threats and the rock incident and asked them to have the FBI conduct an investigation. The Assistant U.S. Attorney assigned to the matter concluded that there was no federal jurisdiction to investigate or provide protection because everything had apparently occurred within the state of Massachusetts.

I was beginning a long weekend on Cape Cod while all this was happening, and it was difficult to reach people. I managed to reach an Assistant District Attorney for Middlesex County, Massachusetts, just as business was closing on Friday. I told him the story and asked whether his office would investigate the incidents and provide protection. He told me that his office could not provide security, but that he would call the Wakefield police and ask them to keep an eye on the Marriott house. That seemed to satisfy Marriott.

But then there were more threats and more violence. As David was leaving a restaurant in Wakefield, two men approached him and started to beat him up, shouting that this was just a preview of what he would get if he continued to make trouble. "If you plan to live a healthy life," they threatened, "you'd better forget about this case."

Marriott called again from the hospital in a panic. "Count me out. I'm not testifying under any circumstances. Claus is going to end up a free man. And I'm gonna end up dead. No way."

Marriott did agree to spend some time quietly looking for other witnesses who might be able to prove drug transactions involving members of the von Bülow household. He told me he had some leads in Newport, in Montreal, and in some other places that he would pursue, but only if he was protected from further violence. And didn't have to "go public." "What do I have to do? End up with a slit throat before you take me seriously?" he asked angrily.

I was taking the threats seriously. Our source in the bathhouse warned us to expect "rough stuff" from Marriott's former associates. "They play for keeps," he told us. "First they threaten, then they hit, and finally they kill." But the police were skeptical. They concluded, after a brief investigation, that there was no hard evidence to substantiate any of the threats or episodes. As the exasperated Assistant D.A. put it: "About all you can say is that David Marriott has made certain allegations, and that these allegations are under investigation. We haven't been able to substantiate any of it, so that's all they are right now—allegations made by David Marriott."

Shortly thereafter Marriott was knifed, his arms deeply cut. After being treated for his wounds, he had them photographed so that he could prove they were deep and serious. He said that "they" were

Martha "Sunny" Crawford at her 1957 wedding to her first husband, Prince Alfred von Auersperg. © *Picture Group*

Right: Sunny and Claus von Bülow arriving at the Newport Music Festival, Newport, Rhode Island, 1979. © *Providence Journal/Picture Group*

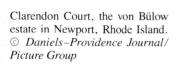

Clarendon Court, the von Bülow estate in Newport, Rhode Island. © *Daniels–Providence Journal/ Picture Group*

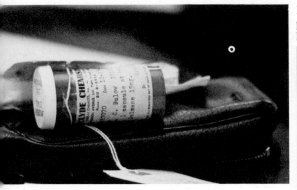

The "black bag." The prosecution contended that syringes and drugs found in this bag were evidence of attempted murder. © *Providence Journal/Picture Group*

Maria Schrallhammer, Sunny's loyal maid. The prosecution's case in the first trial rested largely on her testimony. © *Providence Journal/Picture Group*

Reporters and spectators surround members of the prosecution team on the steps of the Newport County Courthouse during the first trial. © *Providence Journal Company*

Alexandra Isles, soap-opera actress and mistress of Claus von Bülow between 1979 and 1981, who told Claus to "leave Sunny or lose me." © *1982 Bryce Flynn/ Picture Group*

Herald Price Fahringer, chief defense attorney at the first trial, and John Sheehan, co-counsel at the first and second trials, with von Bülow. © *Charles Steiner/ Sygma*

Rhode Island Attorney General and former nun Arlene Violet. © *Jack Spratt/Picture Group*

Claus von Bülow hears the jury foreman deliver two guilty verdicts. © *Providence Journal Company*

Alan M. Dershowitz, *right,* with his research team. © *Steve Hansen 1982*

Dershowitz argues the appeal, 1983.
© *Providence Journal Company*

Dershowitz, von Bülow and Sheehan arrive at the courthouse during the second trial. © *Robyn Wishna/Picture Group*

The Kuh notes contained important evidence withheld from the first trial.

Defense attorney John Sheehan scratched his own forearm to cross-examine prosecution witness Dr. Jeremy Worthington, who had testified that Sunny von Bülow was clawed in a struggle with her alleged assailant. © *AP/ Wide World Photos*

Claus with Cosima von Bülow, Claus and Sunny's only child. © *Providence Journal/Picture Group*

David Marriott, volatile witness who claimed he had delivered drugs to the von Bülow residence. © *Ira Wyman/ Sygma*

Prince Alexander (Alex) von Auersperg and Princess Annie Laurie (Ala) Kneissl, Sunny's children by her first marriage. © *Michael Grecco–Boston Herald/Picture Group*

Thomas Puccio, von Bülow's chief trial lawyer for the second trial, addresses the jury, prosecutors *(from left)* Marc De Sisto and Henry Gemma, and Detective Lieutenant John F. Reise. © *Providence Journal/Picture Group*

Claus von Bülow in court. © *Providence Journal /Picture Group*

Judge Corrine Grande hears testimony.
© *Providence Journal/Picture Group*

Dershowitz debates William Wright, author of *The Von Bülow Affair*, on a Boston-based talk show. © *Kevin Twombly Photo/The Boston Herald*

Andrea Reynolds, Claus von Bülow's constant companion during the appeal and the second trial, leaves the courthouse with a happy Claus after his acquittal. © *Providence Journal Company*

really getting serious about threatening him now because he was getting close to learning who had been supplying drugs to various members of the von Auersperg–Kneissl family.

To complicate things further, Marriott was demanding that Claus von Bülow pay the expenses he had incurred as a result of his involvement in the case. "My coming forward to help Claus shouldn't end up costing me anything," he explained. "I've got an invalid mother to support. I can't pay for these things out of my own pocket."

Marriott complained about losing a printing job he had as a result of his involvement in the case. It was true that Claus was asking for a great deal of his time, and we believed that his dismissal had resulted from our demands on him. He said he was pursuing investigative leads, attempting to prove his story through other witnesses or circumstances. Neither we nor Marriott wanted Marriott to have to testify in court. We all hoped we could prove his story through others. We preferred to use him as a combination investigator and undercover agent. This put Marriott in a difficult situation. He was the sole means of his support for his mother— who was quite sick and in the process of being divorced. Marriott even threatened to sue Claus for his lost wages.

I was asked to give legal advice as to whether it would be permissible to compensate Marriott for his lost wages—or pay some form of living expenses—while he was out of a job he had lost because of his involvement in the case. I consulted with several experts —prosecutors, defense attorneys, professors and Bar officials. The unanimous view of those with whom I conferred was that it is proper for a defendant to treat a defense investigator-witness the way prosecutors treat prosecution witnesses who are similarly situated. Prosecutors do pay for the protection, expenses, lost wages and/or living expenses of witnesses, informers and undercover investigators. The basic rules are that no one may pay a witness to tell an untruth; and if a witness has been paid, all such payments must be fully disclosed if and when the witness testifies. I discussed this issue in a legal ethics class at which several high-ranking federal prosecutors were my guests. They agreed that the rule had to be that defendants should be permitted to treat witnesses, informers and investigators the way prosecutors do.

Eventually, I wrote Marriott a letter expressing my legal opinion on the propriety of paying an investigator who might also be a witness:

Dear Mr. Marriott:

As I have informed you on numerous occasions, it is my opinion, and that of others with whom I have conferred, that it is proper for you to be treated in the way that prosecutors treat their witnesses. Accordingly, it is proper for you to receive protection from threatened harm, compensation for wages lost as a result of your involvement in the case, and compensation for all out-of-pocket expenses connected with the case. It is proper for you to be put in the position you would have been had you not come forward.

You will not, of course, be paid for your testimony, and you are expected to tell the whole truth and nothing but the truth. Moreover, as I have told you, every fact relating to what you have received, or what has been paid on your behalf must be, and will be, disclosed at any court proceeding. You will be asked by Mr. von Bülow's lawyer to make full disclosure and you will do so fully and completely.

Pursuant to that advice, Marriott was paid a small flat weekly sum—at a rate of six dollars an hour—in lieu of his lost wages to cover his living expenses and the time he spent performing investigative tasks. The money was paid by check to a lawyer with written instructions that Marriott *must* disclose every penny he received if called as a witness and that he must tell the truth even if the truth was adverse to Claus von Bülow's interests.

The government was used to dealing with witnesses like Marriott. I was not. But I decided to play by the government's rules. There were no other rules, no guidelines specifically applicable to this situation.*

I hoped that we would never have to use David Marriott as a witness. He was certainly not someone whose testimony I could count on a jury necessarily believing, though I was hoping that his

---

* A recent Supreme Court case disclosed that the United States government has a printed form entitled "Contract for purchase of information and payment of lump sum therefore." The contract promises monetary payment for the witness to "purchase evidence" and to "testify against the violator in federal court." In consideration for these services "the United States will pay to said vendor a sum commensurate with services and information rendered." The Court concluded in that case that the prospect of "a reward" had been held out to the witnesses if their information and testimony led to "the accomplishment of the objective sought to be obtained . . . to the satisfaction of [the government]"—a euphemism for the conviction of the defendant. The court found that a reward dangled in front of the witnesses gave them "a personal stake" in the defendant's conviction. It also found that the contingent nature of the Government's contract to pay them "served only to strengthen any incentive to testify falsely in order to secure a conviction." Despite this incentive, none of the Justices criticized the government for making this deal. Their criticism was limited to the government's failure to disclose it after being asked about any deals.

investigative work might turn up some compelling leads and witnesses.

Nor could I count on Truman Capote, who, despite his fame as an author, would not make the world's greatest witness. The idea of putting on a case consisting primarily of a man who would admit carrying drugs for a gay interior decorator, an author with his own drug problems, and the operator of a bathhouse would not bring joy to the heart of any lawyer. Nor could we use Father Magaldi without David Marriott, because Magaldi's testimony would be largely hearsay. It would corroborate aspects of Marriott's account, but it was no substitute for it. We had a credible story. Now we needed some credible witnesses to tell it.

Probably the next best thing to a clergyman witness is a scientist. And so off we went in search of scientists who could disprove the prosecution's case and lend some corroboration to David Marriott's account. At bottom the case against Claus von Bülow was a scientific case. It would have to be refuted by scientific evidence. The Capote-Marriott-Magaldi information would always remain a sideshow, though a revealing, fascinating and frustrating one.

11

Trial and Error

The Capote-Marriott-Magaldi information raised numerous questions in my mind about the structure of the prosecution's trial presentation. The most damning piece of physical evidence was, of course, the black bag containing both an insulin-coated weapon—the "murder weapon," as the prosecutor called it—and a vial of Dalmane, bearing a prescription label made out to Claus von Bülow. The presence of the prescription vial in the same bag as the insulin needle was like the fingerprint of the defendant on the murder weapon. As the prosecutor put it to the jury: "The only thing in the black bag, ladies and gentlemen, which has anybody's name on it or any indication as to who owns it, is the prescription of Dalmane . . . for Claus von Bülow." There could be little doubt that if both were authentic, then the murder weapon belonged to Claus von Bülow. Nothing could be more damning.

Also present in the black bag were other drugs and pills that—according to the prosecution—could have been used by the attempted murderer to sedate his wife before injecting her. This combination of "weapons" together with Claus von Bülow's telltale prescription certainly contributed to the sealing of his fate.

In light of the Capote-Marriott-Magaldi revelations, I decided to take a hard second look at the black bag and its contents. My first step was to review the testimony concerning the black bag. I had my research assistants gather together in one folder every word that had been said about what was found in the black bag on the day that Alexander von Auersperg allegedly discovered it in Claus von Bülow's closet in Clarendon Court.

I reviewed not only Alexander von Auersperg's trial testimony but the testimony of the private investigator and the locksmith, the police reports, the grand jury minutes and the pretrial testimony. One of a lawyer's most important tools is inconsistency. When the same event is described by several people on several different occasions, it almost never comes out exactly the same. Minor discrepancies merely reflect normal failings of human memory. But major discrepancies in recounting the same event may disclose lies more tellingly than any polygraph.

When I reviewed the testimony relating to the discovery of the black bag, I was shocked by what I discovered. The so-called "evidence" that the Dalmane bearing Claus von Bülow's name was actually found in the black bag was utterly confusing.

There were two witnesses to the events surrounding the discovery of the black bag in Clarendon Court on January 23, 1981: Alexander von Auersperg and the private detective, Edwin Lambert, who accompanied him. (The locksmith had also witnessed some parts of the search, but the prosecution didn't produce him as a witness, claiming that no one had written down his name. Eventually he was found by the defense. And he testified that after the investigator searched the closet he came out and told Alexander, "It's not in here.")

The prosecution had relied on Alex's account in its summation. Alex had testified that among the items he found inside the black bag were "two vials, one containing different types of pills with a prescription on it . . ." He identified the vial with Dalmane prescribed for Claus von Bülow as the one with the prescription.

The other witness to the search for the black bag was the private detective who was hired to conduct the search and who actually conducted it. His job was to find and preserve any and all evidence linking Claus von Bülow to Sunny's coma. And he was extremely well suited by training and experience for this task. He had thirty-three years of experience as an investigator; had served for much of that time as a New York City Police Department detective; had "special training in the handling of evidence"; and was an expert in lifting and preserving fingerprints and photographing, marking and inventorying evidence. Moreover, he had testified at numerous trials about what he had observed during searches and seizures.

I fully expected the detective's testimony to back up Alexander's recollection of what he had seen in the black bag. But it did not. The detective testified that only *he* had handled any of the materials found in the black bag, that Alex did not touch anything at all. The detective remembered finding "two containers containing one a liquid and one a dry substance, a powder." But he did not remember seeing "any containers with pills inside the black bag." Nor did he recall seeing a vial "in the black bag with a prescription on it."

When the detective was shown the pill vial with the Claus von Bülow prescription, he could not identify it as among the items he had found in the black bag (although he was able to identify the other items—the ones without Claus von Bülow's name on them—as having been found in the bag.)

Since the detective's primary task was to find evidence linking Claus von Bülow to Sunny's coma, it would be quite amazing if the detective had actually found a most incriminating piece of evidence —the telltale vial with the prescription for Claus von Bülow—and then proceeded to forget precisely that singularly significant piece of evidence. I believed that the far more plausible explanation was that the detective did not find the prescription vial *in* the black bag at all.

This was likely, because the search was conducted in an extremely haphazard manner. No inventory was made. No photographs were taken. No fingerprints were preserved. And most important, *all* the items found during the entire search—which included items found outside the black bag in various rooms—were "all mixed together" and placed in the black bag for "convenience." No record was made of which items had been found *in* the bag and which *outside it* before they were commingled.

But Prosecutor Famiglietti's representation to the jury that the Dalmane, with Claus von Bülow's name on it, had definitely been found in the black bag had gone unanswered at the trial. It had gone unanswered because the prosecutor had the last word. We would have to answer it now.

Having raised real doubts—at least in my mind, and I hoped in the minds of objective observers—about Alexander's testimony concerning the presence of the telltale prescription vial in the black bag, I began to wonder about the rest of the contents of the bag.

All of the remaining items found in the bag could easily have been used by Mrs. von Bülow if she was injecting herself, as Truman Capote said, with the paraphernalia David Marriott said he had brought to her. Indeed, the detective had testified at a pretrial hearing that he had found Inderal inside the black bag. The police report corroborated that testimony. The significance of this evidence is that the Inderal vial also had a prescription label on it—but the name on that prescription was *Martha von Bülow*.

Thus, if the detective's testimony—rather than Alexander's—

were to be believed, then the "fingerprint" on the "murder weapon" would be that of the victim, Martha von Bülow, rather than that of the defendant. The murder weapon would become a weapon of suicide or accident, but not of murder or attempted murder.

But what about the insulin-coated needle in the black bag? That crucial piece of evidence was not accounted for by the new information provided by Capote and Marriott. Neither of them had seen any insulin nor heard any discussion of it. If Sunny von Bülow was not injecting herself with insulin, who was? That was the remaining question.

But why was I assuming that the needle did, in fact, contain insulin? And why was I accepting the prosecution's theory that it was, in fact, injected into Mrs. von Bülow? If the rest of the prosecution's case—the prescription vial, the claim that no one but Claus had any familiarity with injectable drugs—was so flimsy, why not begin to question the rest of the prosecution's case? Keeping that in mind, I began a second look at the needle itself. With the help of my assistants I started to call experts in forensic medicine, that branch of science which investigates the causes of death, injury and other issues relevant to the law. Television's *Quincy*—based on the real-life medical examiner for Los Angeles County—is perhaps the world's best-known forensic expert.*

We gathered together all the evidence describing the needle, as it was allegedly found in the black bag, and showed it to several of the world's leading forensic experts. Every one of them came to the same shocking conclusion. As Dr. Robert Shaler, who was director of serology for the chief medical examiner in New York, put it: "The needle alleged by the State of Rhode Island to have been injected into Martha von Bülow . . . was not, and could not have been, injected."

If this expert scientific conclusion was valid—and we had no reason to doubt it—the prosecution's entire case collapsed. Without a "murder weapon" there was no crime, and the needle could not be the murder weapon if it "was not, and could not have been, in-

---

* Interestingly, the chief medical examiner for Los Angeles, Thomas Noguchi, has recently written a book entitled *Coroner at Large*, in which he concludes that Sunny's comas may have been caused by a condition called islet cell hyperplasia. He cites a recent Los Angeles case in which a woman with symptoms similar to Sunny's died of excessive insulin in the absence of an injection. Noguchi also dismisses the possibility that insulin allegedly seen in the black bag following Thanksgiving could have been used to inject Sunny a month later, since the kind of insulin in use during 1980 "had to be refrigerated . . . or it would very soon spoil."

jected." It was as if the smoking gun had turned out to shoot only blanks.

But if the needle had not been and could not have been injected, what was it doing encrusted with a lethal solution and lying in the black bag found by Alexander von Auersperg and the detective?

The answer to that conundrum sent a chill down my spine. Its sinister implications were as plain as they were shocking. The expert conclusion was that the needle had "been dipped into solution."

Since the syringe and needle in question were not the kind that would normally be dipped prior to injection—the liquid being contained in the vial of the syringe itself and forced through the hollow needle by the plunger—this expert conclusion raised the specter of a devious plot to make it *appear* that the solution had been injected, when it really had not been.

Why, I wondered, would anyone dip a needle into solution to make it appear that it had been injected? I couldn't come up with an obvious answer. My mind started turning over various theories.

But before I allowed my fantasies to run wild, I wanted to be absolutely certain that the needle had been dipped rather than injected. I insisted that the experts prove their conclusion to me beyond any reasonable doubt.*

They told us that there were four independent reasons why this needle could not have been injected into Mrs. von Bülow. First, if the needle had been injected, any routine examination of it would have disclosed traces of human tissue and blood elements in addition to insulin. But no such material was found on this needle.

Second, amobarbital was found on the needle, but that highly corrosive drug could not have been injected under anyone's skin without leaving enormous and easily visible welts—called barbiturate burns—at the site of the injection. These welts produce oozing and sloughing and could not possibly have escaped detection on even superficial examination. Mrs. von Bülow's body had been searched for injection marks when she was admitted to the hospital and none were found.

Third, Valium was found on the needle in the black bag, but no traces of Valium were turned up on the drug tests performed on Mrs. von Bülow.

Finally, the fact that "crystalline encrustations" were found on

---

* The experts we consulted included the chief medical examiner for the city of New York and the chief toxicologist for Suffolk County, New York.

the outside of the needle near the tip is "inconsistent with injection." They could only have been produced by the needle having been "dipped into solution." The reason for that conclusion is obvious, the experts pointed out, and can be illustrated at home by a simple experiment. When a needle is injected, the experts said, "withdrawal of the needle from under the skin serves to cleanse its surface of drug encrustations." In simple language, the skin surrounding the needle would act like a cotton swab: it would wipe the needle clean—and push all the residue up to the top. "Thus there would be no residue where the needle went in and came out of the skin." The only drug residue that might be visible after injection would be located "at the lever fitting of the needle, that is the point of attachment of the needle to the syringe."

I asked one of the assistants who had interviewed several experts to pretend that I was from Missouri, the Show-Me State, and to prove his point. He took me into a nearby kitchen and looked around for some utensils. He found a barbecue skewer—one of those long round ones that look like an enormous needle. He opened the refrigerator and found some salad dressing. He dipped the skewer into the dressing, took it out and asked me what I saw! At the tip of the skewer there was some liquid residue. Then he placed his thumb and forefinger together. He took the skewer and forced it between the closed tips of his fingers and then pulled it out. Again he asked me what I saw. All the liquid at the tip had been swabbed clean, but there was some residue up near the top, just above the part of the skewer that had touched his fingers. "*Voilà!*" he exclaimed. "Have I proved the point?" He certainly had. There was no doubt in my mind—nor, I believed, could there be any doubt in the minds of jurors—that the so-called "murder weapon" had not been injected into Sunny von Bülow.

With this part of the deck having been knocked out of the prosecution's house of cards, I began to grow even more skeptical of the trial evidence. The only remaining mystery surrounding the needle was the alleged presence of insulin on it. Neither Capote nor Marriott had seen or heard of any insulin. Why was insulin on the needle?

To try to answer that question, we went back to the testimony that had allegedly proved the presence of insulin on the needle. The only scientific evidence of insulin had come from a test conducted by a laboratory called BioScience, an internationally used and highly reputable testing service.

We took the laboratory worksheets and data used by BioScience and showed them to several experts. Again the opinion of the experts was unanimous. The tests conducted by BioScience were inconclusive. As Dr. Steven Flecher, the deputy head of biology in the Central Research Establishment of the British Home Office Forensic Science Service—the English equivalent of the famed FBI crime lab—concluded: "It is my expert opinion that the test results on the needle at trial are consistent with the complete absence of insulin on this needle."

Dr. Flecher's research has demonstrated that when needle washings containing amobarbital and Valium—but no insulin—are placed in saline solution, they often produce a false positive result for insulin—that is, they falsely show the presence of insulin when none is, in fact, there. Dr. Flecher's research was not available when BioScience conducted the test on the needle found in the black bag.

To prove Dr. Flecher's hypothesis, another doctor performed an actual experiment with the BioScience lab. He prepared five different needle washings and sent them to BioScience just as the washing from the "murder weapon" had been sent. Two of the experimental washings contained insulin, amobarbital, Valium and saline solution; one contained only saline solution; the remaining two contained amobarbital, Valium and saline solution—but no insulin.

When the BioScience report came back, it completely confirmed Dr. Flecher's hypothesis: the two washings that contained amobarbital, Valium and saline solution—*but absolutely no insulin*—both came back with *false positive readings for insulin*. One of the false readings was for 93 microunits of insulin per milliliter. The other was for 282 microunits of insulin per milliliter.

The conclusion reached by all the experts to whom we showed these data was that there was no valid scientific evidence that the needle found in the black bag contained any insulin at all. The next card had dropped from the prosecutor's fragile house.

We could now prove that the alleged murder weapon had not been injected into Sunny von Bülow and that the prosecution's scientific conclusion that it definitely contained insulin was invalid.

There was little now left to the prosecution's case, except the fact that Sunny's insulin level was high when she was admitted to the hospital during her second coma, and that her blood sugar was low during the first coma and remained low after she received glucose pushes. (There were no insulin levels measured during the first coma.) These circumstantial facts led the prosecution's expert witness to infer that Sunny had probably been injected with insulin. None of the experts had testified that Claus von Bülow had injected her—indeed, one of them expressed a suggestion that she had most probably injected herself. But the high insulin and low sugar levels were yet another important foundation card for the prosecution's evidentiary house. It was important, therefore, for us to evaluate the strength of this foundation.

We also took the underlying BioScience documents concerning Sunny's blood tests to experts, and again their conclusions were unanimous and devastating to the prosecution's case. Dr. Arthur Rubenstein, chairman of the Department of Medicine at the prestigious University of Chicago Medical School, concluded that it was his expert opinion that the high insulin level found in Sunny's blood "may not be a valid result." And Dr. Harold Lebovitz, professor of medicine and head of endocrinology and diabetes at Downstate Medical Center in New York, concluded that in his expert opinion the insulin reading reported by BioScience "is not a valid result."

These doctors rely on insulin readings every day in their practice and research, and have come to accept certain safeguards. One such safeguard—widely employed in the profession—is that before an insulin level can readily be relied on, the blood sample must be tested several times and the insulin levels obtained must correspond to each other within acceptable limits (plus or minus 10 percent). In the test performed by BioScience, there were four different readings, but no two of them even came close to corresponding within the required percentages. One reading was 216 microunits per milliliter; another was 0.8; a third was 350; and the fourth was recorded as "NSC," meaning "nonsignificant counts." The experts, evaluating these widely diverse results, concluded that "the basis on which they decided what was a valid answer appears to be subject to considerable guesswork," and that "it is impossible scientifically to determine which of the discrepant values is 'correct.'"

The experts thus decided that they would never rely on the "correct" reading given by the lab for their own practice. Yet the prosecution had relied on it in convicting Claus von Bülow and sentencing him to prison for thirty years.

There was one final scientific "fact" that had played a significant role in the prosecution's case. The prosecutor's expert witness, Dr. George Cahill of Harvard Medical School, had been asked hypothetical questions about the causes of the two comas. Hypothetical questions are often asked of experts who did not examine the patient. Since Dr. Cahill had never examined—or even seen—Sunny von Bülow, he could not give an opinion on the causes of her comas. But he could be asked questions about a hypothetical patient *like* Sunny von Bülow. For example, he could be asked, "If you had examined a forty-eight-year-old comatose female patient with a history of reactive hypoglycemia and found a blood-sugar level of 29 and an insulin level of 216, could you give an expert opinion as to the probable cause of her coma?"

If the jurors then believed that the facts contained in the hypothetical question—forty-eight-year-old comatose female patient with blood-sugar level of 29 and insulin of 216—corresponded to the actual facts of Sunny von Bülow's situation, they could extrapolate the expert's hypothetical answer to Sunny von Bülow and conclude that Sunny's coma had probably been caused by the factors contained in the hypothetical answer.

Needless to say, a hypothetical answer can be no more accurate than the underlying facts contained in and omitted from the hypothetical question put to the expert.

With that in mind, we went back to the trial record to take another look at the hypothetical questions put to the prosecution's major expert witness, Dr. Cahill, who had given the hypothetical answer that both of Sunny's comas had been caused by exogenous insulin—that is, insulin that originated from outside her body.

Our second look paid off once again. We discovered that the hypothetical question about the first coma did *not* correspond to the actual facts surrounding Sunny's first coma and hospitalization.

As there was no insulin level, valid or invalid, for the first coma, Dr. Cahill had to rely exclusively on Sunny's blood-sugar readings. He was asked whether he could determine the cause of coma in a hypothetical patient who entered the hospital with low blood sugar that failed to rebound after receiving one glucose push at around 8:00 P.M. and a second glucose push at around 9:00 P.M. Dr. Cahill said that such a patient would probably have been injected with insulin, because in the absence of exogenous insulin, low sugar would rebound after receiving two pushes over a one-hour period.

But we discovered that the actual Sunny von Bülow, as distinguished from the hypothetical patient in Dr. Cahill's answer, had not received two glucose pushes within an hour. Sunny had received only *one* glucose push at 9:00 P.M. The 8:00 P.M. glucose push was a figment of the prosecutor's imagination. Thus, the *hypothetical* patient's *hypothetical* coma might have been caused by an insulin injection, but Sunny von Bülow's very real coma might well have been caused by other factors. Yet Claus von Bülow's very real sentence of imprisonment was being based, at least in part, on the diagnosis of a hypothetical patient who never existed in the real world.

Dr. Cahill's answer to the hypothetical question about the second coma was doubly tainted: it relied in part on the invalid insulin level erroneously reported by BioScience labs, and it relied in part on the conclusion he reached about the first coma, which was based on an erroneous factual premise. Moreover, when the experts gave their various diagnoses they did so under the false belief that the "murder weapon"—a needle with insulin that had been injected into the victim—had been discovered. They would be foolish indeed to ignore such important information in the diagnosis. But this important information, it turns out, may have been false.

Indeed, the prosecution's entire insulin theory was quickly crumbling. At the trial they had presented what appeared to be a scientifically airtight case that both comas had been caused by injections of insulin. Now each of the underlying scientific data—the insulin on the needle, the insulin level of the blood, the evidence that the needle had been injected and the expert testimony—was being challenged by leading experts in their fields.

As we were proceeding to dismantle the prosecution's house of cards, Claus von Bülow kept asking me the obvious question: "How come all these weaknesses in the prosecution's case weren't discovered before or during the trial?" "Why," Claus kept asking, did Fahringer accept the prosecution's lab results "as written in stone"? Claus von Bülow had paid good money for his trial lawyers, and he was certainly entitled to wonder why these avenues of attack had not been used by them.

I tried to explain how easy it is to be a Monday-morning quarterback and criticize what now appear to be errors or omissions by the trial lawyer. But the trial, like the sixty minutes of intense on-field activity during a Sunday football game, is often a frenetic, spontaneous, adrenaline-filled adventure. There is little time for reflection, for careful consideration of all the options, or for putting together all the disparate parts of the judicial puzzle. This is especially true of the defense side of the case, which must react to the ever-shifting sands of the prosecution's presentation.

The posttrial and appellate period is a time for more reflective evaluation of what went wrong. The entire case record is available for careful reading: the police reports, the grand jury minutes, the pretrial hearings, the trial transcript itself. The various accounts of the principal actors—what Alexander first told the police, what he then said to the grand jury, what he recounted to the judge, and what he finally swore before the trial jury—can all be carefully compared and contrasted for discrepancies. It is only after the trial that the prosecution's entire case can be fully known and understood. Only then can its flaws, inadequacies, gaps and contradictions be analyzed.

All this makes it easier to dismantle the prosecutor's case after trial than it is during trial.

But there was one additional factor, other than the timing of the review, that differentiated the trial lawyer in the case from the appellate lawyer. Herald Price Fahringer was a real loner. He tried a case by himself, with the minimal assistance permitted by law. In the von Bülow case he worked only with John Sheehan, the local lawyer who had referred the case to him.

My style is entirely different. I love working with large teams—when that is possible. I try to leave no stone unturned, assigning numerous student assistants to pursue every possible angle. This "overkill" approach leads down a number of dead ends—as I was to learn in this case—but it also assured that there are no open ends.

My secret weapon is my wonderful students—dozens of them clamoring to work on real-life, interesting cases. For them it is an opportunity not only to earn money but also to experience the thrill of breaking open a case by their investigative work or by their legal research.

As soon as I became involved in the von Bülow case, I realized that this was a case requiring a large team effort. As I mentioned earlier, I assembled a group of young lawyers and about a dozen students and eventually set up a series of teams. The teams included the following:

The exogenous versus the endogenous insulin team: their job was to investigate all the medical testimony, evidence and literature, as well as interview doctors and experts, in an effort to determine whether the alleged insulin levels in Mrs. von Bülow's blood were accurate, and if accurate, whether they were produced by her own reactive hypoglycemia or by the injection of insulin.

The self-injection versus other-person-injection team: their job was to explore all the evidence, both old and new, on the question whether, if Mrs. von Bülow had indeed been injected, the injection was self-administered or administered by someone else.

The black bag team: their job was to attempt to reconstruct the contents of the black bag throughout its mysterious history, from its original sighting in February 1980 until its discovery during the search of January 1981.

The needle team: their job was to investigate the needle allegedly found in the black bag to determine whether it was, in fact, the "murder weapon" and what it contained.

The private search team: their job was to evaluate all the evidence surrounding the search conducted by Alexander von Auersperg and the private detective in order to bolster our argument that this warrantless search constituted a burglary whose fruits should not have been admitted at the trial.

The police search team: their job was to consider whether the further searches conducted by the Rhode Island police under the supervision of Lieutenant Reise were constitutionally valid, and if not, whether their fruits should have been admitted at the trial.

The Kuh notes team: their job was to try to figure out what information was contained in the files of attorney Richard Kuh, who had been retained by Mrs. von Bülow's family to conduct the original investigation of Claus von Bülow before the police became involved. It was also their job to construct the legal arguments as to why the Kuh information should have been turned over to the defense for use at the trial.

When it came time to write the appellate brief, we decided to convert my house into a combination law office, dormitory and restaurant. There were so many teams working, and so many issues to be covered, that I wanted everybody under one roof during the final writing phase.

I lived in a mammoth hundred-and-fifty-year-old Harvard-owned house in the Brattle Street neighborhood of Cambridge. I had rented the house when my children—teenage boys—moved in with me following my marital separation. We had installed a sauna, a Ping Pong table and a pinball machine. The backyard was taken up largely by a basketball hoop which had become the locus of some serious family games. My friends had named the house "Camp Dersh," and had even printed up T-shirts bearing that appellation. At the time of the von Bülow case, my boys were both off at college, so that the cavernous twelve-room house was nearly empty during the school year.

Each team was assigned a room—and a tight deadline for completion of its work. The competition became so intense that it even spread to the basketball court. The insulin team divided itself into squads: The exogenous insulin squad competed as ferociously against the endogeneous insulin squad on the court as in the library. The black bag team emerged, however, as the undisputed hoops champs. (Instead of calling an offensive foul, one of the players cleverly demanded the exclusion of the illegally obtained points.)

But it was not all fun and games. We worked long hours, taking turns at kitchen and take-out-food duty. There was at least one secretary available twenty-four hours a day, and the photocopying machine was never turned off. During that one-month period we probably turned out more than two thousand pages of type. The ultimate product—the printed brief itself—would have to be honed down to one hundred pages.

The job of producing and editing an appellate brief is somewhat akin to producing and editing a TV program. Indeed, I once had a long talk with a producer at *60 Minutes* about the similarities. TV producers begin with an unformed mass of data that they eventually reduce to thousands of minutes of videotape. From that tape they must cull a very few minutes that dramatically and accurately reflect the major issues.

The appellate lawyer also begins with a mass of material, in this case a six-thousand-page trial transcript; hundreds of pages of grand jury testimony, police reports, witnesses' statements, hospital records, investigative summaries; five hundred pages of briefs and legal memoranda that have been submitted to the trial judge; and an assortment of miscellaneous material ranging from the black bag itself to numerous photographs of Clarendon Court. The problem of selection was compounded here by the unusual fact that we also had all the material we had recently discovered, developed and noticed in connection with our new-trial motion. We had to make some tough decisions whether, and how, to integrate this explosive and controversial information—some of it not yet corroborated—into our appellate brief.

The most difficult job was deciding which arguments to omit. That's the kind of decision that really keeps you up at night. At least twice in my experience I have come very close to omitting an argument from an appellate brief because I was convinced it was a "loser"; both times my younger associates convinced me to keep it in; both times I listened, relegating the arguments to the back of the brief; both times the court of appeals reversed the convictions on the basis of the ground I had wanted to leave out.

The simple solution is to include every argument, no matter how weak it may seem. But that doesn't work either. Including arguments regarded as losers by the judges tends to weaken your other, stronger, arguments. "If you think your opening arguments are so convincing," I've heard judges ask, "then why do you bother with such a weak closing argument?" Moreover, there simply isn't enough space in an appellate brief—which always has a page limit —to include all the possible arguments.

The perfect solution, of course, would be to include all the arguments that any of the judges might be convinced by, and omit the losers. But lawyers can't read the minds of judges. And the Rhode Island Supreme Court is composed of five very different judges, each of whom may have a different view on which of the arguments, if any, might be convincing.

With that in mind, I studied the judicial opinions of each of the judges in an effort to figure out the kinds of issues he—and in the case of Judge Florence Murray, she—had found persuasive or impressive in past cases. In reading their decisions, I noticed an interesting phenomenon. Most of the judges seemed to prefer rather narrow, somewhat technical legal arguments. They did not like to make new law, but rather seemed to enjoy the process of making small, gradual, incremental changes that flowed almost inevitably from earlier decisions. Rarely were there any discussions of broad legal issues. And almost never did the judges discuss the possible innocence of the defendant.

But between the lines, I could sense (especially in the chief justice and two of the other judges) a real concern about whether the defendant was actually guilty or innocent. This seemed to be the "hidden agenda"—the unspoken premise—underlying some of their decisions. I noticed that sometimes two different defendants would raise very similar issues, but that one would win and the other would lose. These different outcomes could not be understood, or justified, on the basis of the law. But there were hints in the decisions suggesting that the defendant whose conviction was reversed might be innocent. I couldn't prove my hypothesis, but there certainly was enough information to convince me that I had to persuade the judges not only that Claus von Bülow's trial had been inundated with technical legal errors, but that he was an innocent man.

My frequent conversations with other judges (friends and classmates who were serving in the judiciary) as well as my own experience as a law clerk for two appellate court judges confirmed the importance of trying to persuade the court of the defendant's innocence—if you truly believe him to be innocent.

But lawyers and judges speak strange languages to one another in the courtroom, as well as in the legal documents of the courtroom—the briefs and opinions. One of the principal rules of this discourse is "never argue your client's factual innocence, even if you believe it." There are several good reasons for this rule. First and foremost, it would put most lawyers into an impossible fix, since the vast majority of their clients are *not* factually innocent, and an honest lawyer would feel uncomfortable, to say the least, in representing something to the court that he did not believe to be true.

Second, the role of the appeals court is not to second-guess the jury, which has already found the defendant guilty beyond a reasonable doubt. Its sole function, at least in theory, is to consider legal errors. "Factual arguments don't impress us up here, counselor," is the kind of response one often hears from the judges when innocence is proclaimed. "Save that kind of dramatics for the closing argument at your next jury trial" is another favorite.

But many judges care deeply, if quietly, about whether the defendant is guilty or innocent. One very distinguished appellate court judge, known for his scholarly, unemotional legal opinions, recently confided in me that "if I believe that a defendant is innocent—or even if I'm just left in some doubt—I'll do anything to find a way to reverse the conviction and give him a new trial. I'll find *some* legal ground to base it on. But if I'm certain the guy's guilty, it will take one hell of a legal error to get me to reverse." There is nothing surprising about this very human approach to appellate judging. But it is hardly ever discussed openly.

The open agenda of appellate argument is always about legal issues, but the real agenda is often the guilt or innocence of the defendant. This double-think approach poses a real challenge for the appellate lawyer who believes that his client is innocent. My teams and I spent many hours trying to figure out how to select and present our legal arguments in a way that might also persuade the judges of Claus von Bülow's factual innocence. We had already decided to highlight the suppression of the Kuh notes as a vehicle for pointing the judges to old evidence that might have proved the defendant's innocence. But we also needed a vehicle for bringing the new evidence to their attention.

Eventually, we decided on a risky—indeed dangerous—strategy. We decided to play Claus von Bülow's poker hand with all his cards showing. We took his closed cards from the hole and placed them face-up in full view of the prosecution and the Rhode Island Supreme Court. We gathered together all of the diverse evidence pointing to von Bülow's innocence, both the evidence that was presented at the trial and the new evidence that we had uncovered after the trial. Our major point on this appeal would be that the defendant was factually innocent. We would not rely on technical arguments; we would invoke no exclusionary rules; we would not claim constitutional violations—unless those legal arguments supported our major contention that Claus von Bülow was innocent.

Because an appeal is merely a legal vehicle for reviewing the rulings made by the judge at the trial, we had to figure out a way of getting the new information—the evidence not introduced at the trial—before the Supreme Court. A lawyer cannot just hold a press conference and announce that he has found new evidence. He must employ an established legal procedure for introducing the evidence before the court.

Since there is no established legal procedure in Rhode Island for bringing new evidence before the Supreme Court on an appeal, we decided to fashion a new procedure to fit our situation. We opted for a two-step process. First we would try to attach some of the new evidence to the appeal brief itself. We knew this would probably be rejected, but we figured it would be worth a try. Our rationale was as follows: because the state was relying exclusively on circumstantial evidence, it was required to prove that there were no reasonable inferences of innocence that could be derived from its evidence; our new evidence, we argued, showed that the state's evidence gave rise to reasonable, indeed compelling, inferences of innocence. Our new medical evidence told such a different story from the one told at the trial that it would have to shake the court's faith in the correctness of the jury's verdict.

Accordingly, we appended to our legal brief a series of factual affidavits incorporating some, but not all, of our new information. The reason we initially held some back was that at the time we filed our appeal brief we had not completed all of our work corroborating and elaborating our discoveries. We did not, for example, men-

tion the Marriott information, which we were still in the process of
checking out.

As we expected, the state opposed the filing of our new evidence,
arguing that it was not part of the trial record that was the subject
of the appeal. Eventually, the Rhode Island Supreme Court agreed
with the state and ordered most of our new evidence struck from
the appeal. We hoped we had planted a few seedlings of doubt.

Our next step was to try to have these seedlings take root and
blossom. With that in mind, we searched for a legal vehicle that
would entitle us to present our full panoply of new information to
the court.

The usual vehicle for introducing additional evidence after trial
is a "motion for a new trial based on newly discovered evidence."
There were several problems with this avenue. First, such a
motion must be presented to the trial judge before it can be
brought to the Supreme Court. We had no interest in bringing our
new information to the attention of Judge Needham, for the case
was now out of his hands—at least for the moment.

Second, a motion for a new trial cannot be acted on while the
appeal from the old trial is pending before the Supreme Court. The
general rule is that a case cannot be in front of two courts at the
same time. Since our appeal was already docketed in the Supreme
Court, the entire case was now before that court. But that court had
no jurisdiction—power—to consider our motion for a new trial,
since the trial court had not yet passed on it. And the trial court had
no jurisdiction to pass on it, since the case was now in the hands of
the Supreme Court. The usual course of action would be to wait
until the Supreme Court had decided the appeal and then, if we
lost, present our motion to the trial court. But that would be dangerous as well. We feared that the courts might rule that we had sat on
our new information too long—that it had become stale and no
longer newly discovered. We also wanted the information, especially
the medical affidavits, in our new-trial motion to be available to
the Supreme Court justices so that they would have both stories
before them. We decided to fashion our own unusual remedy, designed to serve the particular interests we had in mind.

We faced a real catch-22 situation: the only place we could file
our new-trial motion was in the trial court, but the only time we
could file the motion in the trial court was after the Supreme Court
had decided the appeal. Our only hope of lawfully filing our motion
in the right place at the right time (the Supreme Court before the

appeal was decided) was to engage in some creative lawmaking. We concocted our own motion designed to fit our case between the few existing cracks in the established procedure.

We began working on a traditional new-trial motion to be presented to the trial court while the appeal was still pending; it would include all of our new-trial affidavits and arguments we could corroborate at the time. But we didn't submit it to the trial court. Instead, we would send it to the Supreme Court with a request that the Supreme Court justices themselves decide whether and when to send it to the trial court. This is how we put it in our memorandum:

> This motion for a remand is being filed now in advance of oral argument on appeal in order to alert this Court to the existence of newly discovered evidence and thus to afford this Court maximum flexibility in the ordering of proceedings in this case.

As we were preparing the appeal and the new-trial motion, we learned that a book was about to be published concerning the von Bülow case. Realizing that any account of the case could influence public opinion, and hence judicial opinion, we awaited the publication with anticipation. When we found out what it would say, we became quite worried. When we discovered *why* it took the point of view it did, we became furious and decided to fight back.

The Von Bülow Affair was written by a respected author named William Wright, who had written a biography of Luciano Pavarotti and several books about wealthy socialites. Wright's conclusion was that there could be no doubt that Claus von Bülow was guilty. Only a fool influenced by the media, a "groupie" reflecting sympathy, or a knave sticking up for another knave could believe in von Bülow's innocence. For every doubt there was a certain answer. This wasn't a "Who done it?" or a "Was anything criminal done at all?" mystery. The only real mystery, according to Wright, was why so many otherwise intelligent people would express any doubt about the jury's verdict.

In addition to rehashing the trial—in a completely one-sided manner—Wright crammed the book with uncorroborated gossip, nearly all negative, about Claus von Bülow's background. He trotted out rumors of homosexuality, orgies, necrophilia, pimping and sadism, even incest. He quoted a prominent German as saying that he "did not want to touch [von Bülow] even long enough to shake hands" because his "feeling of evil was so strong." I can understand why this man's feeling of evil was strong; he was, according to Wright, Baron Arndt Krupp von Bohlen, heir to the Nazi munitions suppliers and users of slave labor. (Perhaps it was Claus who didn't want to touch Krupp's hand, a hand that had gladly touched, indeed embraced, the worst evil in history.)

Wright never quite came out and said he believed these rumors, but he obviously knew that by publishing them, even with disclaimers, he would convey a negative impression of Claus von Bülow, whom he characterized as "International White Trash," and support his conclusion that this was a man capable of trying to murder his wife. He even mentioned that Claus had been one of the principal investors in the Broadway play *Deathtrap*, a "thriller about a man who ingeniously plots to kill his rich wife," as if to suggest that life imitated art in the von Bülow case.

Not only was Wright's book serialized in newspapers and magazines, but he went on a national book tour to plug it on radio and TV talk shows. The message was always the same: Claus von Bülow was a wicked man who had twice tried to murder his wife. Wright claimed that he started out doubting von Bülow's guilt, but then—after objective study of the facts—came to the incontrovertible conclusion that he was clearly guilty.

I was equally disturbed with Wright's claim to objectivity and impartiality. Until now everyone who had asserted von Bülow's guilt had a clear interest in that conclusion: the family, Richard Kuh, the prosecutors. But now Wright was claiming to have done a completely independent analysis of the facts and to have reached an entirely unbiased opinion. It had to have a devastating effect on public opinion—unless it was answered.

Claus and I read the book with great care. We found dozens upon dozens of inaccuracies—some minor, several major. For example, Wright emphasized the fact that both comas occurred when hospitals would be understaffed:

> [Prosecutor] Famiglietti didn't add a point brought out elsewhere. Why were both attempts done on a Sunday? This might have been what some call "the Pearl Harbor Strategy": the assumption that manned facilities such as defense installations and hospitals will be operating at partial capacity.

It's an interesting theory, but it simply wasn't true. The first coma occurred on December 27, 1979. A simple check of any 1979 calendar would immediately reveal that December 27 of that year fell on a Thursday. Sunny von Bülow was taken to the hospital when it was fully staffed. The second coma did occur on a Sunday and Sunny was rushed to the hospital just before noon, but there is no evidence that the hospital was in any way understaffed at that time. Indeed, Dr. Gerhard Meier—"one of Newport's most prominent doctors," according to the Providence *Journal*—immediately took over her care and was there to resuscitate her after she suffered cardiac arrest. It is not surprising, therefore, that Prosecutor Famiglietti did not argue Wright's "Pearl Harbor Strategy."

Another striking example was Wright's description of the search for the black bag. He said that Lidocaine was found inside the bag, whereas both witnesses acknowledged that it was found outside the bag. He also said that the searchers put the items they found in the black bag back inside it "and zipped it shut," whereas both witnesses acknowledged that they put *other* items found outside the bag in it *before* they zipped it shut. Wright improved on the family's case in several other significant respects.

What was surprising to me as I read through the book was the fact that no one else had caught these obvious errors and the numerous other equally obvious ones. What made me suspicious was that nearly all the errors reflected *against* Claus von Bülow. There were few, if any, that reflected against Richard Kuh's clients. It was almost as if the manuscript had been read in advance for errors by only one side of the case, but not the other. If that had indeed occurred, it would put the lie to any claim of impartiality or objectivity on Wright's part. I doubted that an author of Wright's reputation would ever submit his manuscript for corrections to one side but not the other.

Soon I learned that it was much worse than that. Claus told me that he had been advised by a confidential source that William Wright had actually signed a formal contract with Richard Kuh. The contract provided that in exchange for interviews with his clients and access to his information, Wright would agree to show the manuscript to Kuh in advance of publication. Kuh and his clients would then review it for accuracy and suggest corrections and other changes. Wright would remain free not to make these changes, but he agreed to consider them in good faith. There was no similar agreement giving Claus von Bülow or his lawyers any opportunity to review the manuscript before publication and to suggest corrections.

If what Claus told me was true, it would explain why the numerous errors were so lopsidedly against his position. I was invited to appear with Wright on several radio and television talk shows. I accepted willingly, eager to confront him and find out about this contract. In May 1983 we appeared together on *People Are Talking*, a one-hour TV show out of Boston. Wright said that in order to interview Kuh's clients he had to enter into a written agreement. He showed me the agreement on the air.* It gave Kuh a contractual right to review the manuscript and point out errors. Wright was not obliged to make the corrections, but of course any author concerned for accuracy (and for protection against a lawsuit) would willingly correct errors pointed out to him. There was no agreement for anyone on our side to point out errors—and Wright did not show us the manuscript—so the errors were almost all in one direction. A newspaper account described Wright as being "on the defensive throughout the hour-long show." I felt that our side's objective had been achieved in raising questions about the Wright book.

I pointed out Wright's one-sided contract on several TV and radio shows, describing it as "a pact with the Devil." Wright was furious and threatened to sue me for libel. In a childish display of venom, he even wrote to the dean of the Harvard Law School urging him to fire me—not the first such letter the dean has received and ignored.

It is entirely understandable why Wright should have been so angry. He had been caught with his impartiality down. The public disclosure of his one-sidedness completely undercut his credibility as an objective chronicler of the von Bülow case. The ultimate proof of his bias was that even after the errors were publicly revealed on television, he did not take the opportunity to correct them in the subsequent paperback edition. And so if you turn to page 134 of the paperback you will find an uncorrected account of the search of the black bag, despite Wright's public acknowledgment that he was in error. And on page 312 you will still see references to "the Pearl Harbor Strategy" and the "fact" that both attempts were made on Sunday.

We regarded the Wright book as the private prosecutor's public brief. It made the family's case even more persuasively than

---

* Wright maintains that his agreement was the standard one "demanded by" Alex and Ala "in exchange for interviews and relevant information," and signed by other authors.

Famiglietti had done, because Famiglietti could be corrected if he made errors, whereas Wright's error-filled book stood uncorrected. We took every opportunity to point out the mistakes and the author's strange one-sided arrangement with Kuh and his clients. We had no choice but to fight back. William Wright—quite understandably—has not sued for libel.

12

Not Guilty by Reason of Innocence

We filed our appeal brief on March 15, 1983—nearly a year after I entered the case. It was the longest and most complex brief I had ever written, consisting of more than fifty thousand words. But then again, this was the longest criminal trial in Rhode Island history. In order not to frighten—or bore—the court away from undertaking the enormous task of wading through the hundred single-spaced pages, we began with an overview that told in simple terms the highlights of the new story we would be telling in the appeal. (The remainder of the story would be told in our new-trial motions.) In our overview, we said:

> Claus von Bülow is facing 30 years in prison for a crime he did not commit. Unable to accept the reality that Martha von Bülow may have destroyed herself, her wealthy family hired a private prosecutor to conduct a vendetta against her husband. The private prosecutor orchestrated a search-and-destroy operation during which evidence was obliterated, lost, or thrown away; that evidence could conclusively have established Claus von Bülow's innocence. On the basis of a needle allegedly found in a black vinyl bag, the private prosecutor . . . convinced the Rhode Island authorities to commence a prosecution—partly financed by his clients' funds—against Claus von Bülow for attempting to murder his wife.
>
> But the facts—some of which were suppressed—demonstrate that the needle was not injected into Martha von Bülow. The facts also establish that the key piece of evidence allegedly linking Claus von Bülow to the needle—a pill vial with Claus von Bülow's name, claimed to have been found *in* the black bag—was actually found elsewhere and *put in* the black bag. Indeed, according to the private prosecutor's own investigator, if any pill vial was found in the black bag, it was a prescription for Martha von Bülow.
>
> Despite concerted and continuing efforts by Martha von Bülow's

family to prevent the truth about her from coming out, it has now become clear that Martha von Bülow was a self-destructive, deeply depressed, and addictive woman who experimented with drugs not prescribed for her, and who continued to engage in life-threatening behavior after experiencing life-threatening emergencies and after being warned by doctors to desist.

Because the jury did not learn the whole truth, it falsely convicted an innocent man. The object of this appeal is to remedy that injustice.*

We told the court that Sunny von Bülow's comas have given rise to

one of the most highly publicized medical and legal mysteries in the annals of American jurisprudence. The von Bülow case is more than a simple "who done it?" It presents the most perplexing question of whether *anything* criminal was done at all. No eyewitness saw anything criminal. The prosecutor acknowledged that the circumstantial evidence "leaves a number of questions which will forever go unanswered . . ."

In addition to the unanswered questions, the prosecution of Claus von Bülow . . . raises profound legal questions, some of first impression, others of long established principle. Each goes directly to the point of this appeal: the total innocence of Claus von Bülow.

We went on to present the court with a description of Martha von Bülow that—though based on the record—was quite different from the one the jury had obviously believed:

Both before and after her [reactive hypoglycemic] condition was diagnosed, Mrs. von Bülow indulged in massive quantities of sweets, though informed that sweets were like poison to her. She was obsessed by her weight, and took twenty-four laxatives a day from the time she was 16.

She also ingested extraordinary quantities of aspirin. Just 19 days before her present coma, Mrs. von Bülow was rushed to the emergency ward with an acute case of aspirin overdose, having voluntarily swallowed more than 60 aspirin. Following this "disastrous aspirin intoxication," her physician of 26 years directed her never again to take aspirin, but instead an aspirin substitute. Mrs. von Bülow continued to take aspirin in massive doses, as evidenced by the 156 mg% of aspirin found in her urine during her final coma.

She also consumed alcohol, despite her knowledge that she had an extremely low tolerance for it, and large quantities of Valium and

* Sunny's family disputes many of the characterizations contained in our brief.

barbiturates. Tests conducted during her second coma established an amobarbital level which, according to the State's principal expert witness, could alone have induced unconsciousness, and perhaps death.

Mrs. von Bülow was a self-destructive woman who, according to the State's own witness, desperately needed psychiatric care and who told the chief psychiatrist at Newport Hospital that she was "almost never happy," "frequently bored," sometimes unwilling "to get up in the morning," and even said "I have often wished myself dead."*

After describing the comas, we turned to the search and seizure of the notorious black bag, and presented our story—one the jury also never heard. We explained to the court how the searchers had

"mixed" together all the drug vials—those found inside and outside the bag—and threw them into the black bag. The searchers obliterated all fingerprints on the vials and the bag, and subsequently lost, threw away or otherwise destroyed crucial evidence which might have proved Claus von Bülow's innocence.

The discussion of the private search inevitably led to the secret notes private prosecutor Kuh had taken of his interviews with the crucial witnesses. We explained how the Kuh notes could be invaluable as fodder for cross-examination:

As is well known, it is often the first contact with a witness which elicits the freshest and most candid observations. By the time [of the trial] their stories had inevitably become honed in the retelling and shorn of any rough edges which did not fit the theory of the case which had developed. Thus, access to these notes was vital both as a source of leads for the defense and as an invaluable source of material for cross-examination and impeachment.

To demonstrate how valuable the material could have been to the defense, we related an episode from the trial that demonstrated its extraordinary usefulness to the prosecution. The defense had called as one of its witnesses a family chauffeur named Charles Roberts, who testified that he had driven Sunny to various doctors and pharmacies for prescription drugs. The prosecution called Richard Kuh, who had interviewed Roberts, as a rebuttal witness.

---

* Sunny was apparently preoccupied with death, asking friends, "Do you think about dying all the time? You don't? How lucky you are. I do."

On the stand Kuh was perfectly willing to refer to his notes and testify that Roberts had told him things during the earlier interview that contradicted his trial testimony. We pointed out that Kuh was thus allowed to use his claim of privilege "as a *shield* against disclosing information when disclosure might help the defense, while at the same time using the allegedly privileged information as a *sword* against the defense when disclosure might serve his clients' and the prosecutor's tactical interests."

We argued that this Kuh-Roberts episode "dramatically demonstrates the sham use—indeed abuse—to which Mr. Kuh put the alleged privileges in this case, and the harms to *the defendant, and the truth-finding process*, that resulted."

Finally, we turned to the exclusionary rule argument concerning the black bag. As I had told Claus, the exclusionary rule is generally the argument of last resort for guilty defendants, because it almost always presupposes that the evidence that was seized improperly is evidence of guilt. We tried to avoid making a guilty-man argument by distinguishing this case from "the usual Fourth Amendment case where the benefits of deterrence must be balanced *against* the loss to society that results from the exclusion of reliable evidence of guilt." We argued that in the von Bülow case, "both sides of the balance support exclusion for, as applied here, the exclusionary rule would result in adjudications based on more reliable evidence, not less."

We explained that the questionable searches had "ignored virtually every requirement imposed on and adhered to by police departments to ensure the proper preservation of evidence." Reminding the court of the absence of any inventory, we argued that the "result is that it is still not clear what was allegedly found in the black bag itself. It is, of course, precisely because individual memories are fallible that photographs and inventories are standard police practices."

We tried to relate the failure to secure a warrant to the contradictions in the prosecution's evidence:

Given the role that the black bag played in the government's theory of this case, our inability even now to reconstruct what was in it is intolerable. No defendant should be subject to conviction on the basis of the location of a pill vial, where neither photographs nor even an immediate inventory attest to its location, and where the searchers themselves are in complete disagreement as to which items were found where.

Turning to the obliteration of fingerprints on the bag and its contents, the brief pointed out the hypocrisy of Famiglietti's jury argument that "there is not one iota or scintilla of evidence which ties in or connects Mrs. von Bülow to that black bag or any of its contents." It reminded the court that "a single fingerprint of Mrs. von Bülow, on the black bag or any of the items within it, would have utterly destroyed the prosecution's theory that the bag and its contents belonged exclusively to Mr. von Bülow. The loss—really, the destruction—of this vital, potentially exculpatory evidence is due directly to [the] deliberate use of private investigative, rather than public police, methods."

We urged the court to apply the exclusionary rule to private searches of this kind, because without such a rule,

> private parties have an incentive to avoid police involvement and to seize evidence for prosecution on their own: free from the warrant and probable cause requirements. And with that incentive, private searches for evidence will continue, and the destruction of evidence— either because the parties lack the knowledge, or the resources, or the desire to preserve it—is virtually inevitable. The "risk to society" that relevant evidence will be excluded is posed not by the application of the exclusionary rule, but by the failure to apply it.

We ended our brief, as we had begun it, with an unequivocal assertion of innocence:

> Because the judge's rulings and the prosecutor's conduct prevented Claus von Bülow from proving his innocence, and because the evidence presented by the State does not even come close to establishing the untrue allegation that he injected his wife with insulin, the defendant respectfully requests this honorable court to reverse his convictions. . . .

Even the simple act of filing our brief on time provided a bit of drama. Because it was so lengthy, we decided to print it ourselves, hoping to be able to squeeze a few thousand extra words into our oversized page and undersized margins. Inevitably, the printing and photocopying process broke down and everything was running behind schedule. I recruited my son Jamin, who was on his school break, to help with the mechanical tasks, and with his first aid we managed to finish the brief at 4:00 P.M. on the day it was due. A quick call to the clerk's office by Terry MacFadyen got us a fifteen-minute extension beyond the usual 5:00 P.M. closing time. We drove down to Providence in record time, with our briefs in the trunk of the car, me navigating and Jamin driving. We arrived just as the doors were closing, heaved a sigh of relief and filed the brief.

On June 16, 1983, the Rhode Island Attorney General filed his 101-page brief in response to ours. He attacked virtually all of our contentions, arguing that "the circumstantial evidence [of] defendant's guilt was overwhelming," that the trial judge had done an exceptionally able job in according the defendant a fair trial, that the Kuh notes were properly withheld, and that the search of the black bag did not violate any constitutional rights. He accused our brief of presenting a "biased and inaccurate portrayal of the facts" and of relying on information "which is blatantly outside the record," referring to our new medical findings.

We then filed our "reply" brief, giving us the final word—or so we thought. In every state which I have practiced, the appellant (the convicted criminal who is bringing the appeal) must file his brief first; the state then responds; and the appellant gets to have the final written say in the reply brief. We were shocked, therefore, when the Rhode Island Supreme Court, in what appeared to be an unprecedented move, allowed the state to reply to our reply brief, thus giving *them* the last word. I wondered whether we were again receiving the Rhode Island Shuffle, or just a benign bit of hometown favoritism.

As various briefs were being filed, a new-trial team—consisting of Jeanne Baker, Susan Estrich, Terry MacFadyen, Joann Crispi, Andrew Citron and several students who were veterans of the appeal brief—was hard at work preparing medical and witness affidavits. My job on the new-trial motion was to write the legal memorandum that would summarize the affidavits and make factual and legal arguments based on them.

We planned to file our new-trial motion early in October 1983. We wanted to get it filed before the oral argument so that if the judges had any questions about it—on either its substance or its unique form—they would have an opportunity to inquire about it during the argument, which was scheduled for October 17, 1983.

I was working on the new-trial legal memorandum over the weekend before we were to file the motion. At that point all the affidavits had been notarized, copied and made ready for inclusion. Suddenly David Marriott appeared at my office demanding to see me, insisting that he had to change his affidavit, that something had been left out. I had been in my private office, working on the legal parts of the motion; I walked outside, where Marriott was loudly complaining to several members of the team that he had to make a change. I asked him whether the change was an important one. "Very important," he responded.

"Is there anything untruthful about the affidavit as it now stands?" I demanded.

"No, absolutely not. Everything there is true, but I left one thing out."

I asked him what it was, and he told me: "You know the part where I say that a woman came out of Clarendon Court and I gave her the box for Alex?" As he was talking, he turned the pages of his affidavit and started to read from it: "The woman did not look like a servant . . ."

"I remember that," I interrupted.

"Well that woman was definitely Sunny von Bülow," David stated, almost defiantly.

"How can you be so sure?" I asked suspiciously.

"She looked just like her pictures and she made it clear who she was." Marriott told me he was so sure it was Sunny von Bülow that he had already told that to the police who had interviewed him.

I told David that if there was even the slightest doubt in his mind, we shouldn't change the affidavit. I explained that he wasn't helping us at all by changing the affidavit because we would tell the prosecutors about the change and they would then be able to argue that there was a conflict between the two affidavits.

"You don't have to tell them," David argued. "Why can't we just say that this is what I always said in the affidavit?"

"Because that's not the way we play the game. If you swear to two different affidavits, we're not going to keep that fact secret." I told Marriott that if he was absolutely certain that the woman was Sunny, we would have to change his affidavit, regardless of the consequences.

"I'm as sure as if she were my mother," he asserted. "I always knew it was her, but I became convinced when I started looking closely at the pictures. Who else could it have been? It certainly wasn't Maria."

I authorized one of my assistants to make the revision and insisted that she have Marriott go over every single word in the affidavit to make sure it was accurate. It wasn't easy to effectuate the change Marriott wanted because it was already late at night when the typing was completed, and there were no notary publics easily available. Marriott solved the problem by telling us that morticians had to be notaries "to do all their official things with the corpses. And they're open all night." And so Marriott and my assistant went in search of a mortician–notary-public and finally found one.

At the very last minute Marriott gave me an affidavit from his mother. We had not asked for, nor expected, one, since he had always said, "Leave my mother out of this." But apparently he had changed his mind and arranged—on his own—to have it prepared and notarized. Mrs. Marriott's affidavit said that while David was in the hospital, a man identifying himself as Alexander von Auersperg repeatedly called the house inquiring about Gilbert Jackson.

Now we had even further corroboration. In order for Marriott to be lying, his own mother and a Catholic priest had to be engaged in a conspiracy to commit perjury. It seemed extremely unlikely.

In addition to the new medical evidence and the Capote-Marriott-Magaldi accounts, we appended affidavits from several witnesses who had observed Sunny at close range over the years and had seen an entirely different woman from the one portrayed at the trial. One close friend of twenty years swore that although "Sunny had many wonderful qualities," her "one failing was that once she took one drink she would not know how to stop." The friend reluctantly described what would happen when Sunny became heavily intoxicated: "Her speech and movements would become completely uncoordinated"; "she would overturn pieces of furniture, bang her head against door frames"; and "simply collapse in the ladies' powder room." Other close friends provided similar accounts: "When I took her hand it was quite limp; she only nodded and had a glazed look in her eyes. I had the impression she did not even know I was there." "She would become intoxicated easily, and I would take her back to her suite." "The effect of alcohol on Sunny was extreme. . . . Sunny simply lost control. I saw this always in her inability to coordinate her movements, in her speech. . . ." "Sunny was sitting on her bed . . . trying to focus [her lipstick tube] on her mouth, making faces, but was so intoxicated that she couldn't get the stick to her lips. Discouraged, she threw the objects in her purse and staggered toward the door, missed it and bumped into the wall." "She would speak with a blurred voice, behave erratically and occasionally faint." "She drank a great deal [and] by the end of dinner her speech had, as a result, become completely incomprehensible."

These descriptions of events, covering twenty years of Sunny's life, bore a striking similarity to Sunny's conduct just prior to her comas and corroborated what Claus had told the doctors. Sunny's friends—many of whom apparently knew about her problems with alcohol and drugs—had tried "to encourage her to go to Alcoholics Anonymous," but Sunny said she would not consider working with "people from such different social and economic strata."

The new affidavits disclosed that "in the circles in which we . . . move, Sunny's problem was, alas, common knowledge." But "Sunny's friends failed to come forward [at the trial because] of emotional and other pressures they have been subjected to, so that the truth should not be known." "Sunny's family and friends only wanted to protect her."

One of Sunny's closest friends, who went to school with her and remained on intimate terms until the very end, originally provided an affidavit about Sunny's drinking problem and then called me on the phone crying hysterically about the pressure she and her daughter were feeling from Sunny's family. She pleaded with me to withdraw the affidavit, claiming that her daughter was being ostracized and snubbed. But eventually she agreed to tell the truth, including the fact of the threats and pressure. "In spite of the threatened consequences to my daughter's and my relations with Sunny's family and other friends," she said, "I have decided that I cannot withhold the truth."

In addition to these revealing new disclosures from Sunny's friends, we also provided an affidavit from a former family servant, who had worked closely with Maria Schrallhammer for five years. Maria had told her about Sunny's drinking and drug problems: how she took "an enormous amount of sleeping pills . . . in a few days, the quantity meant for weeks"; how Sunny had "drunk so much that Maria thought Mrs. von Bülow would never wake up. Maria always tried to hide it from everyone for the sake of Mrs. von Bülow's reputation." The servant had also personally observed Sunny's "binge-purge" syndrome: "Mrs. von Bülow would refuse to eat anything for ten days to keep her figure, and suddenly would start eating huge amounts of food for successive days [in] her bedroom [avoiding] company, even the children's." The servant also revealed that "Maria hated Mr. von Bülow, and expressed her feelings unequivocally," especially after Mr. von Bülow tried to fire her when Cosima was born.

The next day we filed our new-trial motion. It was a blockbuster. After listing the seven new items of evidence—five new medical facts plus the Capote and Marriott-Magaldi allegations—that "wholly undermines the pillars of the state's case," the motion spelled out the ominous implications of the new medical evidence:

> [It] establishes that the "murder weapon" supposedly found by Alex in the black bag could not have been injected into Martha von Bülow; that instead, it was "*dipped* into solution"; and that it may not have contained insulin at all. This new evidence raises precisely the specter of a frame-up that the State itself said would require an acquittal: namely, that the evidence used to convict Claus von Bülow was "planted" in order to convict an innocent man.
>
> But whether or not it can definitely be proved that Alex sought to "frame" his stepfather, any single one of the new facts . . . would be sufficient to warrant a new trial.*

The headlines read: "VON BÜLOW: LEGAL SUCCESS OR MONU-MENTAL FRAME?" "QUESTIONS ARE RAISED ABOUT NEW EVIDENCE IN VON BÜLOW CASE."

We asked the court to order a hearing in order to determine whether the facts alleged in our motion were true. But the court never acted on our motion, apparently choosing instead to focus its attention on the appeal.

A few days after our motion was filed, Marriott decided to hold a press conference in front of his house in Wakefield. I urged him not to do that, explaining that his affidavit was only one out of twenty-six, and by no means the most important one. "The medical affidavits *prove* Claus's innocence. Your affidavits just provide more evidence that other people in the house had access to drugs and injections." I told him that we didn't want all the attention to be focused on his story, especially since there was still no final decision about whether he or Father Magaldi would ever be called to testify. Both they and we strongly preferred to present our arguments without using Marriott as a witness.

Indeed, Marriott said he was busily at work following up leads in various drug locations. He was constantly telling about this courier in Montreal, that dealer in Newport and this organized crime supplier in Florida. We were still hoping that he could find witnesses or documents that could establish Alex's drug use without requiring us to put Marriott on the witness stand.

But there was no stopping Marriott. He convened what was to be

---

* Alex and Ala dispute much of this, but no counter affidavits were submitted.

the first of dozens of press conferences. Standing on the front lawn of his house and wearing his ever-present sunglasses, he simply read his affidavit to the TV cameras. It was little more than a photo opportunity, but Marriott wanted it that way.

By his actions, Marriott made it crystal-clear that he was anything but "our" witness. He was plainly his own person—a loose and extremely loud cannon on the deck, shifting from stem to stern without warning. He would meet with us one day, and then without a word to us, meet the next day with the Attorney General, another day with the Massachusetts authorities, and nearly every day with the press. In addition to his open meetings, he would constantly leak stories about himself to the press. It was becoming clear that David Marriott was a big troublemaker who would be difficult, at best, to deal with. But he was a witness to important events, and if his story was true—and we believed it was—it provided important information relevant to the case. Difficult as he was, he had to be dealt with—honestly and directly.

The other side, of course, made no bones about their disbelief in Marriott's account. Even before the appeal was argued, Richard Kuh told the New York *Times* that Marriott was "a damned kook." Attorney General Roberts publicly declared that "a lot of what he had to say has been contrived . . ." And a police official put it even more bluntly to the Providence *Journal*: "We think he's full of ——."

The justices of the Rhode Island Supreme Court were certainly hearing both sides of the Marriott story even before the oral argument. They would hear yet more before they rendered their decision. Marriott was not making a very good media impression and was exaggerating his own importance to the case; I worried about how this might affect their decision on the appeal. It could hurt us, I speculated, especially if the justices became upset at the media attention Marriott was creating for himself. They might assume —erroneously but understandably—that we were orchestrating Marriott's media blitz.

I wondered whether they would ask any questions about Marriott during the oral argument. I prepared for the argument by convening a moot court. The judges were a group of distinguished lawyers, including John Kerry—now the junior senator from Massachusetts and a former Chief Assistant District Attorney. My entire criminal law class was invited to critique the argument, and critique they did. They tore the argument apart, criticizing my style, my substance and even my grammar. It was a rare opportunity for the students to get even with me for my Socratic style of teaching in which the student is never right. But I benefited enormously from this trial run and changed several planned stratagems.

The real oral argument was held at 10:00 A.M. on October 17, 1983, in the stately courthouse of the Rhode Island Supreme Court. It was telecast live in Rhode Island and several adjoining states. This was the first time that an argument before the Supreme Court of Rhode Island had ever been telecast live, but it was not the first time I had argued an appeal in front of television cameras; a few years earlier I had argued a death case in Arizona that was also televised. My experience is that as soon as the argument begins, everyone seems to forget the cameras. In this case, something would happen at the end of the argument that would remind us all that we were on TV.

As I stepped to the lectern I saw five intense faces staring back at me, almost as if to say, "All right, you out-of-state big shot. Show us why the local folks didn't do the right thing at the trial."

I launched directly into the theme of our entire appeal—that all of our legal arguments "go to the innocence of Claus von Bülow." As I restated the facts in a manner designed to raise doubts in the minds of the judges about the jury's guilty verdict, one particular judge, Thomas Kelleher, kept peppering me with the same question: "Don't you think that could have been argued to the jury?" I explained how the absence of information—including the Kuh notes—had made it difficult for the defense to present certain arguments, and I continued to take apart the state's case. Again Judge Kelleher interrupted me: "You weren't present at the trial, and it seems to me lots of times in these cases, where somebody comes in as appellate counsel . . . they argue a better case than might have been tried." He continued to admonish me: "I think you're arguing the evidence."

He was, of course, absolutely correct. I was trying to get the judges to take a hard second look at what seemed to be an air-tight case for the prosecution, but what was actually a pretty flimsy house of cards. I continued to point out the weaknesses in the state's evidence as to the contents of the black bag, when suddenly a remarkable exchange took place. I was in the process of answering a question and was starting to argue that "to send a man to jail on the assumption that Alexander's observations were more accurate

than those of a trained investigator would raise serious questions of
law." Halfway through the sentence, Judge Kelleher suddenly
shouted at me like an elementary-school teacher talking to a ten-
year-old pupil: "Don't talk to me like that!" It was totally out of
the blue and out of context. I've replayed the tape of that episode
a dozen times to various colleagues and no one can see or hear what
he might have taken offense at. I was speaking softly with a slight
smile on my face. It seemed as if he was waiting for the slightest
provocation to show who was in charge; the provocation hadn't
come and the argument was nearing its end, so he simply attacked.
He seemed embarrassed almost as soon as the words left his mouth.

I explained that I meant no disrespect: "that is simply my style of
argument, I was simply trying to engage the court as the court was
trying to engage me." As we exchanged these words, I wondered
how Claus was feeling back in his hotel room where he was watching the argument. He later told me that his heart nearly dropped
into his stomach when the judge began his unexpected attack.

I moved quickly to the Kuh notes, in the hope that this issue
would be a good bridge between the factual and the legal arguments.
I did not want to argue dry legal principle, but instead to relate this
principle to our claims of innocence. In arguing the importance of
the Kuh notes, I suggested a hypothetical scenario that might have
been supported by the notes. That scenario was later to prove anything but hypothetical. Here is what I argued, before we ever saw
the notes:

> What if this court were to find that in those records there was no
> discussion of insulin, certainly it would be reasonable to conclude
> that the whole insulin case was contrived after the discovery and after
> the witnesses developed an ability to conform their testimony to the
> evidence.

The judges seemed very interested in this argument, but they put
their finger on a serious problem. Herald Fahringer, in seeking the
notes, had never said that he wanted to use them to cross-examine
witnesses during the trial. Had he not waived this argument? The
judges pressed me on this point. I told them that Judge Needham
had ruled unequivocally that he would not allow notes that had
been taken by a lawyer to be used to cross-examine a witness. But
why didn't Fahringer persist in challenging Judge Needham's
ruling? I was stuck for an answer. I knew the whole case could

turn on whether I could persuade the judges that Fahringer hadn't waived von Bülow's rights by not being sufficiently persistent.

Suddenly an idea occurred to me. I reminded the court of the unpleasant exchange I had just had, moments before, with Judge Kelleher: "I think that as my—pardoned, hopefully—encounter with [Judge Kelleher] indicates, I am a bold lawyer, but even as bold a lawyer as I am in the court, I would not have made that argument after Judge Needham had ruled as unequivocally as he did that 'in my courtroom notes are not going to be used to cross-examine . . .' I would not again stand up in court and say, 'Well, your Honor, let's try it again a little bit differently,' after getting a ruling, 'No briefing, no argument, I make those rulings and they are clear and unequivocal.' " I explained to the court how Fahringer might have believed that any further attempt to renew the argument after Judge Needham's firm ruling might have earned him a contempt citation (as it did for William Kunstler in the Chicago Seven case, an appeal I had worked on).

I asked the court to try to "understand the difficulty that a lawyer finds himself in. After all, here I am trying to argue in my best style and I find a judge who found my style somewhat too aggressive. Put yourself in the situation of trial counsel—not wanting to overstep that bound which I have perhaps just overstepped; to now hold counsel accountable for both overstepping the bound and also for refusing to go up to the bound is to put counsel in a very difficult situation." I implored the court not to hold the defendant accountable for any failing of counsel at trial or on appeal.

As I was making this argument several of the judges were nodding —hopefully in agreement rather than sleepiness. I had turned an unpleasant encounter with one judge into what appeared to be a winning argument for several others.

I focused next on the medical evidence against my client. I had been advised that several of the judges were impressed by Dr. Cahill's distinguished reputation and credentials. At the trial his expert opinion had not been seriously challenged. I decided to try to challenge it during the oral argument.

One of the linchpins of Dr. Cahill's testimony was that barbiturates could not have caused Sunny's coma because she had low blood sugar:

Q. But, barbiturates can cause coma, can't they?
A. They certainly can, but not with a blood sugar of 29, sir.

It doesn't take an expert to see how downright silly this answer is, despite the credentials of the expert who gave it. In an effort to persuade the judges that they should not defer to the expertise of the doctors, I offered my own hypothetical case: "Imagine a case where a woman with reactive hypoglycemia deliberately sets out to commit suicide. So she swallows one hundred barbiturates and decides as her 'last meal' she was going to have an ice-cream sundae. What would happen in that case is that the ice-cream sundae would knock down her blood sugar. The barbiturates would put her in a coma. She would be in a coma. She would have a low blood sugar. The barbiturates would have caused her coma. The ice cream would have caused her low blood sugar. Yes, she could have a barbiturate coma *with* a low blood sugar of 29. But the doctor simply failed to consider that common-sense possibility. . . ."

The purpose of this argument was to convince the judges that they should use their own common sense, instead of accepting as gospel everything Dr. Cahill had opined.

After reviewing the remaining legal arguments, I requested the court to grant Claus von Bülow "the tools necessary to establish the whole truth—a new trial with full access to all available information at which the whole truth and not a version edited by interested parties can be heard."

As I sat down, I felt very good. I had withstood the judges' barrage of questions while keeping their eyes focused consistently on the issues of innocence. I knew I had succeeded in setting the agenda for the appeal when prosecutor Famiglietti opened his argument by acknowledging that he "wasn't prepared to stand here and argue the guilt of Mr. von Bülow." But the tone had been set and the court continued to question Famiglietti about the facts. It was obvious that at least several of them were concerned that a possibly innocent man had been convicted. Famiglietti went on for nearly an hour, but he was plainly on the defensive both legally and factually. I was enjoying every minute of it.

As Famiglietti was nearing the end of his argument, I turned to Susan Estrich and Terry MacFadyen and whispered, "I've never in my life declined the opportunity to have the last word in rebuttal, but I think we've won, and I don't think there's anywhere else to go but down at this point. So unless either of you thinks I should get up and give a rebuttal, I'm gonna keep my mouth shut."

This was a difficult judgment for me to make. Lawyers love the rebuttal. It's the part of oral argument I've always been best at. A lawyer can try, in a very few minutes, to tie the case together, to explain to the judges where the two sides agree and disagree, and why they should resolve these disputes in his client's favor. I always teach my students about the importance of rebuttal. Now here I was rejecting my own teaching, but not everything; I also urge my students to develop the art of quitting when you're ahead. I tell them about the lawyer who was defending a wrestler in a suit charging him with biting off his opponent's ear. "Did you actually see my client bite off his ear?" the lawyer asked a witness. "No, I didn't," answered the witness. Instead of quitting when he was ahead, the lawyer put the next question. "Then how do you know he actually bit it off?" he asked triumphantly. To which the witness responded, "Because I saw him spit it out."

My associates agreed that this was a good time to quit. "I know how difficult it is for you to keep quiet," Susan whispered mockingly. "But if there ever was a good time, this is it," she said, holding on to my jacket as if to prevent me from rising.

But I did rise, simply to say: "Unless the court has any questions, we will rest."

The judges looked surprised. "You don't wish to use up the ten minutes now?" the chief justice asked. They certainly expected a rebuttal. But their surprise was nothing compared to that of the television people in the courtroom, who had been given a schedule and were counting on a rebuttal to fill the allotted time. The camera director looked at the chief justice, who shrugged as if to say, "Nothing I can do about it." The director quickly switched back to the studio, where a couple of "talking heads" nervously filled the time by speculating about why I had waived my rebuttal time and why I had spent so much time on the facts.

That's what happens when show biz goes to court.

Within days of arguing the appeal, we began to hear rumors that we were going to win. Not surprisingly, Sheehan reported that the word around the court was that the justices had not liked my argument about the Kuh notes, but they had been convinced by the search-and-seizure point. We even learned which justice would be writing the decision—Florence Murray. I had my doubts about the accuracy of these reports, for the past track record of Claus's local sources was not very convincing. But I was amazed at the specificity of the information. When I told some of my student assistants about the local prediction that we would win the case on the basis of the search for the black bag, one paraphrased the information with a clever double entendre: "So it's in the bag."

It may be difficult for a nonlawyer to appreciate how extraordinary it is for a lawyer to learn in advance how an appeal is going to be decided. The inner workings of the appellate courts are among the most closely guarded secrets of the law. When I was a law clerk —an assistant to a judge—on the United States Court of Appeals and then on the Supreme Court, the first rule was "absolutely no leaks." Although that is supposed to be the rule in other branches of government, everyone recognizes that executive and legislative leaks are part of the game. But a judicial leak is high treason— punishable, when I was clerking, by immediate dismissal. And there are very good reasons for this rule of secrecy. Although information is always power, advance knowledge of how and when an appeal will be decided is great power indeed. A person with advance knowledge of how a corporate case will turn out can parlay that information into quick profits. In the criminal law context, a defendant who knows that he is going to lose his appeal may flee the country; a prosecutor who knows he is about to lose may be able to strike an unfair deal with a defendant who lacks that information.

I was still doubtful, even as the rumors became more and more specific about the result and the legal grounds. At one point Claus was told that Count I of the conviction—the first coma—would be reversed and dismissed for insufficient evidence and that Count II —the second coma—would be reversed for a new trial because of the illegal search of the black bag. "The justices don't want to take the political heat," we were told, "for throwing out the whole thing. They want the Attorney General to have to make the decision whether to try Claus again." It all seemed so logical. The only surprise was that anyone outside the court would *know* what the judges were thinking and discussing in their secret conferences.

We were told that the Attorney General's office also knew they were going to lose the appeal, and was lobbying the justices to change the outcome or at least some of the language so as to give them a better chance on a retrial.

I was still skeptical and somewhat nonplussed at these leaks. Obviously, we were all thrilled at the information. I was the only one who still expressed doubt about their reliability. I also thought we had won the appeal, but my optimism was based more on the courtroom reaction of the justices to the oral argument. My uncomfortableness about receiving inside information was relieved somewhat by the knowledge that the other side also had access to the same rumors.

Every week or so, we would hear a report that the decision was coming down next week, usually on a precise day. On the eve of the expected decision, we would be told of some small problem or delay, nothing that would change the outcome, but some of the justices were disagreeing on the wording or on a legal point.

I was planning a week-long Caribbean vacation during the early winter, but I was hesitant to leave Claus to face a possible loss of the appeal alone. Claus assured me I could go. The decision wouldn't come down until after I returned. Still skeptical, but looking for any excuse to get the sun, I went—carrying my portable shortwave radio with me at all times to hear if the decision came down. It didn't.

I returned to the freezing climes of New England to wait out the decision, but even the waiting was not uneventful. David Marriott was waiting too, and he had some disturbing surprises in store for us.

13

Reversals of Fortune

In early Febuary 1984, after the appeal was argued and the new-trial motion submitted, I received a phone call from a lawyer named Roanne Sragow. "David is hinting that some parts of his story may not be entirely true," she said with anger. Sragow is a friend of mine who practices law in Boston. A former prosecutor and former law partner of Senator John Kerry, she has a well-deserved reputation for integrity and brilliance. Her most recent victory at that time was the release from prison of a man named George Reisfelder, who had been convicted of a murder the police knew he didn't commit. But the cover-up had been so thorough that Reisfelder had served sixteen years before Sragow and Kerry had successfully argued for his release. They had performed nothing short of a legal miracle.

When David Marriott had asked to be paid for his expenses and lost wages, I turned to Sragow. I wanted the payments to be approved by and to go through a lawyer of the highest integrity, so that Marriott would know that everything was being done by the rules and that there was absolutely no room to cut corners. Marriott had his own personal lawyer to whom he went for confidential advice and counsel. Sragow would not serve in that capacity. She would be the lawyer responsible for validating any payments to Marriott. Marriott understood the role Sragow would play and agreed to it. He would submit all bills, vouchers and proof of expenses to Sragow. Claus then sent his check to Sragow, who would send her check to Marriott. This arrangement was designed to assure that Marriott would have as few direct dealings with Claus as possible, as well as to prove some independent check on the validity of Marriott's expense claims. It also created a channel of communications through which Marriott was expected to direct any complaints or messages (though Marriott frequently circumvented the channel by calling me and Claus directly or suddenly appearing at one of our doorsteps at all hours of the day and night).

Marriott spoke to Sragow on a regular basis about his expenses and payments. He was always complaining about small items that were questioned or refused. Sometimes he threatened to disappear. "I wish I had never gotten involved in this whole mess," he complained frequently. "I can't get a job. Everybody knows I delivered drugs. It was because I came forward that I got fired from my old job. It's all Claus's fault and now he's nickel-and-diming me about my expenses. I don't need any of this. I drove around in limos and wore nice clothes before I came forward. I don't need Claus's money. I've got other sources of money, but it's the principle of the thing. I shouldn't be suffering because I was a good citizen." Occasionally Marriott threatened to sue Claus for lost income or for uncompensated expenses. Once he sent his gargantuan security guard to my office damanding payment for an overdue security bill. My secretary boldly advised him that he would have to wait for the check to be processed through the proper channels.

Marriott's anger often turned against Father Magaldi. "The father's got his rectory. They take care of everything for him. Nobody's calling him a drug-pusher. He's the guy who made me do it. And he hasn't suffered."

On a few occasions Marriott subtly threatened that he would change his story unless Claus authorized more money: "I can always say I didn't remember something. It was a long time ago."

Whenever he made any such threat, I gave him what he came to call "the speech." It went like this: "Look David, you're not anyone's witness. You're a witness to the truth or you're no witness at all. You told your story to the Attorney General, to the police, to the press and to us. If you want to change it, go right ahead. As long as it's the truth. That's all I'm interested in. You're not being paid one penny for your testimony. You're getting reimbursed for your expenses and for the wages you have lost as a direct result of coming forward and spending so much time on the case. You will continue to get that—and no more than that—whether you testify for or against Claus or at all. And if anyone asks, you should tell them exactly how much you've received. There are no secrets, and you're expected to pay taxes—both state and federal—on every penny you have received in lieu of your lost wages. Check with your lawyer and accountant."

At the mention of taxes, Marriott would always bristle: "I never pay taxes. Can't you work it out that the money is tax-free?" My response would be as predictable as his question: "We're sending you 1099 forms for the money. You take them to your lawyer and accountant and pay what you owe."

I always tried to discourage him from holding his press extravaganzas, because inevitably some people would assume that we were orchestrating them. But I never discouraged him from meeting with the police, prosecutors or his own lawyer. Since Marriott had such a big mouth, we figured he would tell us what they seemed interested in. He rarely disappointed us in that regard.

It was always a tense relationship, much of the tension caused by my insistence that we play by the rules and pay by check.

When Sragow called, I fully expected more of the same. But this time her tone was different. "David insists on talking to you. He says he has some tapes that will prove that certain parts of his story are false." I asked Sragow to arrange for an immediate meeting with Marriott in her downtown Boston apartment.

At 4:00 P.M. on that Sunday, the three of us met. David brought along a mini-cassette recorder and some small cassettes. "Alan, you're going to be in for the shock of your life," he declared. "You've really been hoodwinked."

"Tell me exactly what you're talking about," I insisted. "I don't want you to hold anything back. I must know the truth, and I must know it right now. I don't care whether you think it hurts or helps my client. Tell me everything." I took out a small spiral notebook, expecting to take notes, but Marriott started to get vague.

"There are certain things I can't tell you. At least not yet. You'll have to ask Father Magaldi. What I can tell you is that not everything in our affidavits are true."

"What part of it isn't true? Did you or did you not deliver drugs to Clarendon Court?" I demanded in the tone of a cross-examining prosecutor.

"Oh, that part of it is true, all right. The basic story is the way it happened. But the way Father and I said we met, that's a different matter."

"What do you mean, the way you met?" I asked incredulously. "Didn't you have a counseling relationship with Father Magaldi?"

"You can call it that if you like, but you don't know the whole story. It's here on these tapes," he said, holding up three cassettes in a passive manner.

"Let me hear them now."

"I'll let you hear enough to know that it's really Father I have on tape, but I'm not playing you any more. Not now. These are the ace up my sleeve," said Marriott suggestively. "And these aren't the only tapes I have. I have Claus, Andrea, Joann Crispi, the Assistant District Attorney of Middlesex County and the state trooper who interviewed me. I have an attachment on my home phone and a pocket recorder I strap to my leg. These tapes are my protection."

I was reminded of my first major case, which is described in the opening chapter of *The Best Defense*. My client Sheldon Seigel had surreptitiously recorded police and prosecutors who had made him promises, and we had used the tapes to help win the case. Now the tables were being turned. The witness had taped my client. And I had no idea what my client had said, though I was confident Claus had said nothing incriminating, since he always asserted his complete innocence.

I asked Marriott whether he was taping *this* meeting. "How can I? he responded unconvincingly. "Here's my tape recorder." He proudly held up his tiny machine. There was, of course, the possibility that he had another machine hidden somewhere on his body.

To this day I don't know whether he recorded this or other meetings. I hope he did, so that there may exist a full account of my discussions with him. I know that he did record some of our phone conversations. Again, I hope he recorded them all, so that he cannot lie about what was said. In any event, I was careful to have witnesses and keep notes of our meetings and phone calls. During one meeting at a bar I had a male and female student planted at the next table, pretending they were whispering sweet nothings to each other while they were really taking notes. At another meeting I had one of my sons and a woman friend at the adjoining table.

Marriott put one cassette into his machine and started searching for a particular spot. He had difficulty locating it, but as he paused to listen to snippets of conversation, I recognized his voice, a voice that sounded like Father Magaldi's and lots of crowd sounds. Finally he landed on the portion he wanted me to hear. He played the tape for about twenty seconds, and then replayed it. I couldn't hear what was being said because of the background sounds. The discussion sounded like it was occurring over dinner. David was talking about a prior meeting in a bar. There was a brief response by Father Magaldi.

"There it is. You heard it with your own ears!" Marriott shouted. "You hear, he's admitting it. We met in a bar, not in the rectory like it says in the affidavit. He was lying. He admitted it on tape."

I turned to Roanne Sragow and asked her what she had heard. "Sounds like they once met in a bar. But I didn't hear anything inconsistent with the affidavit. Why don't you call Father Magaldi?"

I started toward the phone, but Marriott reached out as if to grab me. "No, don't do that. I have to call him first. He won't talk to you unless I tell him what it's about."

It sounded suspicious, and I decided to wait until Marriott left, but before he called the priest, to place my phone call.

Suddenly Marriott's entire tone of voice changed. "Alan," he said nervously, "don't worry. It's just a small detail I'm talking about. You don't have to worry, and you certainly don't have to upset Claus. The basic story is true. It happened the way we said it did, I just have to straighten a few things out with Father. It's between me and him. It doesn't involve you."

"It certainly does," I responded. "Anything having to do with the truth of those affidavits I care about. Even if it's just one word. You are not going to testify to one falsehood, if you testify at all."

I told Marriott that I wanted to hear everything he had on his tapes that might bear on the affidavits or the case. Marriott said he would play them for me soon, but not now. In the meantime, "Don't worry. There are no problems."

But I knew there were problems. I was not going to put my credibility behind any witness who wasn't telling the whole truth.

As soon as Marriott left, I called Father Magaldi and told him what Marriott had said and had played on his tape machine. The priest seemed unconcerned. "Of course, I've met with him at bars and restaurants. He always insists on meeting at places that he picks. I come to Boston quite a bit, and when we meet here it's usually over dinner."

I asked Father Magaldi directly, "Is every word in your affidavit absolutely true?" I felt as if I were challenging the authority of the Church by my question. The idea of asking a respected priest whether he had lied under oath was upsetting to me. I know how I would feel if someone asked me such a question. But I explained to Father Magaldi why I was obliged to ask it.

He said he was not angry at me for asking. "You're doing your job. Just like I was doing when I insisted that David come forward. He's an impossible person. Always trying to find villains everywhere. But everything I have said in my affidavit is the truth. I just hope that everything he told me was true, but I'm not swearing to that. I'm just swearing to what I saw and heard with my own eyes and ears."

I told Father Magaldi how much I appreciated his candor with me and told him that he would probably be receiving a call from Marriott. He should feel free to tell Marriott about my call or not, as he wished, I told him.

"I'll tell him," Father Magaldi said. "I don't like beating around the bush."

Shortly after the meeting, Marriott called with another bombshell. "You know those threats and assaults I told you about? Well, some of them happened the way I said, and some of them didn't."

"What do you mean, some of them didn't?" I demanded. "Did you make them up?"

"Well, I exaggerated them," he said defensively.

"Look, either you were knifed, or you weren't. Let's not play games."

"That one was real, but some of the others didn't happen exactly the way I said," he admitted unconvincingly.

"So you lied to us and to the police!" I shouted angrily.

"I had to. I was afraid that the organized crime people were after me for what I was doing, but I didn't want to mention that because their influence goes high into the police, especially in Rhode Island. I really needed protection, so I changed things a little."

"I must know exactly which threats and acts were real and which are phony," I demanded.

"All right, I'll give you a list by Tuesday." He also told me that by that time he would have proof that Father Magaldi "is the world's biggest liar."

Marriott insisted again that the basic story was absolutely true: "The stuff about drugs and Clarendon Court is all true. It's the stuff about Father Magaldi and the threats that aren't completely true."

When I told him that he had said enough to make me decide that I would never call him as a witness or ask him to execute another affidavit, he seemed relieved. I also told him that if after a thorough investigation we concluded that either his affidavit or Father Magaldi's were false, we would notify the court and seek to have them withdrawn.

As soon as Marriott started telling me about possible falsehoods in the affidavit, I conferred with Terry MacFadyen and several other members of my team to discuss what course of action we should take.

The options were limited, the issues complex. Here we had a witness who was telling us that his basic story was true, but that some of the important details he had sworn to were false and that his corroborating witness—a priest—was "the world's biggest liar." The priest was standing behind his story with absolute certainty. We believed the basic story, but we knew one thing for sure: the prosecution was absolutely correct in publicly characterizing David Marriott as a man who doesn't always stick to the truth. And I was becoming more and more convinced that Richard Kuh, the private prosecutor, was right in calling Marriott "a damned kook."

When Marriott called, he seemed more and more out of control all the time. Sometimes he said the stories were all true. Other times he charged that Claus von Bülow and Andrea Reynolds had put some of the words in his mouth.

I wrote a long letter to a friend of mine who was a member of the Standing Committee on Legal Ethics of the Massachusetts Association of Criminal Defense Lawyers, spelling out in detail the twists and turns in the different Marriott stories. I sought his advice on various ethical questions growing out of Marriott's machinations. I also turned to several other colleagues and experts in legal ethics, as did Terry MacFadyen and his partner in Rhode Island.

As our responses were coming in, the whole story changed again in several ways. First, Marriott called me on February 24, 1984. He seemed rational and calm during the call—which I assume he taped. He told me he was "terribly sorry for making up accusations against Claus and Father Magaldi," that all the "threats against him and Magaldi were true." He explained that he had been under enormous psychological strain and that he concocted his lies in the desperate attempt to make sure that I did not call him as a witness, because he was scared. He really was receiving threats; the most recent, he claimed, was a warning that he would be "sorry" after someone "blows your head off."

Marriott told me that he did not want to be called as a witness, but that he was willing to continue to gather evidence for Claus and try to find other witnesses, mentioning some names in Montreal and Newport. He asked me to draft a letter for him to send to the court, withdrawing his affidavit. I drafted a letter and gave it to him; he said he would decide whether and when to send it.

At this point it was impossible to know when Marriott was lying or telling the truth. Our ethics experts were advising us that the government faces this kind of problem all the time. Many of their most important witnesses are consummate liars and con men who agree to tell an occasional truth for their own benefit, parlaying their fortuitous knowledge of relevant facts into a personal bonanza. I had considerable experience with the phenomenon from the perspective of defending persons accused by such selective liars. The experts we spoke to, some of whom were high-ranking government prosecutors, advised us that we should follow the guidelines under which the government deals with similar informer-witnesses. We were not obliged to disclose every twist and turn in Marriott's story as it occurred, so long as the entire story would come out if he took the witness stand. This was especially true here, because Marriott himself was talking directly to the prosecutors, and to the press. The prosecutors could, if they wished, formally advise the court of Marriott's new claims. The experts also advised us that Marriott could continue to be paid out-of-pocket expenses and his small compensation for lost wages. Indeed, one expert advised us that the only thing that would be wrong was to terminate all payments as soon as he changed his story. Such an abrupt cutoff would suggest that he *was* being paid for the content of his story and that as soon as the story was not to our liking the payments would stop.

As all this was going on, Marriott took still further actions that effectively mooted some of the ethical issues. While the appeal was still pending, he held another of his press conferences. The Associated Press reported that Marriott "is withdrawing his affidavit on the convicted socialite's behalf because he is no longer convinced von Bülow is telling the truth." Marriott labeled Claus von Bülow "a liar and a con man." He continued: "There is nothing these people wouldn't do, legally or illegally," and added suggestively, "and there's a lot more to it."

Before the appeal was decided, Marriott made even more public accusations about Claus von Bülow, claiming that Claus and Andrea Reynolds had given Marriott narcotic drugs and that he and Claus had an association—a sexual one was implied—dating back nine years. I checked each of these accusations with Claus, who denied them categorically.

Marriott also remained in communication with the Rhode Island authorities and the state police—who kept Kuh apprised. The prosecution was conducting an investigation of Marriott. They could have submitted counter-affidavits but chose not to. Their tactic may well have been to try to surprise us at a hearing or new trial. Virtually everything Marriott did became the subject of one of his news conferences and was widely reported in the media.* The Supreme Court of Rhode Island was being exposed to all the variations on this bizarre theme as it wrote its opinions in the von Bülow case. Any possibility that the justices could somehow be misled by the Marriott-Magaldi affidavits was obviated by the fact that well before they rendered their decision, Marriott had publicly turned against von Bülow and Magaldi. It was anybody's guess what David Marriott would say next, and to whom.

In the meantime, the rumors about the progress of the Supreme Court's decision were continuing. Every report of the imminence of the decision would be followed by a delay: "They're having a little problem about the language." We began to worry that internal dissension might be slowing up the decision—even changing the result. If the rumors were accurate about the result, they might also be correct about the Attorney General's efforts to lobby the court to change that result. This was an election year in Rhode Island, and if the popular Democratic Attorney General, Dennis Roberts—whose father had been Chief Justice of the Rhode Island Supreme Court until 1976 and whose uncle had been governor— lost the biggest case in Rhode Island history, he would suffer at the polls. Was he urging his Democratic colleagues on the court not to ruin him politically? Were they listening? It all sounded like *Alice in Wonderland* justice, but this was Rhode Island—a small-town state whose level of political and judicial propriety seemed at least a decade behind Massachusetts. One of my colleagues quipped that he now understood why Rhode Island used to be called "Rogues Island."

On Wednesday, April 25, I was on my way to New York to give a talk and visit my ailing father, who was in the geriatric ward of a hospital suffering from Alzheimer's disease. As the Eastern Shuttle began to land, an announcement came over the speaker: "Will Professor Dershowitz please identify himself to a flight at-

* We often learned about Marriott's disclosures from reporters, who had already called the other side for comments. Sometimes we were—quite literally—the last to know what "our" witness was saying.

tendant." When I did, the attendant told me that my office was trying to reach me for an emergency message. My first thoughts turned to my family. I knew my secretary would not go to such efforts to tell me about a legal decision—no matter how important. I hoped it was a professional message, but I feared it was not. I raced off the plane and called my office. "Call your mother," my secretary told me, unwilling to give me any further information. I reached my sobbing mother, who told me that my father had died peacefully that morning. I went directly to their apartment in Brooklyn and tried my best to comfort my mother, who had ministered to my father during his five-year deterioration from Alzheimer's. At the end, my father could recognize only my mother, and his sole remaining memory was of portions of the prayer book from which he had read—*davened*—every day of his life. My father's peaceful passing after so many difficult years was both a blessing and a poignant reminder of what a wonderful man he was.

As I was making arrangements for my father's funeral the next morning, the phone rang. It was Claus. "This is it. The decision is definitely coming down tomorrow." Claus asked me to come to his apartment so that when the opinion was read over the phone, I could explain its implications to him—and to the press. I told Claus about my father's death and explained that I could not join him in celebrating the news. Claus understood.

By this time there was absolutely no doubt in any of our minds that we had won. The only remaining questions were on which legal grounds, whether a retrial would be possible, and whether the prosecutors could appeal their loss to the Supreme Court. I wondered to myself how I could have become so certain of the outcome, despite my skepticism about the inside information. Repetition has a way of easing doubts and confirming certainty.

Later that afternoon, another delay. The decision was put off one more day: typing and proofreading problems. But this was the last delay, we were assured. Even the Providence *Journal*—the local newspaper power—was given an embargoed, off-the-record advance copy of the decision. When we found out about that, we asked to see a copy on the same basis. It was important, we explained, for the lawyers to see the opinion at the same time the newspapers did, so that we could be prepared to answer press inquiries. No, we were told. We would have to wait for the general release. Only in Rhode Island, I thought, would a favored newspaper get to see the opinion before its competitors and before the lawyers *and before the client.* Another variation of the Rhode Island Shuffle.*

On Friday, April 27, at 9:00 on the morning after my father's funeral, the decision was announced. My office phone began to ring off the hook. "We won," my secretary said. "That's all I know." I was sitting *shivah*—the Jewish ritual of mourning for seven days— in my mother's apartment in Brooklyn. I took a short break from our collective sadness and drove from Brooklyn to Fifth Avenue— a ride of half an hour and half a world. By the time I arrived at 960 Fifth Avenue, the street was filled with TV cameras and reporters.

"No comment until I see, or hear, the opinion," I responded to the mikes being shoved under my chin.

"Can we come up with you?" "When will Claus be down?" "What is Claus going to do now?" "Is Andrea with him?" "Does Cosima know?"

I apologized for not being able to respond, and raced through the lobby to the same elevator that Maria was in when—so she said—she opened up the black bag for the last time, saw there were insulin and syringes in it, and failed in her final opportunity to warn her lady. I instinctively counted the eight seconds it took to get to the von Bülow apartment, as if to confirm to myself that Maria couldn't possibly have done all she claimed to have done during the brief ride.

When I opened the door to the large foyer, the dog was barking, but nobody was around. Claus was in the library quietly listening to Terry MacFadyen reading him the fifty-eight-page opinion over the telephone. Andrea Reynolds was in a guest room, recording Terry's mellifluous, if by now somewhat weak, voice. Joann Crispi was filling a notebook with media calls to be returned.

Claus motioned to me to pick up another receiver. Terry was reading away. I stopped him and said: "Bottom line, what did they do?" Terry told me that the court had reversed both counts on legal grounds and had expressly said there could be a new trial.

"State or federal grounds?" If the reversal was based on federal grounds—the U.S. Constitution—then the state could appeal to the U.S. Supreme Court, which is the highest authority on interpreting the U.S. Constitution. If it was based on state grounds—

---

* I later learned that one of the justices had consulted an experienced journalist several weeks before the decision was rendered, told him that the conviction would be reversed and solicited his judgment about how the press was likely to react.

a violation of the Rhode Island Constitution or statutes—then the state would be barred from appealing to Washington, since the Rhode Island Supreme Court is the highest authority for interpreting its own constitution and laws.

"Both," Terry said with an air of bemusement. "They really covered all the bases." That was wonderful news to me. Because the Rhode Island Constitution provided an *independent* basis for reversing the conviction, the U.S. Supreme Court had no power to interfere. Claus von Bülow's conviction was reversed. He was an innocent man—at least for the moment. The state could not appeal the reversal any further, but it could try him once again.

I asked Terry to tell me, in shorthand, what the grounds for reversal were.

"The first ground was the Kuh notes."

"The Kuh notes? But we were told they didn't like that argument," I said with a note of self-satisfaction.

"Maybe they changed their minds," Terry said dryly.

The other ground was more surprising. It was one of the issues we had nearly left out of our brief: "The second ground was that the state police should have gotten a search warrant when they sent some of the pills from the black bag for lab testing."

"But what about the bag itself?" I inquired.

"That's okay," Terry responded. "A private search. Alex and the investigator weren't bound by the Constitution. But the police officers were, and they should have gotten a warrant when they sent the pills out."

"Somewhat narrow and technical," I observed. "Those pills are going to be awfully hard for the media to swallow, especially since they weren't all that central to the prosecution's case. I wonder why the court relied on so narrow an argument."

Terry reminded me that the Rhode Island Supreme Court had written several opinions on the issue of evidence which private parties turn over to the police for further investigation. I still wondered whether the justices would have found this ground sufficient for reversal if they had not felt some twinge of doubt about von Bülow's guilt.*

---

* In a recent case before the New York Appellate Division, the same ground was presented for reversal of the defendant's conviction. Although the facts surrounding the search in the New York case were somewhat stronger for the defendant, the judges unanimously affirmed his conviction, without even pausing to write an opinion.

But if they felt it, they certainly didn't express it. The chief justice filed a separate opinion concurring in the reversal of the second count but arguing for dismissal of the first count. In that opinion the chief justice did find that there was not enough evidence for a conviction on Count I, the first coma. He concluded that the "facts surrounding Count I at most support a conclusion that the defendant acted in an unhusbandlike, rather than a criminal manner." The chief justice's dissenting view provoked the following response from the majority:

> With all due deference to the Chief Justice, we believe that when one views the evidence [in "the light most favorable to the prosecution"] the reasonable inferences drawn from such evidence support a reasonable conclusion that in late December 1979 the defendant, mindful of the ultimatum of his intended bride, decided to take matters into his own hands, one of which held a syringe containing a copious quantity of insulin, and so injected the contents of the syringe into his wife with the intent that she should expire so that he would be free to marry Alexandra.

But despite its conclusions about the sufficiency of the evidence that was presented against von Bülow, the court expressed grave doubts about some of the evidence that was not presented, namely the Kuh notes. The court ruled that the withholding of that material created an "injustice and hardship to defendant" and its effect "was to block the flow of potentially relevant evidence that may have been vital to his defense." Since the judges themselves had not seen the Kuh notes, they could only surmise how vital these notes indeed were.

> On the basis of the record before us, we have no way of knowing to what extent information obtained by Kuh from interviews with prospective witnesses was disclosed to the Rhode Island authorities. We do know, however, that from the outset Kuh and his clients, by choice, selectively disclosed information sufficient to help the state build its case against defendant while relying on one privilege or the other to prevent the flow of potentially relevant evidence to defendant. This selective use of allegedly privileged material cannot be said to have promoted the interests of society or defendant in reaching a fair or accurate resolution of the question of guilt or innocence.*

---

* Despite its favorable ruling on the Kuh notes, the court said there was nothing wrong with Kuh having served as a private prosecutor.

The court went on to illustrate the "unfair use" of the Kuh material by referring to the very episode we had highlighted in our brief—the use of Kuh's testimony as a rebuttal witness against Charles Roberts. The court specifically noted that "there is also evidence that Kuh [in his testimony] relied upon the very interview notes that he had previously refused to disclose." The "selective use" of the Kuh materials constituted a clear "injustice and hardship to defendant." It "blocked the flow" of potentially relevant evidence.*

But then the court itself blocked the flow of some relevant evidence. It held—as its second ground—that the state police violated both the federal and the Rhode Island constitutions when they subjected certain pills found in the black bag to chemical analysis without a search warrant. In our brief we had argued that the contents of a person's medicine cabinet or case may reveal as much about his or her most intimate secrets as a diary. They may disclose sexual, emotional and other aspects of life that one wishes to keep private. Hence a warrant should be required before the state is permitted to "turn the pages" of this "pharmaceutical diary." The court agreed with our somewhat novel argument and ruled that the "state's failure to procure a search warrant here . . . cannot withstand constitutional scrutiny." Because the "state's entire case is predicated upon circumstantial evidence," the chemical tests conducted without the necessary warrant "formed a significant part of the state's case," suggesting that "defendant may have anesthetized" his wife before injecting her.

Having heard the basic outlines of the opinion, we were ready to talk to the press. In a continuing case—with the likelihood of a new trial—a lawyer must constantly remember that he or she is talking to the press *for his client's interest* and not for his or her own interest. It is certainly tempting to go out there and claim all the credit for the victory (or—as Sheehan had done after the first trial—place the blame on the evidence). But every word has to be calculated to have a positive impact on the client's legal interest. Nor are the interests of the lawyer and the client always in tandem. Sometimes the guiltier the client is made to seem, the smarter the

---

* There is no inconsistency between the court's finding enough evidence for a jury to convict and also finding that potentially relevant evidence had been excluded. In evaluating the sufficiency of the evidence, the court looks only at the evidence actually before the jury and draws all reasonable inferences favorable to the prosecution.

winning lawyer looks. Conversely, the more innocent the client, the easier the lawyer's job in winning. Every word uttered by the lawyer or the client must be calculated to further the client's case —or at the very least not to damage it.

The moment the Rhode Island Supreme Court decision was rendered, the next phase of the case began. All of our strategic decisions would now be focused on trying to persuade the Attorney General—or trying to persuade the people to persuade the Attorney General—not to subject Claus von Bülow to a second trial. Not only is it perfectly proper for a lawyer to go public in an effort to influence a prosecutor to drop the charges against his client, but it is, at least in my view, improper to neglect this important forum of advocacy—especially when the private prosecutors are using every technique at their disposal to try to influence him to go after that client. Nor are there any canons or rules of the profession that prohibit lawyers from trying to influence prosecutors in this manner. The only prohibitions are designed to prevent *juries* from being improperly influenced on the eve of the trial. And retrial in this case—if there was to be one—was at least a year away.

With that in mind, Claus and I both accepted invitations to appear on various TV interview shows. That evening on *Nightline* I explained our understanding of the decision and Claus talked about his ambivalent feelings concerning a retrial: on the one hand, he wanted total vindication; on the other, he wanted to put the entire matter behind him so that he could devote more time to his daughter, Cosima. The next day we made similar points on the various morning news programs.

The story of the von Bülow reversal was front-page news. Even the staid New York *Times*—which does not generally report on soap-opera trials in detail—put the story on page 1: "APPELLATE COURT VOIDS VON BÜLOW CONVICTION." The tabloids, of course, ran racier headlines: "ANOTHER SHOT AT FREEDOM FOR RICH ARISTOCRAT," "DAPPER DANE LIKELY TO WIN: LAWYERS." Several media accounts characterized the reversal as based on "technical" grounds, implying that the court was deliberately reversing the conviction of an obviously guilty man. This, of course, ignored the court's express finding that the suppression of the Kuh notes prevented "a fair or accurate verdict."

To our considerable surprise, the Attorney General of Rhode Island decided to seek review of his own state Supreme Court's decision in the U.S. Supreme Court. He had to know he didn't have a ghost of a chance. Any first-year law student could have told him that the U.S. Supreme Court only has the power to interpret the U.S. Constitution. Even if the Rhode Island Supreme Court was wrong in its interpretation of the U.S. Constitution, von Bülow's conviction would have to stay reversed because it was based—independently—on the Rhode Island Supreme Court's interpretation of the Rhode Island constitution. As to its own constitution, the Rhode Island Supreme Court—like the Pope in relation to his ex cathedra pronouncements on divine law—is deemed to be infallible. (Unlike the Pope, it is not the Supreme Court *because* it's infallible; rather, it's infallible because it is the Supreme Court.)

We surmised that the Attorney General might have appealed for political reasons. Dennis Roberts was running for reelection right after losing his biggest case. There was a chance the U.S. Supreme Court might sit on the case until after the election. If so, he could hold out the prospect of vindication from on high.

For whatever reason, he asked the Supreme Court to review the case. Joining him were Richard Kuh on behalf not only of Sunny's children, but also of Sunny herself! How Kuh got the authority to speak for Claus's comatose wife, he never explained. But he wrote a brief that attacked the Rhode Island Supreme Court's opinion in the von Bülow case in the most vitriolic terms. In arguing that the United States Supreme Court should recognize the rights of victims, Kuh characterized the decision reversing von Bülow's conviction as "preposterous," "absurd," "whimsical," "aberrant," "unreasonably irresponsible" and "frivolous." He said that the justices had gone "haywire" and had brought "dishonor and ridicule upon our American system of criminal justice" by making themselves "partners in Claus von Bülow's deprivation of [Sunny's] 'life, liberty and property.' " It was quite an attack, not designed to make friends or influence justices on the Rhode Island court.

Other briefs in support of review in the Supreme Court were filed by the Attorneys General of Connecticut and Arizona* as well as organizations called the Victims Assistance Legal Organization, Americans for Effective Law Enforcement, Inc., and the International Association of Police Chiefs.

We filed a brief advising the Supreme Court that it had no power

---

* I later learned that Attorneys General of several other states refused Roberts's request to file *amicus* briefs, advising him that the Supreme Court had no power to review the case.

to review the Rhode Island Supreme Court's interpretation of its own constitution:

> The Rhode Island Supreme Court's decision according Claus von Bülow a new trial at which an "accurate resolution of the question of guilt or innocence will be possible," was based on independent state grounds, was correct as a matter of fact and law, and should be deemed final under principles of federalism, constitutional restraint, and fairness. Accordingly, respondent respectfully requests this Court to deny the petition for a writ of certiorari.

On October 1, 1984, the first Monday in October, when the U.S. Supreme Court opens its session, the justices unanimously declined to review the von Bülow case. Again there were headlines and media attention. "U.S. SUPREME COURT BACKS VON BÜLOW" read the headline to a full-page story, with Roberts expressing "disappointment" and vowing that he would "immediately begin preparation for a new trial." If Dennis Roberts had sought further review for political reasons, his decision had backfired. Five weeks before his reelection bid, a unanimous Supreme Court decision reminded the electorate of his big loss.

Several months later, one of the Justices of the U.S. Supreme Court, in an opinion, described the Attorney General's attempt to obtain review of the von Bülow case as "frivolous." It is unprofessional conduct for a lawyer—especially a public official—to file frivolous lawsuits. The Supreme Court's rebuke of the Rhode Island Attorney General was complete.

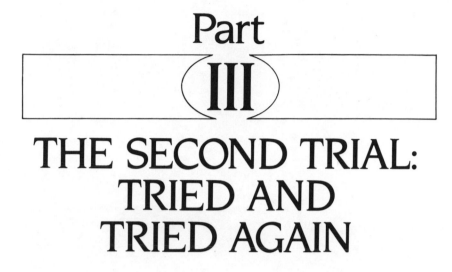

Part

III

THE SECOND TRIAL: TRIED AND TRIED AGAIN

14

Preparing for the New Trial— with the Kuh Notes

A month after the U.S. Supreme Court denied review of the von Bülow case, the voters of Rhode Island denied Dennis Roberts the office of Attorney General. In his place they elected a former nun named Arlene Violet, who had campaigned on a platform of victims' rights—a current euphemism for what used to be called "law and order." So tough did she promise to be that she became known as "Attila the Nun"—a label she apparently delighted in. (One of my sons dubbed her "the Frying Nun" after hearing her views on the death penalty.) Her election as the first woman Attorney General in the country became a media event. Violet was profiled on *60 Minutes* and in the New York *Times* and other newspapers and magazines—and the von Bülow case was at the center of every story.

Among the specific cases about which she had criticized her opponent during the campaign was the von Bülow case. Roberts should not, she insisted, have wasted the taxpayers' money by filing such a foolish appeal to the Supreme Court. This criticism encouraged us to believe that the new Attorney General might have an open mind about whether to retry von Bülow.

We were encouraged even further when she announced that she would conduct a full-scale review of all the evidence before deciding whether to reprosecute. She criticized her defeated opponent for referring to von Bülow as a "guilty man" even after his conviction had been reversed. "I suppose Mr. von Bülow will be particularly happy . . . that there is a change," the new Attorney General declared, seemingly turning the possible retrial into a political issue. "VON BÜLOW CASE MAY BE DROPPED," read the headlines.

In the meantime, of course, we had to act as if there was going to be a new trial. We had to assemble a trial team and turn our newly discovered medical evidence—which was now in affidavit form—into live testimony. We also had to get what we were now finally entitled to: the Kuh notes.

I told Claus that I couldn't take the responsibility for trying the case if there was to be a retrial. As I had told him from the very beginning of my involvement in the appeal, my teaching schedule always comes first. The retrial was scheduled to begin during the middle of my spring semester, and I had a full load of courses. (In one of my courses—legal ethics for criminal lawyers—we spent quite a few hours discussing all the implications of the Marriott-Magaldi situation; it was an invaluable educational experience for my students to be thrust into the vortex of an ongoing ethical dilemma.)

I told Claus that I could remain in Cambridge and continue in the role of strategist and legal writer. Two of my former students and research assistants, Joann Crispi and Andrew Citron, could be at the trial on a day-to-day basis and serve as conduits for my input. Claus was agreeable but pleaded with me to play as active a role as my schedule would permit. He also asked me to remain in charge of all the pretrial motions and legal issues and to help him select a trial lawyer.

Claus had certain specifications in mind for a trial lawyer, and he asked me to prepare a list of excellent criminal lawyers who fit them. He wanted a fighter, preferably a former prosecutor who could put the state and its witnesses on the defensive. He wanted someone with street smarts who could fight it out with a local favorite like Steve Famiglietti. Although we knew that Famiglietti—who had left the Attorney General's office for private practice—would not be retrying the case, we did not know who would. Claus wanted someone who could go head to head with the likes of Famiglietti. Reading between the lines, I interpreted that to mean that Claus preferred someone whose ethnic background was compatible with the likely backgrounds of the jurors, prosecutors and judges. My interpretation was corroborated when Claus peremptorily struck several lawyers from my list.

The first person on both of our lists fit none of these descriptions, but he was so good, and so highly regarded, that Claus wanted him anyhow. He was Edward Bennett Williams, a Washington lawyer who had defended Jimmy Hoffa, Joseph McCarthy, Texas Governor John Connally and a legion of other defendants. His partner Vince Fuller had just secured an acquittal by reason of insanity for attempted presidential assassin John W. Hinckley, Jr. I called Williams and spoke to him and one of his senior litigation partners, Robert Weinberg, whom I knew from law school. I was enthusiastic about working with the acknowledged master of criminal trials. Claus went down to Washington to meet with him. But in the end, it didn't work out. Williams could not commit himself to become personally involved in a day-to-day manner in the case; his partners, Vince Fuller and Bob Weinberg, would handle much of the work. Claus balked at that delegation of authority. Despite the brilliance and experience of Williams's partners, von Bülow wanted the master.

We bandied about several names, but Claus had objections— some more persuasive than others. It was his life. He would have to make the decision.

Claus asked me about a lawyer who had been mentioned by Joann Crispi. His name was Thomas Puccio, the recently retired prosecutor who had gained fame by prosecuting the Abscam defendants—Senator Harrison Williams of New Jersey and several congressmen. I knew Tom quite well because I had taught the Abscam cases in my law school classes, and he had come up to Cambridge to "retry" them in front of my class (I played defense counsel). Shortly after he had gone into private practice I had recommended him to a client of mine, and we were working together on a case. Tom certainly fit all of Claus's categories. He was a street-fighter, a former prosecutor, smart, and came from the same ethnic background as many of the jurors, prosecutors and judges in Rhode Island. (I had wondered about the latter once when I called his house and was told he was at the synagogue; it turned out that he was there with his Jewish wife.) Tom had been born and raised in the same Boro Park neighborhood of Brooklyn where I had spent my youth, but he came from the Rome side of what we used to call the Rome-Jerusalem border. His grandparents had migrated from Sicily, and Tom was—according to the Providence *Journal*—a "fresh-mouthed, fast-talking former prosecutor with a heavy Brooklyn accent." The papers also called him a "glory hog," as they call most good criminal lawyers. Some of his detractors think that he is not a team player: "All he thinks about is number one." But I liked Tom, and Claus was very pleased that we had worked together. The only thing that worried us about Tom was that he had never tried a case as a defense lawyer. There are enormous differences between prosecuting and defending a case. Most prosecutors develop an expertise in putting on a direct case, but not in cross-examining. Most defense attorneys learn how to cross-examine, but not how to put on a direct case. This was a heck of a case in which to "learn—while you earn." But Tom had considerable experience trying cases as a prosecutor.

I welcomed Tom onto the team and began to work with him. My former assistants Joann and Andy became his right and left hands. Claus referred to them as Tom's "human computers." They knew every fact, every piece of new evidence, every medical expert we might consider using. They were young and inexperienced in the courtroom, but they were an indispensable part of the team—the critical link between the appeal and the new trial.

Our first task was to get the Kuh notes. Despite Richard Kuh's personal written assurance to me that "there is not a scrap of paper in my files that might even arguably be viewed as exculpatory," I was as certain as anyone could be that his notes would contain important material. I had suggested to the Rhode Island Supreme Court during the oral argument that if the notes did not mention insulin, then that would support our theory that the entire insulin story had been contrived. I had predicted to my co-counsel exactly what I thought the notes would show. "I'll bet you my fee in this case," I rashly boasted to Susan Estrich, "that nobody ever mentioned seeing insulin in the black bag until *after* they found insulin in Sunny's body or on the needle."

When we finally got the Kuh notes, I pored through them to see when insulin was first mentioned. The notes were in Kuh's handwriting and nearly impossible to read. The judge had tried, but couldn't make heads or tails out of them. Several of the other lawyers had similar problems. But I was able to read them as easily as if they were typed. The reason was simple: every year I grade several hundred handwritten exams. The handwritings come from all over the world. Some of them seem indecipherable. But we *have* to read them, and so we learn. After I'd spent twenty years of decoding more than a hundred thousand pages of chicken scratches, the Kuh notes were a piece of cake.

Kuh's first interview was with Alexander von Auersperg and his sister Ala. It took place on January 5, 1981—two weeks after the final coma. Sunny's children discussed their suspicions, especially after the maid Maria Schrallhammer discovered the black bag. The children mentioned that "Valium and several prescriptions" and "bottles" were "found by maid in his travel bag." There was no mention of insulin or syringes at this first meeting.

I quickly turned to Kuh's notes of his first meeting with Maria Schrallhammer three days later. What I found was absolute dynamite. It confirmed my most optimistic predictions—and more. Maria described in detail what she had found in the black bag the first time she opened it in the February after the first coma: "Valium," "several bottles." She took out "powder, liquid and pills." Maria described the bottles and their labels with precision: "The original bottles all were from Zitomer Pharmacy then on Madison and 75th; now on Madison between 77th and 78th. Physician: Dr. Rosenberg. Name on one prescription was for Leslie Baxter. One had Claus von Bülow but a phony address."*

So far the notes of this first interview were entirely consistent with Maria's trial testimony. Even the fact that there was no mention of insulin during the February sighting was consistent, since she had testified at the trial that she did not see the insulin and syringes until the Sunday after Thanksgiving. Her trial testimony was that when she opened the black bag that day, she was surprised to see insulin and syringes because she knew Sunny was not diabetic. She testified that immediately upon discovering the *new* items in the black bag, she summoned Alex, held up the insulin, pointed to the syringes and exclaimed: "Insulin, for what insulin?" On cross-examination Maria repeated her reaction to seeing the insulin: "I asked Alex, 'For what insulin?' because Mrs. von Bülow is hypoglycemic. She doesn't need insulin." Maria was certain that she had read the word "insulin" clearly on the label.

> Q. Did it have a label on it?
> A. Yes.
> Q. And did you read the label?
> A. Yes, that's where I read insulin, because I never saw insulin before.

It is unlikely that Maria would forget so dramatic a discovery and exclamation just six weeks after it happened—*if* it happened. What the notes disclosed cast grave doubt, to put it most generously, on whether what she had testified to so dramatically at the trial had happened at all.

This is exactly what the January 8, 1981, notes say about what Maria had seen on the Sunday after Thanksgiving:

---

* The address, it turned out, was not phony; it was one of Claus's clubs.

In November 1980 (Thanksgiving)—Sunday after in New York City.
In Claus' black case, saw same and called Alex attention to same But
no labels—all scraped off!!

Thus the notes show that Maria told Kuh that during this crucial
post-Thanksgiving sighting Maria saw the "same" items she had
previously seen in February. In February she saw no insulin or
syringes, only prescription vials and bottles for Valium and secobarbital. Moreover, during the Thanksgiving sighting all the labels
had been scraped off, so she could not identify what they said. The
great significance of Maria's trial testimony about the Thanksgiving
sighting was precisely that the bag did *not* contain the same items
she had seen in February. Maria's crucial trial testimony was that at
Thanksgiving she had seen—for the first time—insulin and syringes.
This new material had prompted her to summon Alex and show
him the new items, not the "same" old items. And she swore at the
trial that she had read the word insulin on the label.

Every important part of Maria's trial testimony concerning the
post-Thanksgiving sighting was thus specifically contradicted by
Kuh's notes of what she said when her memory of the events was
freshest—about two and a half weeks after the coma—and before
there was any family theory into which the Thanksgiving sighting of
insulin and syringes neatly fit.

It was better than we could hope for. It was certainly better than
Kuh had led us to believe by his lawyerly representation that there
was "not a scrap of paper in my files that might even arguably be"
helpful to the defense. This information not only would be useful,
it would undercut the entire basis of Maria's crucial testimony about
insulin. No jury would now credit the maid's trial testimony that
she saw insulin and syringes on the Sunday of Thanksgiving weekend, because we could now prove that she had specifically told
Richard Kuh that all the labels had been scraped off and that the
items in the bag during the Thanksgiving sighting were the "same"
as the items in the bag in February. The sightings of the unexplain-
able insulin and syringes was just too important to be totally forgotten in just six weeks. And the specific mention of labels being
scraped off—a fact never mentioned at the trial—was completely
inconsistent with her trial testimony that she read "insulin" on the
label. These major discrepancies could not be excused as mere innocent changes of memory. If Maria's memory had changed, it was

far more likely that it would have lapsed—and not improved—with the passage of time.

My theory was strengthened even further when we proceeded through the notes and discovered *when* Maria and Alex first "remembered" their discovery of insulin and syringes. It was on January 20, 1981, that Kuh's notes first mentioned that Maria found insulin and "a hypo needle" in Claus's bag. Everything began to fit neatly into place when we found out that just days earlier the family first learned that a high level of insulin had been found in Sunny's blood. But even then the family hadn't yet gotten its story straight. Alex told Kuh that the insulin and syringe had been found in "December 80 or early January 81 in the bag." A son who found insulin and a syringe *before* his mother went into a coma would remember that it was before, and not say that it might have been afterward. Again, hazy contemporaneous memories were improving considerably with the passage of time—and with the emergence of the family's theory of guilt.

The Kuh notes also revealed how the insulin theory had come together for the family during the early weeks of the investigation. After the finding of the black bag at Clarendon Court on January 23, 1981, Kuh's notes disclose that the needle was sent out for testing. But the test was not a general one to find out what was on the needle. It was specifically sent "to check for insulin." There was insulin in Sunny's blood. There might be insulin on the needle. How important it now became to "remember" seeing insulin in the black bag a few weeks before the final coma. By January 30, 1981, Maria "was certain it was insulin." She had a "vivid recollection" of it. Why that recollection had not been communicated to Kuh *before* the insulin theory had materialized, and how Maria could have read labels that had been "all scraped off," was never alluded to in Kuh's notes.

There was more—much more—to be gleaned from the Kuh notes. We learned for the first time that Alex had told the family banker within days of his mother's coma that Alex was "ready to provoke fight with Claus"; that Alex was "eager not to lose [Clarendon Court]—which was willed to Claus—under any circumstances"; that Ala "has never gotten along with Claus"; and—most important —that before the family decided to prosecute Claus, they discussed buying him off and getting him to renounce all interests in his wife's will.

Finally, the Kuh notes showed that Claus had discussed with Ala the question of terminating her mother's life-support system just two weeks after the second coma. They suggest, moreover, that Claus had told her that "he (Claus) will *not* make decision; kids must." Finally, they show that Ala was "uncertain what to do," in light of the fact that "Sunny had made it clear she would *not* want to 'live' this way [emphasis in original notes]." This was important because the stepchildren had repeatedly told the press that it was Claus who insisted on turning off Sunny's life support and that they had resisted this barbarous suggestion: "Claus von Bülow wanted to pull the plug on his wife's life-support system after her second coma, but was blocked by her two children," read one story, headlined "VON BÜLOW WANTED TO PULL PLUG ON WIFE." The contemporaneous notes suggested a more complex exchange between Claus and his stepchildren over this emotionally difficult question.

A whole other story was being told by the Kuh notes, and it was an original story, an unrehearsed story, a story based on "just the facts" without theories. It was a story that was far less certain, far more ambiguous than the one told at the trial by witnesses who had become more certain of their memories as time went by and as witnesses spoke to one another and to their lawyers, the police and prosecutors. "VON BÜLOW RETRIAL EXPECTED TO HINGE ON LAWYER'S NOTES" read a full-page headline in the Philadelphia *Inquirer*.

The new story—which was really the oldest story—strongly confirmed the approach we had taken in our new-trial motion and were planning to reassert on the retrial. At the retrial, we would attack the entire insulin theory head-on. We would challenge each of the four independent bases the insulin theory had relied on so successfully at the first trial. We would prove that Maria and Alex had *not* seen insulin and syringes in the black bag after Thanksgiving. We would prove that Sunny's blood did *not* contain high levels of insulin. We would prove there was *no* insulin on the needle found in the black bag in January. And we would prove that the prosecution's doctors were *wrong* in concluding that exogenous insulin had caused Sunny's comas. It was a tall order, but we had to confront the state's case directly. No more multiple-choice defense. Our defense was becoming single-focused: there was no exogenous insulin involved in this case. The Kuh notes were the Rosetta stone, containing the raw information needed to unravel the mystery.

My experiences with the Kuh notes certainly confirmed my view that all evidence should always be turned over to the defense for its independent evaluation. Here was a situation where the lawyer in sole possession of the notes was prepared to make an unequivocal representation that he was "satisfied" that his secret notes contained "not a scrap of paper" that could "even arguably be viewed as exculpatory." Kuh may honestly have believed that. Even a judge, unfamiliar with our other evidence and information, might not have discerned the significance of the Kuh notes upon a quick reading. But any defense lawyer, familiar with the entire defense strategy, would immediately see the exculpatory relevance of the very different story told in the Kuh notes and in the in-court testimony by the same witnesses.

Our big problem now resulted from the manner in which the first trial had been conducted. Fahringer had never disputed the presence of insulin on the used needle found in the black case in January. Indeed, he had gone so far as to stipulate that "fact." Could we now unstipulate it and contest it? We set out to persuade the judge that we—the lawyers on the retrial—were not bound by or stuck with the stipulations of our predecessor. Of course, Sheehan's presence at both trials would make that argument a bit more difficult to put forward with an entirely straight face. But in the end Tom managed to convince the judge that we should be free to introduce the new medical evidence that cast doubt on the laboratory tests purporting to find insulin on the needle. The new disclosures contained in the Kuh notes gave us the right to try our case differently this time around.

In our new-trial motion—the technical part that had been downplayed by the press in favor of the more racy Marriott-Magaldi affidavits—we had laid the foundations for our retrial strategy. Indeed, every major aspect of the medical and forensic defense that was eventually presented at the second trial in 1985 had been outlined in our new-trial motion filed in 1983. We had taken a calculated risk by showing all of our cards well in advance of a possible retrial. Normally, the defense in a criminal case has the advantage of surprise. It generally does not have to disclose much of its case in advance of trial. Few defendants can use this advantage to their benefit, since most simply don't have any defense. But the few that do can employ the element of surprise, even though some parts of the defense case—such as an alibi—generally have to be disclosed before trial.

We had given up this advantage by laying out just about all of our evidence in advance. We felt that we had no choice. We had to protect against the possibility of losing the appeal and having our client sent to prison before we could file our new-trial motion. I had discussed at length the pros and cons of this decision with Claus and with my team and we had all decided to take the risk of disclosure. If we had known for sure that we were going to win the appeal, obviously we would have kept our down cards closed to maintain our advantage in a retrial. But despite Sheehan's "inside information," we could not know for sure.

In poker it is impossible to bluff with all your cards showing. In law it is difficult, but not impossible. We had shown the prosecution all of our evidence, but we had not disclosed our theory. A theory requires a culling and a shaping of the evidence. We didn't tell the prosecution which parts of our evidence we were planning to discard and which we were planning to employ.

The prosecution knew, of course, that we would not use Marriott or Magaldi. Indeed, *they* were threatening to use Marriott as a prosecution witness against Claus, even though they had previously declared their disbelief in his credibility. We have no idea what Marriott might have said as a prosecution witness, but he had now told the press that the drugs he delivered to Clarendon Court were for Claus rather than Sunny and Alex. Marriott was recanting everything he had sworn about his contacts with Alex. The prosecution didn't know whether we planned to try to introduce the affidavit of Truman Capote or the testimony of several of Sunny's friends and acquaintances who knew about her use of alcohol and other stimuli. Nor did they know whether we would ask Alex if he had received drugs. Indeed, at one point when the court was considering whether Kuh should be excluded from the courtroom as a potential witness, Kuh submitted an affidavit containing the following statement: "Moreover, in light of the wholly false allegations made in affidavits submitted by the defense in the fall of 1983, concerning alleged criminal conduct on the part of my client, Alexander von Auersperg, his attorney's courtroom advice may also be necessary concerning issues involving the constitutional privilege against self-incrimination during his testimony." We considered this a faux pas because it in effect acknowledged that Alex might have a problem answering questions about his contact with drugs.* Shortly after this blunder, Kuh withdrew from the

---

* Invoking the privilege against self-incrimination might, of course, generate a public perception that the person invoking it had something to hide.

case and was replaced as counsel for the von Auersperg family by another lawyer.* Our tactics seemed to be working. The other side seemed to have been thrown off guard by our multiple-choice *evidence*. We would not tell them which of the multiples we would choose for the trial—until the trial.

Law is not a game, but the adversary system requires that defense lawyers not give up any advantages. *Trade* some for a counter-advantage—maybe. But give up anything in exchange for nothing —never!

As we were poring over our case for trial, we were also proceeding with our campaign to try to persuade the new Attorney General not to proceed with a retrial. We learned that she had met with Richard Kuh prior to his withdrawal as counsel. We believed that fairness required that she meet with us as well to hear all sides of the story. There were risks for us involved in such a meeting. We would have to lay out our case in the most persuasive manner, thereby disclosing our theory of the defense and our strategy. There were no risks for her. She could sit back and listen to our whole case. If we persuaded her that we were right—that von Bülow was innocent—ethics required her not to subject him to a retrial. If she remained convinced of his guilt but concluded that she would probably lose the case, considerations of priorities and resources might compel her to drop it. If she felt she could win, then she could proceed to retry von Bülow with the advantage of knowing what our case would be.

Most prosecutors jump at the opportunity for a "sit down" with the other side. Indeed, in my twenty years of experience I had *never once* been turned down for a requested meeting. But Attorney General Violet refused to meet with us. The Providence *Journal* reported, "She said she refused to meet with Dershowitz and other defense attorneys . . . because she did not want to be put in the position of learning things that might never be put in writing in the court file as part of the pretrial discovery in the case." This argument is preposterous, especially since we would have been prepared to stipulate in writing that the meeting was not for the purpose of formally discovering the other side's evidence, but rather for the purpose of trying to persuade her to drop the case.

At first I thought Violet's decision was simply a blunder resulting from her inexperience. She had never been involved in criminal

---

* The judge excluded Kuh, and Kuh claims that he asked to be relieved because he would be "at best of extremely limited value in light of the judge's ruling."

cases. But I later learned that although she had never met me, Arlene Violet had a real "thing"—as someone who knows her put it—about me. It was, according to my source, a combination of fear, jealousy and unspecified antagonism. She told several people that she wasn't going to be "pushed around" by Dershowitz, that he had finally encountered someone who was not going to be "overwhelmed" by his "aggressiveness." Not only hadn't we met, but I had supported her candidacy because I had liked what I had heard about her. Her apparent antagonism took me by surprise. Whether her attitudes toward me had anything to do with her refusal to meet in advance of her decision to retry von Bülow, I will probably never know. But in retrospect it seems clear that her decision cost the citizens of Rhode Island dearly. I am convinced that if we had met with her and explained our new evidence, particularly the medical and forensic case, she might very well have realized that she was going to lose. Even if she decided to proceed, it would have been with the considerable advantage of having learned our theory and strategy in advance.

Instead, Violet announced that she would decide whether to reprosecute von Bülow the day after I was scheduled to cross-examine Richard Kuh about his notes at a pretrial hearing on January 4, 1985. It was all calculated to draw maximum media attention to her decision.*

On Friday, January 4, I confronted Richard Kuh in a courtroom for the first time. The purpose of the hearing was to determine the nature and extent of the Kuh notes and to obtain an order from the court requiring the full disclosure of notes he was still withholding. Kuh was a formidable opponent—and an opponent he was. Much had happened between us since that exchange of polite letters back in 1982, in which he had praised my book and my integrity. Now he was calling me a liar and a scoundrel on the airwaves. There was an air of anticipation as I stepped up to the lectern to examine him.

The examination was recorded by the television camera that is permitted into Rhode Island criminal courts. At one point I began to read from Kuh's notes of his first meeting with Maria, which said that all the labels were "scraped off," and reminded Kuh that he had represented to me in a letter back in 1982 that there was nothing in his files that could possibly be deemed exculpatory. The

---

* I also learned from unimpeachable sources that Violet had made the decision to retry von Bülow—and indeed had drafted her prepared statement—before my examination of Kuh.

cross-examination was punctuated with sharp exchanges. In the end, the judge ruled in our favor, requiring Kuh to turn over nearly all the notes that he had continued to withhold.

As we left the courtroom, representatives of the media surrounded me. Several TV reporters asked me to summarize what I had said in the courtroom. Other reporters were circling Kuh. One newspaper reporter, Tracy Breton of the Providence *Journal*—a particularly shrewd reporter with excellent sources—asked me to show her the Kuh notes. I told her that I wasn't sure I was allowed to because they were not part of the public file. Breton raced off in the direction of the judge's chambers and quickly returned to tell me that she had asked the judge, who said there would be nothing wrong with showing her the notes, for they were not under seal or a gag order. We decided, however, that for tactical reasons we would not show anyone the complete notes until the second trial.

As I stepped outside, I paraphrased, in somewhat more colorful language, what I had just stated in court: "The notes produced by Dick Kuh are dynamite. They blow the prosecution's case out of the water." I also explained that Maria and Alexander had testified the way they did "because they were not confronted with prior inconsistent statements they had made to Kuh." Kuh told the press that my statements were "garbage" and he continued to claim— despite the clear language of the notes—that his notes "didn't contradict a single thing in the testimony." Since the reporters had not seen the Kuh notes, they couldn't ask him about Maria's statement in the notes that the labels were "all scraped off" and the bag contained the "same" material at Thanksgiving that it had earlier when no insulin was seen.

The next day the Attorney General convened a major press conference. Every national and local network and station was invited; dozens attended. The conference was purposely scheduled for early Saturday afternoon, because that was the time for maximum coverage of this kind of story in the Sunday papers. At the press conference Violet announced that she had decided to retry Claus von Bülow. It was her belief, she said, that "there is sufficient probative evidence which, if believed by a jury, would result in conviction. This should be submitted to a jury of Mr. von Bülow's peers and that's what we will do."

Then she went on to level a personal attack against me. I still had not met her, so the ferocity of her criticism surprised me. "Obviously, Mr. Dershowitz is also Mr. Showman." Later she elaborated:

"Dershowitz has had one shot to shoot his mouth off. From this point on if he persists in making statements [about the case], I will move to have the court exclude him" as one of von Bülow's lawyers.

She then expanded on her views about von Bülow in an interview with the New York *Post*, which reported that "the new prosecutor announced yesterday that she is 'absolutely convinced' he twice tried to kill his wife, Sunny."

What offended me most was that Violet picked up Kuh's tune and charged me with distorting the Kuh notes: "I have reviewed the Kuh notes and [Dershowitz's] representation of Maria Schrallhammer's comments is erroneous and false. Totally false." When I heard those words, I wondered whether Violet and I had reviewed the same notes. I could not understand how anyone who read the Kuh notes and compared them with Maria's trial testimony could escape the conclusion that the former contradicted the latter—as would become demonstrably clear at the second trial.

Several members of the press expressed surprise at what she had done. As one journalist put it: "It's the first time I've ever seen a prosecutor convene a press conference with the media to criticize a lawyer for responding to the media." Violet's behavior gave new meaning to the word *chutzpa*.* A lawyer who knows both of us characterized her threats against me as a "preemptive strike," a desire on her part "to strike the first blow in what obviously is going to be a long war. When she has something against you," warned my source, "she never lets go."

I was in Florida on a speaking tour when she held her press conference and utterly unaware of and unprepared for her attack. I learned of it when I routinely called my answering service for messages. "You have about forty calls from the press," I was told, "something about some trouble you're in with the Attorney General of Rhode Island." I thought about getting on a plane and returning home, where I could fight back with my full array of weapons, but the sun was too beautiful. I decided to go back to my hotel and take a swim. When I got there I realized there was no choice but to fight back, right there and then. Several cameras were pointed at the front entrance waiting for me. The result was a full-fledged media battle with charges and countercharges.

I followed up this skirmish with a long letter to Attorney General

---

* The traditional illustration of *chutzpa* is the defendant who killed both his parents and then threw himself on the mercy of the court because he was an orphan.

Violet outlining my position on the role of a lawyer in dealing with the press.

I reminded Violet of her own press conference and comments on her belief in von Bülow's guilt, which were far more dangerous to a fair trial than anything I had said. I referred her to cases that held that the kind of out-of-court comments I had made, which essentially repeated the substance of what had already been said in the courtroom, were constitutionally protected exercises of free speech, as was my right to respond to what she and Kuh were saying. I ended my letter on a conciliatory note:

> Because of my client's visibility and because of the media interest in the first trial, the retrial of Mr. von Bülow is certain to generate enormous publicity. My co-counsel and I are eager to sit down personally with you to work out reasonable guidelines to govern the comments of the defense, the prosecution and Mr. Kuh in the coming months. My primary concern is, I believe, the same as yours: a fair trial, in which all the evidence is heard.

This time she agreed to meet. When we arrived for our meeting, I got a better sense of what my source meant in describing Violet's complex attitudes toward me. Throughout the meeting she seemed to wear an artificial smile, while at the same time trying to show who was in charge.

We reached an oral understanding that we would both comply with certain agreed-upon rules in dealing with the press during the remainder of the case. She accepted the responsibility of trying to, as she said, "keep control over" Kuh—who was still in the case at that time—so that he didn't present the prosecution's side of the case to the press without our having an opportunity to respond. And finally, she acknowledged that her statements about me were based on a "misunderstanding" and some "misquotations" by the press. She agreed to put all of this in writing so as to avoid the necessity of continuing the acrimonious debate in public. Although Violet did eventually write to me, her letter did not contain the acknowledgments she had promised.

When I deal with a prosecutor, I quickly decide whether she is a woman of her word who can be trusted over a handshake. I decided that when dealing with Arlene Violet, one puts everything in writing.

The Boston *Globe*, in a rare editorial about an upcoming case, sought to portray it as a personal clash between "the showman lawprofessor" and "Attila the Nun." Entitled "As Newport Turns . . . ," the editorial acknowledged that Violet's decision to retry von Bülow "may be political, as defense attorney Alan Dershowitz has charged," but concluded that Violet really "had no choice." The courts must resolve "the real-life legal questions in a case as compelling as any melodrama seen on afternoon television."

Jury selection for the trial was scheduled to start in the beginning of April 1985. A new judge had been assigned to preside over the case. In typical Rhode Island fashion, several decisions were made internally. First the trial was moved from Newport to Providence. Neither side had asked that it be moved. But the chief justice of the Superior Court—the trial court—decided by himself to move it; he was not even directly involved in the case. His decision caused a furor. The restaurateurs, hostelers and merchants of Newport went bonkers over the decision. It was bad enough the Australian yachtsmen had taken away the America's Cup. Now the second biggest Newport spectacle was also being moved, and this would destroy the tourist business. A local legislator even introduced a bill to return it to Newport, but to no avail.

The informed speculation was that the chief judge wanted to replace the trial judge who had originally been assigned to retry the case, Alberto DeRobbio, a smiling old-timer from Newport with a reputation as a tough, efficient and fair-minded judge. Some observers thought that Judge DeRobbio had been ruling too favorably to the defense. He had given us just about everything we had asked for in relation to the Kuh notes, and he had given me wide latitude in cross-examining Kuh. The effect of moving the trial to Providence was to leave the kindly and level-headed Judge DeRobbio back in Newport to deal with drunken yachtsmen, while the real action was taking place forty miles to the north.

In place of Judge DeRobbio the chief justice appointed Corrine Grande, a judge whose last name describes her well. She conducts court grandly, with quiet dignity and respect for all participants. Though occasionally allowing a certain pedantic quality to show through her controlled demeanor, she was otherwise highly regarded. She seemed to deserve her excellent reputation as a thoughtful judge who is cautious about what she allows the jury to see and hear.

On the evening before jury selection was to begin, the defense team assembled in Providence. I asked Claus to arrange a meeting time. His response reflected a tension. "What's wrong?" I asked.

"Sheehan doesn't want you to come for the opening of the trial," he said apologetically.

"The Rhode Island Shuffle again?" I asked.

"Well, you know how he is. He'll walk out of court if you're there."

I was surprised that Claus would succumb to this kind of pressure. After all, it was our team, not Sheehan, that had produced the appellate victory, the denial of further review by the United States Supreme Court, and the new evidence. All through the preparation for the trial, Claus had pleaded with me to be in Providence as often as my schedule allowed. I did not teach on Monday, and so it was natural for me to be there on the opening day to meet the judge and become a part of the team. Claus told me that Sheehan was once again blaming it on the judge. "She doesn't want the first day to be a media circus, and if Alan's here, she thinks it will attract media attention."

The argument was absurd on its face. Hundreds of reporters and TV crews had descended on Providence—to see Claus von Bülow, who had generally stayed out of the public eye since his first trial. No one would notice my presence. Indeed, if anyone noticed anything about me, it would be my *absence*. The press was referring to me as the "legal mastermind," the "player-coach," the "backbone" of the defense, the "unseen force behind Claus's new defense," the lawyer who "will direct the von Bülow defense from his law school office" and even "the most important person in von Bülow's life." There was every reason to believe that I would be present on opening day. But Claus was terrified of losing whatever clout Sheehan might provide. The word was that Judge Grande liked Sheehan; they had been friends for decades. "I just can't afford to risk alienating the locals, certainly not now."

I decided not to cause a flap. After all, my involvement in jury selection would be minimal. I really wanted to be there just to see the beginning of the trial, to get a feel for what was going on. That could wait for a less divisive occasion.*

At this juncture, my first disagreement with Tom Puccio about strategy emerged. Puccio and Claus were adamantly opposed to the sequestration of the jury. Somehow they had gotten it into their heads that a sequestered jury—kept in isolation in an uncomfortable

---

* As soon as the first court day was over, I received four press calls inquiring why I was not in court.

hotel away from friends and family—would take out its resentment on the defendant. I didn't know where they got that idea. Tom said that he had conferred with several experienced defense attorneys, all of whom recommended against sequestration.

Tom's argument that the vast majority of sequestered juries convict the defendant may well be true, but it is also true that the vast majority of unsequestered juries convict. Most juries convict most defendants—and for a very good reason: they're guilty. Even if it were true that sequestered juries have a higher rate of conviction than nonsequestered juries, that might reflect the obvious fact that juries generally tend to be sequestered in cases involving notorious defendants—alleged organized crime members, mass murderers, sex perverts. It should not be surprising that these kinds of defendants are convicted more often than the norm, whether the jury is sequestered or not.

I was convinced that a sequestered jury would be best for von Bülow. There were so many nasty stories circulating about him, so much misinformation that would never be admissible into evidence. But all of that would be reported gleefully by the press. Moreover, there was the whole Marriott sideshow. Marriott—who would never be called as a witness by anybody, because at this point nobody could believe anything he said—was desperately trying to get himself into the case. He was calling press conferences, phoning the media, playing his tapes for anyone who would listen.* Although to my knowledge Claus had done nothing wrong, who knew what Marriott might say, and who knew what an individual juror might believe.

I just didn't understand why *we* were arguing against sequestration. Fortunately, we lost. I cheered loudly when I heard that Judge Grande had decided, on her own motion, to sequester the jury. "Sometimes you gotta lose to win," quipped my son Elon.

After several days of questioning, a jury of ten women and four men was picked. Only twelve would eventually decide von Bülow's fate, but all fourteen would hear the entire trial and two would be dropped before deliberation. The trial began on Thursday, April 25, 1985.

---

* Additional mystery was added to the Marriott sideshow when we learned that he was beaten up—sustaining a broken nose and black eyes—during the trial.

15

The Multiple-Choice Prosecution

The prosecution's witnesses at the second trial were essentially the same as at the first. And their direct testimony was similar. This is not surprising, because the defense has a transcript of the first trial, and if witnesses depart from their earlier testimony, they can be cross-examined about inconsistencies. So consistency becomes the rule. Sometimes details are added or forgotten, but the gist remains the same.

There were, however, significant differences in the cross-examination, and these differences reflected primarily what we had uncovered during the appellate process.

The first witness for the prosecution at the retrial was the star of the first trial, the maid, Maria Schrallhammer. "You lead off with your strongest witness," observed one of the prosecutors. Her direct examination was like a video replay of her testimony at the first trial. Her voice cracking, her eyes filling up with tears, she told the attentive jurors how she had tried to get Mr. von Bülow to call the doctor as her lady sank deeper and deeper into a coma. She related her discovery of the black bag in February with certain prescription vials in it. Prosecutor Marc DeSisto, the thirty-year-old lawyer who had taken over when Stephen Famiglietti entered private practice, began to ask her about the crucial sighting on the Sunday after Thanksgiving—the sighting where, according to her testimony at the first trial, she first saw insulin and needles. We waited anxiously for her answers, wondering whether she would change her testimony to conform to the newly revealed Kuh notes. DeSisto asked her what she had found after Thanksgiving. She replied:

Well, I saw vials again in the little black bag . . . There was another little bottle which I took out and looked at.

DeSisto asked her if it had a label. This was the testing question, for she had told Richard Kuh six weeks after the event that "all" the labels were "scraped off."

SCHRALLHAMMER: It did, yes.
DESISTO: Did you read the label?
SCHRALLHAMMER: Yes, I did read it.
DESISTO: And what did the label say?
SCHRALLHAMMER: It said insulin on it.

Maria was testifying in direct conflict with the Kuh notes. We wondered what the prosecution's strategy was. How did they plan to have Maria handle the anticipated cross-examination based on those notes? We would have to wait for Tom's cross-examination to begin.

In the meantime, almost as if to show contempt for the Kuh notes, Maria blurted out, "And there was a syringe." She had, of course, not mentioned any syringe to Richard Kuh during her first interview.

Maria then went over her familiar "Insulin, for what insulin?" testimony, claiming that she had showed the vial of insulin to Alex and asked that question. Reporters noted that at the first trial this testimony was given with "a tone of genuine bewilderment," whereas at this trial it was uttered in a "flat" tone. This slight change in delivery subtly suggested how Maria was planning to parry Tom's cross-examination questions.

Maria concluded her testimony by describing the events leading up to the second and final coma. It was a superb repeat performance, but she was not off the stand yet.

Her cross-examination began on Monday, following the weekend recess. After some preliminaries, Tom went right for the jugular: "The first time you spoke to Mr. Kuh, you didn't tell him about the insulin. Is that correct?"

Suddenly for the first time Maria became evasive and a bit defensive: "That's could be. That could very well be, since I was not concerned so much about the insulin."

Here it was, her explanation why she had failed to mention insulin or syringes at her first interview with Kuh. She was telling the jury that finding the insulin had no significance to her because she was not aware of its potential use as a murder weapon. "I was not aware of the danger," she elaborated. Now we understood her subtle change in delivery between the first and second trials. At the first trial she had dramatized her discovery of the insulin by expressing bewilderment and surprise. At the second trial—realizing that she would have to explain away her silence about insulin during her Kuh interview—she downplayed the discovery by describing it in flat tones conveying the sense that it was simply another unimportant item in the bag. Maria admitted as well that she didn't make any mention of needles or syringes, despite their obvious relevance to any suspected criminal activities. And she was evasive to the point of confusion when asked about her statement to Kuh that all the labels were scraped off: "Yes, that could be if the labels were scraped off at that time, because the note I made earlier."

We had all noticed that during both trials Maria used her "difficulty" with the English language as a shield against probing cross-examination. When she wanted to be understood, she was perfectly capable of Germanic precision, even in English, as her direct examination revealed. But whenever she was boxed into a corner, she used awkward, ungrammatical phrases to avoid giving clear answers. As one of the lawyers noted, "When the going gets tough, Maria's English goes sloppy."

As I sat in the courtroom watching Tom Puccio cross-examine Maria Schrallhammer, I felt a mixture of pride and frustration. I was proud of the role my team had played in securing the Kuh notes and in focusing on their importance from the beginning of the case, but I was frustrated by the way Tom was using them. Claus characterized me as the playwright in the audience watching an actor who was very good but who was not reading the lines quite the way they were intended. Every lawyer has his or her own way of cross-examining a witness who is believed to be lying. My way is to zero in on the inconsistencies repeatedly and to focus the jury's attention on the impossibility that they could have been inadvertent. Tom's way was very different: he would bring out the inconsistency and then pass on to something else. I felt he was letting Maria off the hook, that he wasn't pressing hard enough about why—if she had indeed found insulin and syringes—she had never told her lady; the family doctor, Richard Stock; or Sunny's mother about her discovery, and why she had failed to mention it during her initial interview with Kuh. Her excuse that she didn't realize its significance until she learned of the insulin in Mrs. von Bülow's blood sounded lame to me, but I didn't know how it would sound to the jury.

Before the cross-examination Tom and I discussed his approach. "I don't really believe that prior inconsistent statements impress a jury all that much," said the former prosecutor. Prosecutors are always trying to explain away inconsistencies because their witnesses have generally testified in front of a grand jury and given a police or FBI statement before they finally testify to the trial jury. The inconsistencies among these statements are generally minor. Yet defense attorneys, with little else to go on, tend to hammer away at even the most minute grammatical variation. Naturally, that tactic rarely succeeds. But here we had major variations. As Maria left the witness stand I had the frustrating feeling that we had not done all we might have with the striking inconsistencies.

The press reports the next morning confirmed my worst fears. "STEELY MAID MARIA COOL UNDER PRESSURE," read one headline. "DEFENSE UNABLE TO SHAKE MAID'S TESTIMONY," blared another. The stories themselves reported that "Puccio did score points in a few big areas, thanks to notes that Richard H. Kuh was forced to turn over to the defense earlier this year. The fact that the defense did not have the Kuh notes at the first trial was one of the reasons the State Supreme Court overturned the guilty verdicts."*

Having observed the cross-examination myself, I did think that Tom had scored significantly in attacking Maria's account of seeing insulin in the black bag, but not significantly in other areas. As we left the courthouse that day, my son Elon characterized Maria's account—which he was hearing for the first time—as the "maid-up story."

To my mind the cross-examination of Maria Schrallhammer was not an auspicious beginning for the defense case. I worried—and indeed wrote a memorandum to Claus—about Tom's approach to cross-examination. But there's only so much a coach can do when the athletes are out there doing their thing on the playing field. I hoped Tom would become more aggressive with the state's next witness, Alexander von Auersperg.

Alex, like Maria, reiterated the critical testimony he had given at the first trial: Maria's calling him in to show him the bottle of insulin and the syringes she found in the black bag on the Sunday after Thanksgiving; his search for the bag in Claus's closet at Clarendon Court after his mother's final coma; and the discovery of the needle that was found to contain traces of insulin.

---

* In a widely covered trial, the reporters tend to discuss their perceptions among themselves. The resulting stories often represent the group-think approach of the reporters, and rarely convey an accurate juror perspective. It would be interesting for a newspaper or network to employ a mock jury—three or four typical citizens selected like the real jurors who would listen *only* to what the real jurors heard and then convey their impressions to the reporters at the end of the day.

But, like Maria's, his cross-examination was entirely different. Holding the Kuh notes in one hand, Puccio pointed his other hand at Alex and asked him about the meetings with Richard Kuh that were never disclosed to the first jury. He focused on a meeting that had been held four days after Alex and the investigator had searched the closet at Clarendon Court and found the bag with the insulin-encrusted needle. Present at the meeting were Alex, his sister Ala, Sunny's mother and stepfather, the family banker Morris Gurley, and Richard Kuh. Puccio asked Alexander, "One of the things you discussed at that meeting was a desire on the part of some of the people present to pay your stepfather some money to have him renounce any interest in your mother's estate. Isn't that correct?"

Faced with the incontrovertible new evidence contained in the Kuh notes, Alex had no choice but to admit what the first jury never heard: "That's correct."

Puccio continued, "The idea of paying your stepfather to get rid of him, so to speak, was after you went to Clarendon Court and gathered all of these belongings from various places [and placed them into the black bag]. Isn't that right?"

Of course it was right. The Kuh notes established the precise chronology.

"I believe so," answered Alex.

Thus, the Kuh notes proved that just weeks after learning that Sunny would never recover and days after finding the black bag and needle, the family was actively discussing the possibility of buying off the man they suspected of trying to murder their comatose loved one.

The Kuh notes further revealed the depth of the financial motive. Again referring to the notes, Puccio asked Alex about discussions he had had with Kuh concerning Sunny's will a few days after she had become comatose.

After a long pause, Alex responded, "I don't recall that specifically."

Puccio then asked him about Clarendon Court, the fabulous family estate: "Am I correct in saying that at that first meeting with Richard Kuh in early January of 1981 you discussed . . . Clarendon Court?"

Again Alex could not remember: "I don't recall if it was during that meeting."

Here's where the suppressed notes really proved their worth. It is understandable that a witness would not remember with precision events and discussions that had taken place more than four years earlier. It is especially unlikely that he would recall the precise chronology and words. But contemporaneous notes rarely lie and they never forget.

So Tom walked over from his lectern, Kuh notes in hand, placed them in front of Alex, directed him to certain portions, and asked, "Now, having read that, does that refresh your recollection that [in] early January of 1981, during a meeting with your sister and Mr. Kuh, you discussed your mother's will?"

Confronted with his own words, in his own lawyer's handwriting, Alex responded, "Yes, it does."

Puccio refreshed Alex's memory about Clarendon Court by again showing him the Kuh notes. "I don't really recall the meeting, but if it's in the notes then it's—it may have come up," acknowledged Alex. The rest was easy. Tom got Alex to admit that he had told Kuh—as quoted in the notes—that he would not want to lose Clarendon Court "under any circumstances."

Finally, Tom got Alex to make some damaging concessions about the sighting of the insulin and the seizure of the black bag. Alex acknowledged that he had only a vague memory of what Maria showed him: "I heard her say something." He did not remember her "words" and his memory was "vague." Now Maria's testimony about seeing insulin in the black bag was corroborated only by some "vague" four-year-old recollections and contradicted by specific contemporaneous notations. Tom also proved that Alex had thrown away some of the drugs he had gathered in his search of Clarendon Court.* The private investigator who conducted the search along with Alex admitted at the retrial that he was "confused" about what he found in the bag and what he found outside it—a point we had emphasized during the appeal. At one point during Puccio's cross-examination, he seemed to admit that the Inderal with *Sunny's* prescription on it was found in the black bag, but then he said he couldn't be sure, because he had failed to take an inventory. The Kuh notes, and the new story they told, were quickly becoming the star witness at this retrial.

The newspaper headlines next morning demonstrated their impact: "FAMILY AIMED TO CUT CLAUS FROM WILL," "SUNNY'S KIN SCHEMED TO CUT CLAUS FROM WILL," "VON AUERSPERG TELLS OF

---

* Alex's lawyers claim that he threw away only unimportant drugs, such as aspirin. But of course in the context of this case, no drugs—regardless how "innocent"—could be deemed irrelevant.

HIS INTEREST IN CLARENDON COURT." The attention was being focused away from Claus's behavior and onto the behavior of his accusers. Richard Kuh, no longer in the case but still an interested bystander, commented defensively that the plan did not actually constitute "blackmail" because "there was never any discussion with Claus."

All of these new revelations had been stimulated by the Kuh notes. Not surprisingly, the news reports focused on their importance:

> The defense learned of the family meeting from handwritten notes taken by the family's New York lawyer, Richard Kuh, who engineered what the defense had called "a private prosecution." Lawyer Alan Dershowitz, who masterminded von Bülow's appeal, has said the notes "would blow the prosecution's case right out of the water." Yesterday, some of the first explosions were heard.

Even the staid New York *Times* characterized the cross-examination based on the Kuh notes as "a bomb shell . . . that apparently shifted some of the appearance of greed from the defendant to the family."

After the completion of Alexander's testimony, several reporters asked me why there were no questions about the Marriott charges. Even though we were not going to be calling David Marriott to the witness stand, we could still have used the information and leads we had as a basis for asking Alex questions about drugs.

The law requires an attorney to have a "good-faith basis" before asking any question on cross-examination. This important rule is designed to prevent the irresponsible prosecutor or defense attorney from planting a fictitious accusation in the minds of the jurors by the framing of the questions. Without this salutary rule, a lawyer could ask all kinds of variations on the "When did you stop beating your wife?" theme. For example, if a respectable-looking prosecutor asks a seedy-looking defendant or defense witness whether he has ever been convicted of perjury, even a denial will not completely erase the thought by some jurors that maybe there is fire behind the smoking question. The rule does not require that the cross-examining lawyer must have proof of the assertion underlying the question, but simply that there must be a good-faith basis—a concept difficult to define.

We believed we met that test, despite Marriott's recantation of his affidavit. Among our bases were the following: Father Magaldi was sticking by his story. Alex's own lawyer had submitted an affidavit implying that Alex might have to invoke the privilege against self-incrimination if asked about Marriott's "wholly false" charges. Alex's stepfather, Claus, though an obviously interested party, had told his lawyers from the very beginning, even before Marriott came along, that his stepson sometimes used marijuana and cocaine, and had provided some specifics.

We thought long and hard about the pros and cons of opening up this can of worms. In the end, the judge made the decision for us. She ruled that the evidence of Claus's having used syringes in Majorca in 1969 would not be admitted at this trial. She disagreed with the ruling of Judge Needham at the first trial to let the jury hear the evidence and to let the prosecutor argue in his summation that the only person in the household who had any familiarity with injections was Claus von Bülow. Judge Grande ruled that since the last evidence of administration of injections by Claus was more than ten years before the alleged injections in this case, it was "too remote" and hence inadmissible. Its prejudicial impact, she ruled, would outweigh its probative value.

If we were to cross-examine Alex about *his* alleged drug use, we might lose the fruits of this victory. The judge might rule that we had opened the door to the old evidence of Claus's familiarity with injections by asking Alex questions about drugs.

Moreover, there was always the risk that such accusatory questions directed at a young man could backfire and engender sympathy, especially since we had no evidence to corroborate the Marriott allegations relating to injectable drugs, and it was impossible to credit anything Marriott had said by this time.

Finally, there was the possibility—remote as it was—that by asking Alex questions based on Marriott's allegations, we might invite the prosecution to introduce Marriott as *its* witness in rebuttal. This risk was remote because neither side wanted to be tainted by Marriott's character and history of contradictions. But we did not want to take the chance of diverting the jury's attention away from the real issues and onto the Marriott sideshow.

Considering all these risks, there was no real advantage in putting questions to Alex about any alleged drug use. The judge had excluded any evidence that Claus had administered injections, and there was nothing to rebut. So Alex left the stand without having to invoke the Fifth Amendment or answer any questions about drugs.

The David Marriott charade had indeed become a freak sideshow with no relevance to the retrial.

The soap-opera part of the state's case was now two-thirds complete. The only witness necessary to fill in the missing pieces of the emotional puzzle—before the state would begin the medical part of its case—was the real-life soap-opera star Alexandra Isles. But she was nowhere to be found. The judge directed the prosecutors to keep looking, while the jurors began to hear the parade of doctors and technicians who would try to persuade them that Sunny's comas were both caused by exogenous insulin.

The state began its medical case with a bolt of lightning from the blue. Its first three witnesses—doctors who had treated Sunny von Bülow in the Newport Hospital Emergency Room during her final coma—tried to offer new evidence that Sunny's body had multiple bruises, scratches, abrasions and lacerations. The state was attempting to prove that these marks had been caused by a struggle. For the first time in this four-year-old case the state was suggesting that Claus von Bülow might have forcibly injected his struggling and resisting wife. Throughout the first trial and the appeal, the state had always maintained that Claus had administered the insulin injection "surreptitiously"—while she was sleeping or unconscious. Now they were trying to raise the specter of a life-and-death struggle between the six-foot-three-inch defendant and his smaller and weaker wife. This is how Judge Grande summarized the struggle theory in making her ruling on whether to allow the jury to consider it:

> Here is a woman drugged, partially drugged, in her own home, where she would be safe, secure, with a husband she's come to rely on, care for, be concerned about, and she suddenly awakes from this drugged condition . . . It is in the middle of the night. No one else is around. She awakens to find her husband injecting her. And she struggles, struggles for her life. And in the struggle—the state's theory—she is scratched.

It was dramatic, but was it docudrama or melodrama? The state was not contending this was what definitely happened, only that it "may" have happened. Now it was the state's turn to try a multiple-choice offense: it was accusing Claus of either "surreptitiously" or "forcibly" injecting her.

But try as they would, they were unable to prove the struggle theory. In a dramatic demonstration outside the presence of the jury, John Sheehan put one of the doctors to a difficult test. The doctor had testified that he could determine, "with a reasonable degree of medical certainty," that Sunny's scratches "did occur secondary to a struggle" rather than by some other innocent cause. During the hearing to determine whether the jury should be able to hear this struggle testimony, Sheehan walked up to the doctor on the witness stand, rolled up his sleeves and showed the doctor some scratches he had suffered over the weekend. Thrusting his arm under the doctor's nose, Sheehan defiantly asked the expert whether he could say what caused them: "Is that a struggle?" The doctor examined the scratches and the judge awaited his answer. After a long pause, he responded, with some embarrassment, "I cannot say, sir."

Sheehan continued, "Well, how did I get my scratches?"

The doctor responded, "I don't know."

Sheehan then went in for the kill: "Yet you do know how Mrs. von Bülow got hers, is that what you're saying to me?"

The doctor backed down completely: "No, I do not know how she got those scratches." It was Perry Mason cross-examination at its best, and showed why Sheehan had such a high success rate in front of juries.

Following Sheehan's masterful performance, the judge ruled that the doctor was "unable to state with a reasonable degree of certainty the origin of the trauma he testified to." She excluded all reference to the struggle theory, thus eliminating the state's "multiple choices" about how Sunny ended up in a coma. After the day's proceedings had ended, reporters asked Sheehan how he had, in fact, gotten the scratches. Sheehan smiled and declined comment. Later he admitted to me that his scratches were "self-induced" by a nail file. "Sometimes a lawyer has to go a bit beyond the call of duty to make a point," Sheehan said modestly. The point he had made was a sharp and painful one indeed. It showed the savvy courtroom lawyer at his best.

The judge was obviously concerned about the prejudicial impact of this and other testimony that she had ruled irrelevant. In addition to the struggle evidence, she had also forbidden the prosecutor from further describing the bloody scene following Sunny's aspirin overdose. (Some evidence of Sunny's bleeding head had already been presented.) The prosecutors were trying to imply without coming out and saying so—that Claus had assaulted his wife with a blunt object. The evidence pointed to a self-induced overdose followed by a fall that caused the bleeding, so the only purpose of telling the jurors about the blood was to suggest another possible choice: that Claus was somehow responsible for that episode.

After denying a defense motion for a mistrial following this bloody testimony, Judge Grande told the prosecutors in a private conference in her chambers that she was "holding this case together with baling wire" and that her decision to deny a mistrial might well be reversed on appeal. When Claus learned about this comment, he called and gleefully instructed me to keep a running list of issues on which Judge Grande might be reversed on appeal. We both laughingly expressed our hope that we could soon tear up our list.

During the state's medical case, a bizarre incident in the courtroom momentarily deflected attention from the testimony. A regular at both trials placed an envelope on the defense table marked "Escape and Supplemental Plan." Inside was a dollar bill, a hand-printed passport and a set of escape instructions for asylum in El Salvador in case "things go bad." The sheriff seized the material and took the man into custody. Eventually he was released but barred from the courtroom.

Throughout the second trial, a strange assortment of characters found their way into the courtroom: an actress who wanted to play Sunny if a movie were to be made of the trial; several "witnesses" who offered to testify about anything that would help Claus; and, of course, a number of women volunteering to become Claus's lovers.

Before long the prosecution suffered yet another major setback in its medical case. This one came from a most unexpected source: its own witness, Doctor Janis Gailitis, the sixty-nine-year-old Soviet émigré who had saved Sunny's life when she went into her first coma, and who had provided important evidence for the prosecution at the first trial.

During a luncheon recess, the garrulous Dr. Gailitis talked to lawyers on both sides of the case. He told the defense that prior to the first trial he had told the prosecutors "with clarity" that the first coma—the one he had personally observed—was caused by factors other than insulin: "My conclusion, as her attending physician, is that the basic medical problem at that time was caused by airway obstruction, secondary to vomiting, and aspiration of gastric contents." He told the prosecution that "there is absolutely no question in my mind" that the coma was caused by factors other than insulin. And he told them in certain and graphic terms: "I don't know how more graphic I could describe it." Yet the prosecutors had instructed him not to "volunteer" that information or opinion during his testimony at the first trial. The first jury, thus, never heard the medical opinion of the doctor best qualified, by personal observations, to give it: the doctor who actually saw the first coma in progress and saved the patient's life.

A hearing was immediately convened outside the presence of the jury, and Dr. Gailitis made further discosures about how he had been "prepared" for his role as state's witness. He described his meeting with prosecutors and with Professor William Curran— the lawyer hired by Richard Kuh to help prepare the state's medical case—as a "rehearsal." Prosecutor Famiglietti would ask questions, Dr. Gailitis would offer an answer, and Professor Curran would either approve or disapprove of the answer. Dr. Gailitis was not aware that Curran had been hired by Richard Kuh on behalf of the family. But he did know that he "just hated the whole thing." He characterized it as a "stage production," like "being prompted for TV appearance. . . . The questions which apparently didn't fit very well in Mr. Famiglietti's scheme later were not asked . . ."

Puccio then asked Dr. Gailitis what the prosecutor told him when he described his opinion that the coma was caused by factors other than insulin. He replied: "We have experts who are going to discuss clinical details. All *you* have to do is answer our questions and not volunteer any information."

Finally, he was asked whether anyone told him that his views on the cause of the first coma would be passed on to the defense lawyers. His answer was "positively no." And, of course, his views, which supported the defense contention, were never made known to the defense team at the first trial—or to the jury. Thus, in addition to the Kuh notes, other dramatic evidence supporting the defendant's innocence had been withheld from the jury that convicted von Bülow.

In a criminal trial, the prosecution has a constitutional obligation to disclose all evidence that might support the defendant's claim of innocence. This obligation is codified in a series of rules, the most prominent being the *Brady* rule (named after the case in which the Supreme Court articulated it). Failure to provide *Brady* material—information in the possession of the prosecution that may be favorable to the defense—can result in a reversal of a conviction and a new trial.

Had we known about Dr. Gailitis's newly disclosed information, and the failure of the prosecution to turn it over to the defense, we might have added that to our argument for reversal of Claus von Bülow's conviction. But the conviction was reversed on other grounds and we were now in the midst of a new trial. Moreover, we now had the information. So it was difficult to use Dr. Gailitis's bombshell to any specific tactical advantage at this late date. Tom Puccio moved for a mistrial, but after a hearing Judge Grande denied it, stating that "the implications of what were being raised were enormous [and had] a rather sinister sound . . ." But she went out of her way to absolve all the Rhode Island prosecutors and police of any wrongdoing, though the credibility of the Attorney General's office suffered a severe blow in the minds of many. Dr. Gailitis's revelation showed how far they had been willing to go to secure Claus von Bülow's conviction—even to the point of suppressing medical evidence that might help prove his innocence. It was a bad day for the prosecution. Prosecutor Henry Gemma, who was participating in the presentation of the state's case along with Marc DeSisto, declared that "a black cloud has descended over the case."

At about the time this black cloud was hovering, Gemma began to discuss the possibility of a plea bargain. Claus had always been open to the prospect of pleading guilty to—as he put it—"a parking ticket." By that he meant that he might consider pleading guilty to a misdemeanor that suggested a slight degree of culpability or negligence on his part. "Negligent failure to call the doctor"—or some other such violation if it existed under Rhode Island law—might be acceptable. He would not, under any circumstances, plead guilty to any crime suggesting that he had deliberately tried to kill or injure his wife, since he had done nothing of the sort. But in order to put the matter behind him, and to avoid the roulette-wheel risk that a second jury might convict him (as the first had already done), he was willing to acknowledge that he might, in retrospect, have acted more quickly in summoning help during Sunny's 1979 medical crisis.

Eventually, Arlene Violet—the newly elected and inexperienced prosecutor—rejected any deal that would not mandate a prison term for von Bülow, and the negotiations broke down.

The remainder of the state's medical case was presented to the jury in pretty much the same way as the first case. Tom effectively used the medical information developed for our new-trial motion to cross-examine the state's experts.

He kept Dr. George Cahill, the state's star medical witness, on the stand for three hours, shooting question after question at him based largely on the additional medical information we had dug up for the new-trial motion and some additional material our two assistants had discovered in preparation for the second trial. By way of contrast, Fahringer had questioned Cahill for only twenty minutes, and had done no damage to his testimony.

While Puccio certainly didn't destroy Cahill's testimony, he weakened it considerably. Puccio got him to admit that factors other than insulin alone could account for the second coma. Cahill acknowledged that prescription drugs called sulfonylureas—never mentioned at the first trial—could have caused it.

> PUCCIO: Now, at this point, Doctor, you've changed your testimony, because you can't testify to a reasonable degree of medical certainty that it wasn't sulfonylureas. Is that right?
> CAHILL: Correct.

Cahill acknowledged that "one can never testify to one hundred percent certainty," but he placed his degree of certainty at 90 percent. This led Tom to shoot back, in typical Brooklyn fashion, "This is not a crap shoot."

At one point Dr. Cahill became so exasperated with Tom's barrage of questions that he blurted out: "I'm sorry; it's just so difficult for me to answer inane questions all of the time." But neither the judge nor, apparently, the jury regarded Tom's questions as inane. Indeed, Judge Grande rebuked Dr. Cahill for his "extremely inappropriate" and "gratuitous" comment and told the jurors to ignore it.

At the end of the three-hour grilling, Dr. Cahill grudgingly admitted that he had been given a much harder time by Puccio than by Fahringer: "The questions were so much shrewder" this time, but he did not think he had contradicted himself. The jury would decide that in good time.

The state presented one brand-new medical expert, Dr. Robert Bradley, a distinguished-looking sixty-five-year-old man who headed the Joslin Diabetes Center in Boston—the leading center for research on blood sugar in the world. Dr. Bradley was asked to "quantify" how certain he was that the first coma was caused by an injection of insulin. With an arrogance that only a Boston doctor could muster, Dr. Bradley—who had never examined Mrs. von Bülow—declared, "One hundred percent."

What he was saying, in effect, was that the team of doctors who had examined Sunny at Columbia University between her two comas were a bunch of incompetents guilty of malpractice. If he, who had never even seen her, could be one hundred percent certain that an insulin injection had caused the first coma, then any examining doctor who had not even suspected an insulin injection was missing the only obvious diagnosis.

When asked about the second coma, Dr. Bradley modified his views a bit: "Ninety-nine percent."

There's an old story about the student at a supermarket in Cambridge who brought his dozen items to a checkout counter marked "5 items or less." The gruff cashier looked at the kid and then at the items and growled: "Hey, are you from Harvard and can't count, or from MIT and can't read?"

I felt the same way about Dr. Bradley's "100 percent" and "99 percent" testimony. Did he not understand probabilities? Or medicine?

As the state was nearing completion of its case-in-chief, speculation became rampant about the whereabouts of Alexandra Isles, Claus's mistress, who had provided much of the motive testimony at the first trial. The word spread that she had fled the country to avoid testifying. The prosecution made a motion to allow a transcript of her damaging testimony from the first trial to be read to this jury. The defense objected, arguing that the state had not satisfied its burden of proving that they had tried everything to bring her back so that she could give live testimony. The issue was compounded by the refusal of Fahringer to cross-examine her at the first trial—the chivalry bit. The defense at the second trial wanted to cross-examine her vigorously. The judge ruled in favor of the defense, agreeing with its contention that the state had not done enough to try to bring her back. But she gave the state the long Memorial Day weekend to find Isles and get her to court.

I smelled a rat. I suspected that the state preferred to use her un-cross-examined testimony from the first trial, but if they failed at that, then they would really try to find her. I thought Alexandra Isles might feel the same way. She would rather not have to testify if her transcript could be used to convict Claus, but if it couldn't, then she'd be raring to go.

Another theory being circulated by some cynics was that Alexandra Isles had always intended to testify; she just wanted the tension to build for her dramatic entry. Corroboration for this theory was provided by a report that Mrs. Isles had been beautifying herself at Forest Mere, an exclusive English "fat farm," for several weeks prior to her appearance.

In any event, her entry could hardly have been more dramatic—or better staged. An airport rendezvous with prosecutors in shirt-sleeves—cameras recording every moment of it—and then a police escort to Boston's ritziest hotel. Round-the-clock guards to "protect" her! From whom? Were the police worried that Claus would break into her unguarded room, insulin needle in hand, and try to put her into a coma? It was all preposterous. But the media loved it. Fortunately, the sequestered jury was spared the entrance spectacle and heard only her courtroom testimony.

But the in-court testimony was a shocker, providing one of the few real surprises at the trial. Isles supplemented her account at the first trial with the following melodrama. Prosecutor DeSisto asked Isles about a telephone conversation she had had with Claus von Bülow shortly after Sunny's first coma, which she had not disclosed at the first trial:

DeSisto: What did he say?
Isles: Well, he told me what had happened in more detail that led to Mrs. von Bülow's [first] coma. . . . He said they had been having a long argument, talking about divorce that had gone on late into the night. She had drunk a great deal of eggnog, and then he said, 'I saw her take the Seconal.'
   And then he said the next day when she was unconscious that he watched her, knowing that she was in a bad way, all day. And watched her and watched her.
   And finally when she was on the point of dying he said that he couldn't go through with it, and he called and saved her life.

The prosecution was thus offering another option in its multiple-choice offense: in addition to the possibility that Claus might have administered insulin surreptitiously, or perhaps forcibly, there was also the possibility that he might have passively allowed his wife nearly to die after watching her ingest a deadly combination of drinks and drugs.

Tom was unable to shake Isles's testimony about this call, though he did manage to expose her bitterness toward Claus for spurning her. At one point he asked her about a letter she had written to Claus after the first trial asking him to continue the relationship:

ISLES: Have you ever been in love? I doubt it! But you do some crazy things.
PUCCIO: Maybe I should have my wife speak to you about that.

With that exchange—right out of *Dark Shadows*—Tom's cross-examination ended.

Emotionally, and perhaps even morally, Isles's new testimony was devastating to Claus. "BOMBSHELL BY BÜLOW BEAUTY," read the headline. The entire front page of the New York *Post* consisted of a picture of Isles with the quote "You do some crazy things when you're in love." But the bombshell actually *helped* Claus's legal case. After all, Alexandra Isles, a state witness against von Bülow who obviously despised him now, was corroborating the defense contention that Sunny's first coma had *not* been caused by an injection of insulin, but rather by self-administered Seconal and alcohol. If the jury believed Claus told Alexandra the truth about nearly watching her die, it would be difficult to disbelieve the rest of what he allegedly told his mistress.

It may be immoral—perhaps even criminal—for a man to sit idly by and watch his wife slowly die from self-administered drugs, but it is not the crime of assault with a deadly weapon, the only crime for which Claus von Bülow was standing trial. Neither unhusbandly conduct toward a comatose wife nor caddish behavior toward a naive mistress could serve to convict von Bülow of that crime. As Tom told the press after his exchange with Alexandra: "She proved he was a cad, but not a wife-killer." (Andrea Reynolds immediately denied that Claus was a cad: "He has been absolutely perfect and charming and good to me and to my daughters and to my dogs." Alexandra, on the other hand, is not "what I call marriage material," because she "had men . . . two or three at a time [and] there's no safety in numbers as far as men are concerned . . ." Claus's diplomatic response to this verbal squabble between his past and present lovers was: "I know that cockfighting is illegal, but I see that hen fights still are permitted.")

The defense motion to exclude Isles's transcript had backfired when she showed up. Then the backfire backfired when she ended up supporting the single important defense contention. "Sometimes you gotta win to lose and then win," to paraphrase my son. Although the headlines may have read "ALEXANDRA'S BOMBS," a more realistic appraisal from the prosecution's point of view was "ALEXANDRA BOMBED."

The prosecution's case was ending as it had begun—with emotional testimony about Claus von Bülow the man. Sandwiched in between the soap-opera witnesses—the maid and the mistress—had been a vast array of doctors, technicians and scientists. The prosecutors had tried to include the testimony of Morris Gurley, the banker who had provided the financial motive evidence at the first trial. But Judge Grande, in a controversial ruling, prohibited him from testifying as part of the prosecution's opening case (leaving open the possibility that he might be heard as a rebuttal witness). When Alexandra Isles heard that Gurley could not testify, she reportedly said to him: "I can't believe they're not letting you testify. I wasn't the motive, Morris. The money was the motive. He had me for free." Judge Grande also ruled that Claus's famous "cover-his-ass" letter—highlighted by prosecutor Famiglietti at the first trial—could not be heard by the jury. In general, Judge Grande tended to control tightly the evidence admitted in her trials. Some judges have a philosophy of letting almost anything go before the jurors; they leave it to the jury's common sense to evaluate the worth of questionable evidence. Other judges edit far more aggressively, cutting out everything but the most relevant evidence. Judge Grande tended toward the latter pole. She wanted a quick sequence of relevant scenes. The result was a film edited far more heavily than at the first trial.

16

The True-or-False Defense

The prosecution's case was now over, and it was time for the defense to put on its case. Our case was to be entirely medical and forensic. We would make no effort to rebut the negative character and behavior evidence provided by the state's nonmedical witnesses. If our medical case was as powerful as we thought it was, then the jury would believe that there had been no crime: in the technical parlance of the law, no *corpus delicti*. No crime means no criminal, regardless of how unhusbandly or caddish the jury might believe von Bülow to have been.

I was anxious to see how our medical case would make the transition from our paper affidavits to Tom's live witnesses. It had been my job, with the help of my team, to provide the information for our medical and forensic case. We had found the best people in the world—on paper. Now it was Tom's job to find the best live witnesses to present this information to the jury. Claus kept using the theatrical analogy: it was as if I were the playwright and Tom the director.

The measure of a witness's persuasiveness is not only his academic credentials, but his poise, his likability and his ability to withstand withering cross-examination. Tom did a masterful job of casting and directing the medical production.

The state had three basic building blocks to its insulin case: that there was a high level of insulin in Sunny's blood; that there was insulin on the needle found in the black bag after the second coma; and that some of the world's leading experts had given their medical judgments—to a high degree of certainty (and in Dr. Bradley's case, perfect certainty)—that both comas had been caused by insulin.

This had all been made even more convincing by Maria's claim, corroborated by Alex, that a vial of insulin and syringes had been seen in the black bag just three weeks before Sunny's second coma. Maria's testimony was attacked on cross-examination by reference to the Kuh notes. The other building blocks were challenged by the defendant's direct case.

The defense's first witness was Dr. Leo A. Dal Cortivo, chief forensic toxicologist for Suffolk County in New York. We had found Dr. Dal Cortivo while we were researching the new-trial motion. His affidavit had been heavily relied on in that motion, and even in helping us formulate the arguments in our appellate brief. As a live witness, the expert toxicologist bolstered the defense contention that Sunny had taken "at least sixty-five aspirin tablets" during a half-hour period just three weeks before her final coma. He also employed his experience in forensic examinations to demonstrate why it was extremely unlikely that the needle found in the black bag could have been used to inject Sunny. If the needle had been injected, he explained to the jury as he had explained to us two years earlier, any residue would have been "wiped clean" when the needle was extracted from the skin. It was exciting to see the real expert show the jury what my assistant had shown me in the kitchen using a barbecue skewer and salad dressing.

The next major forensic witness was the noted endocrinologist Dr. Arthur Rubenstein, chairman of the medical department at the University of Chicago. He was an eminent doctor whose major contribution was in assessing the validity and reliability of the insulin readings upon which the prosecution had relied so heavily at the first trial: the extremely high insulin level (216) found in Sunny's blood when she was admitted for her second coma, and the traces of insulin found on the encrusted needle discovered in the black bag during Alex's search of Claus's closet at Clarendon Court. These two scientific conclusions were among the most important building blocks of the prosecution's case.

Dr. Rubenstein had concluded in his affidavit for our new-trial motion that the 216 reading was scientifically invalid and should not have been relied on. At the trial he reiterated that conclusion, stating that it was "impossible to assess the validity" of a reading that could not be duplicated and that produced such discrepant results. "I personally would have no confidence in any of these values," he told the jury. "There is no way of saying which of the three independent values is correct. They could all be incorrect."

If an experienced doctor would have no confidence in the 216 reading, how could a lay jury send a man to prison on the basis of that uncertainty?

During our research for the new-trial motion, we had also asked Dr. Rubenstein to assess the reliability of the finding that traces of insulin were present on the needle found in the black bag. That was perhaps the most important scientific conclusion in the case. It was that finding that cemented the family's determination to prosecute Claus von Bülow. After receiving the confirmation that the needle was encrusted with insulin, Dr. Stock had threatened to call the police if Kuh did not. That evidence seemed so uncontestable that the defense at the first trial had stipulated to the presence of insulin on the needle.

But in doing our research for the new-trial motion, we had learned about a technique for distinguishing true findings of insulin from false positive readings. Based on this technique and his own experience, Dr. Rubenstein told the jury that it "is impossible to interpret" the insulin reading for the needle. The state's so-called murder weapon, it turned out, may have been loaded with blanks.

The remaining defense witnesses reiterated the conclusions we had argued for in the new-trial motion: namely, that neither coma had been caused by insulin, but rather by combinations of drugs, alcohol, hypothermia and apoxia. It was all very complicated, but the bottom line was that some of the world's most renowned experts were disputing, with equally impressive credentials and logic, the 100 percent and 99 percent conclusions of the state's experts. The case had shifted from a soap opera to a battle of the experts. And in a close battle of equally persuasive experts, the side that has the burden of proof generally loses. We were happy to see the focus shift from Maria's description of Claus von Bülow's behavior to the complexities of testing for insulin and diagnosing coma.

As the defense case was winding down, speculation focused on whether Claus would take the witness stand. From the moment he lost the first trial, Claus had regretted not testifying. He had repeatedly stated that he wanted to testify at a retrial. He told that to Barbara Walters in a highly publicized TV interview, and he told the press: "I am convinced it was a mistake that I didn't [take the stand at the first trial]. My counsel felt that there wasn't a case to answer. I probably didn't exercise sufficient judgment to recognize that I should have my way."

One of the reasons he had been advised not to testify at the first trial was no longer valid: at the first trial, Richard Kuh's investigatory material had been kept from the defense and Richard Kuh was in the courtroom ready and willing to provide additional information to the prosecution that might be useful in cross-examining or rebutting Claus and other defense witnesses. Now that we had much of Kuh's file, we had a far better assessment of the prosecution's arsenal for cross-examination.

Moreover, Kuh's clients, Alex and Ala, were publicly goading Claus to testify. By this time they had hired a professional public relations firm to handle the media for them. They had appeared on *60 Minutes* and various other TV shows, as well as in *People* magazine and other print outlets. One headline challenged: "CLAUS IS A 'LIAR': STEPKIDS: 'IF HE HAD THE GUTS, HE WOULD TESTIFY HIMSELF.' "

Claus wanted very much to testify at his second trial. His friend Andrea Reynolds also wanted him to take the stand. They constantly called me for advice on that crucial issue.

Whether or not to put your defendant on the witness stand is among the most difficult decisions a defense lawyer is asked to make. In *The Best Defense* I mentioned a lawyer who charges $50,000 for trying a criminal case; he says $5,000 of that is for his preparation and trial work and the remaining $45,000 is for his expertise in advising the defendant whether to take the stand.

Lawyers who are not privy to the deep, dark secrets of the defendant's life are generally not in a very good position to evaluate the decision whether or not to testify. But that doesn't prevent them from offering advice. I don't know a single criminal lawyer—present company explicitly included—who doesn't second-guess the way other lawyers handle their cases. Numerous defense attorneys were interviewed by the press about what they would do in the von Bülow case: "If the guy's guilty, you don't put him on," said Melvin Belli, describing his "cardinal rule." But "if he's not guilty, generally you put him on." F. Lee Bailey said he would prefer to try the von Bülow case without putting the defendant on the stand, but speculated that Alexandra's damaging evidence "may force him to the stand to deny it." Grant Cooper agreed that unless Claus explained his conversation with Alexandra, "he's sunk." William Kunstler said that although he thought von Bülow might seem "too smart for his own good," he would probably have him testify. Barry Slotnick, the excellent lawyer who represented subway vigilante

Bernhard Goetz, surmised, "I think he'll probably have to take the witness stand," especially to rebut the damaging testimony of Alexandra Isles. "I think the jury needs to hear it from his own mouth."

Many defense lawyers operate by standard rules. One prominent attorney says that he always puts his defendants on the stand unless they have a prior criminal record. Another says he never puts on his defendant unless the jury looks like it's "tying the knot in the hang-man's rope" even before the close of the case.

My own view is that any standard rule is wrong. Every case must be decided individually by reference to the strengths and nature of both the prosecution and the defense presentations.

Another myth is that the decision can be a "snap" one, made suddenly at the end of the prosecution's case, or even at the end of the defense case. I'm certain that many such decisions are, in fact, made at the last moment. But that, in my view, is often a serious mistake. The decision, at least preliminary, should be made at the very beginning of the case, even before the trial begins. Every action taken from the very first moment the lawyer enters the case should be considered with a view toward whether the defendant will take the stand.

If the defendant does take the stand, he waives a considerable number of his rights. For example, evidence illegally seized in violation of the defendant's Fourth Amendment rights cannot be used against a defendant who does not take the stand, but that same evidence can be used to impeach a defendant who testifies in his own behalf. The rule is similar for confessions or admissions illegally secured in violation of the *Miranda* rules. Evidence of a defendant's prior convictions cannot generally be introduced against him if he doesn't testify, but if he does, it can. Other evidence that is usually inadmissible becomes admissible when a defendant exercises his right to testify in his own behalf. And in so testifying, he may open up the door to issues on which the judge had previously slammed the door shut.

On the other hand, a defendant who exercises his equally legiti-mate right not to testify risks a great deal. Despite the constitutional presumption of innocence and the privilege against self-incrimina-tion, most jurors believe that if a defendant doesn't take the witness stand, he must have something to hide. And they are absolutely right about that. The question is, *what* is he or she hiding? Often it is guilt, but sometimes it is something equally sinister but less

relevant to the trial: a prior conviction, a fraudulent business trans-
action, a sordid sexual experience, or a shameful background of
some other kind.

Defendants who *don't* take the stand rarely win. But that's because defendants as a whole rarely win. If it is true that defendants
who take the stand win more often than defendants who don't, that
may be largely because the former includes a "better class" of
defendants than the later—more articulate individuals with fewer
prior convictions and more savory backgrounds. There is no way of
conducting a controlled experiment under which identically situated
defendants are divided into two groups—one of which does, and
the other of which does not, take the stand—and then comparing
the outcomes. Absent such an experiment, most lawyers will continue to rely on their own incomplete experience. (As someone once
put it, "Twenty years of experience is often one year of mistakes
repeated twenty times!")

When you win a case, you think you made the right decision;
and when you lose, you suspect you might have made the wrong
one. That is not necessarily so. A losing lawyer who put his witness
on the stand might have strengthened his case by so doing, but not
enough to overcome other problems. The winning lawyer might
have weakened his case, but not enough to undercut his other
strengths. Even after the most careful and thoughtful calculations,
the decision whether to call your defendant to the witness stand is
an extremely subjective one that can always be second-guessed on
Saturday morning.

The decision at the von Bülow retrial was one that I thought
about from the day I entered the case. It was one of the issues we
had discussed at our first meeting in the Carlyle restaurant. Our
entire strategy was geared toward the possibility of calling Claus as
a witness at any retrial. That was certainly the correct strategy in
trying to obtain a retrial, since we wanted to present only "innocent
man" arguments. An innocent man is supposed to want to take the
stand in order to tell the truth and vindicate himself. He certainly
had nothing to lose by *saying* that he wanted to take the stand.

After we won the appeal, Claus persisted in his insistence that
he must testify at any retrial. Indeed, among the factors he wanted
me to consider in advising him on a new lawyer for a retrial was
making sure he did not pick a lawyer who would foreclose that
possibility. Edward Bennett Williams has a reputation for putting
his clients on the stand, and he told Claus he should have testified

at the first trial. Tom Puccio had an excellent reputation as a prosecutor for putting on a good direct case and preparing his witnesses effectively. That boded well for Claus's wish to be put on as his own principal witness.

At Claus's first meeting with Puccio, Claus said, "Look, I didn't take the stand at the first trial, and I was convicted. I'm convinced I must take the stand at this trial or I'm going to be convicted again." But as our preparation for the trial progressed, it was becoming clearer and clearer that our best defense would be a medical one. If Claus did not inject his wife with insulin, then he would have no particularly useful information as to the causes of her comas.

He could, of course, testify about what he had *not* done. He could dispute the damning testimony of Maria and Alexandra and deny that he had placed insulin in the black bag or in the needle. The necessity for him to do so would depend, we advised him, on how strong the state's emotional case—or, as we called it, the soap-opera portion of their case—turned out to be.

In preparation for his possible testimony, I had Claus relate to me the entire story of his life. Claus's story was entirely convincing, answered many of my persistent questions, and put everything into a coherent context. I became convinced that *substantively* Claus would make an excellent witness, though I still had some doubts about how the jury would respond to his somewhat haughty manner.

We approached the trial with Claus ready to testify if he had to, but hoping that he would not have to expose himself to the risky shoals of cross-examination.

As the time came for him to make the decision, Claus and Andrea called me daily for my ongoing judgment. Finally, on the weekend before the final decision had to be made, he asked me to come down to Providence for a summit meeting. "Would you be kind enough to play the devil's advocate," he asked me, "and argue in favor of my taking the stand." Since I was somewhat more open to that possibility than Tom was, I agreed. But by that time I had pretty much decided what my own advice would be.

I drove down to Providence with my older son, Elon, who always advises me on my tough cases. He is a professional magician and entertainer and has excellent insights into audience reaction. "You and I both do the same thing," he would chide me, "sleight of hand —making things appear to be what they're not."

Early on in the case, I had taken Claus to watch Elon perform at the Legal Seafood restaurant. As Elon was making coins, silks and cards disappear, Claus bellowed in a loud voice that brought looks and laughs from our neighbors: "Do you think you could make a little black bag disappear?"

I asked Elon for his "audience reaction" to Claus's not taking the witness stand. He told me why he thought Claus would make a much better silent witness than talking witness.

"There's a certain aloof mystique about him. He seems impenetrable, unflappable. I think he's made a relatively good impression on the jury just sitting there, reacting. Once he testifies, the mystery's gone, and everyone loves a mystery. His not testifying confirms all the doubt swirling around this case. It emphasizes the uncertainties. If he were to take the stand, everything that came before his testimony would be relegated to an opening act, and whoever remembers the act that opened for the Rolling Stones? If you want this to become focused completely on Claus von Bülow, let him testify. If you want to focus the jury's attention away from him, you have to use the kinds of illusions and misdirections I try to use in my magic act. Let the jury think they know what von Bülow would say. But don't give it to them directly."

It was excellent advice, but I would still argue the opposite— the devil's advocate point of view—at our meeting that night.

When we arrived in Providence, Claus, Andrea, Claus's daughter Cosima, my son and I all went to dinner. As a gesture of defiance, Claus insisted that we go to one of the "banned" restaurants on "Arlene's hit list." The reference was to a list of restaurants that Attorney General Arlene Violet had declared off limits to her staff because they were allegedly under Mafia control or frequented by members of organized crime. It had been alleged that several judges and prominent public officials—including the chief justice, who was then under investigation—could also be seen at these restaurants. As soon as the list was made public, it immediately became a kind of informal gourmet guide to downtown Providence, with everyone clamoring for a reservation. "Those guys really know how to eat" was a common refrain. It did almost as much for the restaurateurs on the list as a "banned in Boston" label used to do for racy films.

We had an informal and pleasant "family" dinner with little discussion of the case. My one job over dessert was to report to Claus my conclusions from listening to some tape recordings David Marriott had surreptitiously made of conversations with Claus and Andrea Reynolds. Prior to the trial, Marriott had completely changed his public posture. After Claus refused his demand for extortionate payments of money for photographs he had taken from Claus's apartment—"Claus and Cosima in their underwear," he claimed, but they turned out to be in bathing suits—Marriott threatened to sell his story to the highest bidder. We refused to enter into the bidding. Marriott told us he had offered his photographs, surreptitious tapes and "memory" to Richard Kuh, the Aitkens, the Rhode Island prosecutor, *People* magazine, *60 Minutes* and others. The only apparent taker was the Attorney General's office, who "paid" Marriott by granting him immunity from prosecution in exchange for his tapes, his testimony and his promise not to hold any press conferences. The District Attorney of Middlesex County refused, however, to grant him immunity for the crime of secretly recording the conversations of another person without knowledge and permission. Nevertheless, Marriott decided to become a witness for the prosecution.

Prior to the trial we demanded and received copies of all tapes Marriott had made of conversations with Claus. When the tapes arrived, I was asked to listen to them. It was crucial for us to know what was on them *before* we could advise Claus whether or not to testify, because his taped conversations could be used by the prosecution to cross-examine him. We had to be sure Claus had not said anything to Marriott that could come back to haunt him if he took the stand.

Never have I been so bored since the time I had to sit through the screening of six dirty films in a row for a case. The tapes droned on for hour after hour. I began to hate the sound of both Marriott's and von Bülow's voices. Marriott was at his most sycophantic, constantly trying to impress Claus with his contacts and knowledge within the drug community. Claus was at his most pedantic, regaling Marriott with tales of European royalty, architecture and culinary delights. Neither seemed to understand, or pay much attention to, the other. It was a meeting of mutual convenience between two different worlds.

But the tapes were important for one reason. Marriott's latest machination was his public claim, made after extortionate demands were repeatedly turned down, that he had known Claus for nine years before any drug deliveries; that he had actually delivered the drugs to *Claus* von Bülow at Clarendon Court; and that Claus had concocted the whole story about the drug deliveries to Alex and Sunny.

The tapes proved unequivocally that these latest claims were utterly false. Had any of them been true, it would have been easy for Marriott, who knew he was taping an unsuspecting victim, to mention something consistent with his allegations: "Hey, Claus, remember the time . . ." Not only is there no such reference during the many hours of tapes ranging over numerous subjects and time frames, but all the tapes—every word—are consistent with Claus's account and Marriott's *original* story: that the two met in April 1982 and that Marriott said he could prove that he had delivered drugs to Alex and Sunny.

Moreover, there were other tapes that demonstrated Marriott's ability to get someone to say what he wants them to. Marriott also recorded conversations with Father Magaldi in which he apparently got the priest to acknowledge that when they first met, the priest was using a different name.

MARRIOTT: I knew you before the accident as Paul Marino.
MAGALDI: I knew you did.
MARRIOTT: I would never tell that I knew you as Paul Marino.

The "accident" apparently refers to an automobile collision in which Father Magaldi was involved in 1978. The tapes apparently show that Marriott and Magaldi originally met under circumstances different from what they stated in their affidavits (a fact of which we, of course, were unaware at the time we submitted the affidavits). The tapes do not make clear the nature of the Marriott-Magaldi relationship. But they do show how Marriott could use his secret tape recorder to elicit admissions from his unsuspecting parties in conversation. The fact that every single word on his tapes—both von Bülow's words and Marriott's—confirms *Claus's* account of the circumstances of their meetings was devastating proof that Marriott's latest revelations to the press were pure fiction.

This was an important piece of information to put into our calculations on whether Claus should take the stand. We now knew that he was in no danger of being blind-sided by the Marriott tapes. Marriott was becoming more and more of a noisy irrelevancy to the case as every day passed.

I told Claus that I had listened to the tapes "and you are at your absolute worst." He gave me a quick, troubled glance as if to ask, "What do you mean?" But I quickly added, "You're an insufferable bore on the tapes, droning on and on about castles, barons and

Bordeaux wines. You helped put me to sleep on at least three occasions." I asked him to remind me "to bring a pillow the next time we have a long talk about anything but law." My description brought laughs from everyone at the table, especially Andrea and Cosima, who knew exactly what I meant.

"Now you see what we have to go through at dinner parties and long evenings at home," Andrea quipped. "These damn castles. That's all he ever talks about."

Claus, looking a bit sheepish, promised to begin a moratorium on "castle talk," at least until the trial was over.

After dinner we had our summit conference. Tom argued forcefully against Claus taking the stand: "Look, this is a medical case. No insulin on the needle. No insulin in the blood. No insulin in the bag. No insulin, period. The comas were caused by drugs, booze, sweets and vomit. That's all there is to it. What does Claus have to add? Is he some kind of doctor or expert on insulin? I sure hope not," he added cynically.

I was reminded of the time we had dinner together in Bravo Gianini, a somewhat pretentious Italian restaurant where the maître d' gives every guest a title. "Professor"—he motioned to me. "Countess"—he pointed to Andrea. "Doctor von Bülow," he said deferentially, as Claus responded, "They accuse me of giving two injections, and already I've become a doctor!"

When my turn came, I argued that Tom would be right only if the jury didn't focus on the soap-opera testimony: "My fear, Tom, is that all this medical stuff is so complicated and boring, that the jurors might say, 'Look, what do we know about blood sugar and insulin levels; what we're experts on is life, love and the motives people act on.' If they focus on the 'people' part of the case—the maid, the mistress and the son—there are lots of unanswered questions, questions only Claus could answer."

Tom asked me to list the questions:

"All right, here's what I'd be asking myself if I were a juror:

"One: Why didn't Claus call the doctor sooner? Was he just sitting around watching Sunny die as Maria said she saw, and Alexandra said he admitted? What was going through his mind at the time? Did he tell Alexandra what she said he had told her about not being able 'to go through with it'? What was that referring to?

"Two: Whose black bag was it, anyhow? Why was he getting Valium with Leslie Baxter's name on the prescription? What the heck were those other drugs for—the papavoritum, the Lidocaine, the ground-up Valium of different colors? Was he giving himself injections? Was he giving her injections? Of what?

"Three: What happened in the bedroom just before the second coma after Alex carried Sunny to her bed? Did she say anything?

"Four: Was Sunny suicidal? Did she know what was in the gifts that Alexandra Isles had delivered to the house before the first coma? Did you ever try to get Alexandra not to testify?

"Five: What's the real story behind David Marriott and Father Magaldi? Did you really believe Marriott's story? After all, you knew your wife and stepson: *were* they getting drugs from Marriott or anyone else? Do you really believe that your stepson may have planted or tampered with evidence in an effort to 'frame' you? Did you make any promises to Marriott that you didn't tell your lawyers about?"

As I was continuing my litany of questions, Tom cut me off. "I thought you were supposed to be arguing *for* Claus to take the stand. These questions are the best argument against it. Look at what you're opening up. If those are the questions the jurors are thinking about, don't you think the prosecutors will be trying to ask them? Sure, Judge Grande may keep some of them out, but who knows what she might let in?"

I countered with the suggestion that if we were to decide to put Claus on the stand, we could ask Judge Grande for an advance ruling about what lines of cross-examination questions she would allow. Some judges will give advance rulings as a guide to the direct questions that should be put to the defendant by his own lawyer, without risk of opening up other issues.*

But a consensus was quickly emerging. All the lawyers agreed that in light of the way the case had been going, the jury would probably go into the deliberation room with the medical testimony on its mind. "I'm going to ask them in my closing argument," Tom said, "to follow a certain order in their deliberations. First, were the comas caused by insulin? And only if they decide that in the affirmative, who administered the insulin? I hope they never reach the second question."

I said that I wished the jury could be sent out first to decide the insulin question alone. And if they were to decide that the comas

---

* For an example of how that advance request strategy backfired against F. Lee Bailey in the Patricia Hearst case, see *The Best Defense.*

had been caused by insulin, we could then decide to put Claus on the stand.

"Dream on," Tom said, "That's not the way the system works. You've got to make all the decisions now, without knowing what the jury will be thinking or doing. And I'm ready to decide that Claus doesn't testify."

"That's my vote too," I chimed in. There were no dissents, except for a regret from Claus, who said he had no choice but to follow his lawyers' advice. Andrea Reynolds responded with an angry glare, signifying that she wouldn't try to fight the entire legal team, but that if she had her way, Claus would be testifying. But the decision had been made; the jury would never hear Claus von Bülow's story.

As we drove back to Cambridge, my son Elon asked me about Andrea Reynolds. He was utterly fascinated by this dynamo of a woman who seemed to have so much influence over Claus's life. I told him what I knew about her background and current life.

Andrea Reynolds traveled in the same social circles as Claus and Sunny. In fact, Andrea had known both of them from their St. Moritz vacation days. But she became Claus's companion and lover only after the first trial. Since that time, Claus and Andrea have become nearly inseparable, though she says that "friendship" plays no part in the relationship. "Good friends are terribly unromantic," and romance is everything to her in a relationship. They engaged in what she calls "a ballet of seduction" before they became lovers, and that "seduction dance" still keeps the romance alive. "He's a good lover," she says of Claus. "I wouldn't be around him if he weren't." And she is around him twenty-four hours a day. She never allows him to be alone. "He needs a witness to account for his every move," she says. She answers his phone calls, attends his meetings, participates in—some say makes—his important decisions. "I'm a pussycat," Claus has said. "I do anything she says." Andrea has added, "Claus hates arguments, and I don't." It was she who insisted that Claus lighten up his image for the second trial, commenting that at the first trial he looked "like a mortician who had swallowed an umbrella."

It was she who handled most of the dealings with David Marriott and Father Magaldi. About Marriott she now says, "Don't talk about him when I've just eaten." About Marriott's claim that "he was on very, very close terms with Claus": "That's obscene." And

Andrea ought to know, since she was with Claus at almost every meeting. Claus has only praise for her efforts: "I realize that that Hungarian hussar has, often to one's total exhaustion, whipped everybody, including me, into total activity."

It was Andrea who made the final decision to hire Tom Puccio to represent Claus at his second trial "because I thought he was totally the antithesis of Claus," she explains. "Claus is a born gentle *man* and gentleman, while Puccio is a bull in a china shop." (Claus says he "concurred" because "if a defendant believes he's innocent and believes he's being framed, he'll hire a prosecutor [to go] after the culprit.")

During the second trial Andrea frequently regretted her decision to retain Tom. "They draw away from him when he approaches the jury box. . . . He's screwing up our case," she would say, especially when the decision was made not to call Claus as a witness. "He must tell his story," she insisted, and after Claus reluctantly concurred with the lawyer's judgment not to testify, Andrea was heard to say, "Okay, so I'll tell his story. Somebody's got to do it." Andrea was also furious at Puccio for not going after Maria and Alexandra aggressively enough on cross-examination.

Many court observers wondered who this mystery woman was who spent her days in the television trailer of the Cable News Network, watching every minute of the trial proceedings, and her nights counseling and comforting Claus. Although she never appeared in the courtroom until the verdict was announced, she was regarded by the press as "clearly the star of the second trial."

Andrea Miloš was born in Budapest, Hungary, in 1937, on the eve on the Second World War. When the Russians entered Hungary, her father, a banker and world-class chess player, was kept under house arrest. After the war her parents were divorced and young Andrea moved to Geneva with her mother. But Andrea's adult life would reflect her father's passions for banking and chess. She calculates every move with an eye toward the bottom line and the endgame.

After attending finishing school, she married, and quickly divorced, an Italian banker and shortly thereafter met and married the man who would father her only child, Caroline. Her thirteen-year marriage to Pierre Frottier was glamorous and affluent, marked by lavish parties, jet-set vacations and extravagant living.

When it ended, Andrea quickly married an American TV producer, Sheldon Reynolds, whose name she still carries; they were in the process of divorcing at the time of the trial. Andrea, unlike Alexandra Isles, is giving Claus no ultimatums about marriage. As her daughter Caroline, now herself a mother, puts it: "I don't think the institution of marriage is important to her" right now. Andrea does not want Claus to divorce Sunny: "Divorcing someone who's in a coma is like divorcing someone who's in an insane asylum. It's absolutely horrible." Though her daughter says she is "very religious" and attends Catholic mass regularly, Andrea openly lives with Claus, sharing the apartment at 960 Fifth Avenue, which she has redecorated since moving in. They attend the opera together and share a common passion for beautiful dogs and expensive wines. They both speak numerous languages and often communicated with each other during the case in a series of incomprehensible tongues. (When they lapsed into their strange languages, I was reminded of my grandmother, who spoke a combination of Yiddish and Polish when she didn't want me to understand.)

When her friends are asked why this glamorous woman was attracted to a man facing life imprisonment, they respond that she is an inveterate ambulance-chaser who loves to "care for people" who really need help.

Between 1978 and 1980, Andrea and her husband Sheldon lived for long periods of time in Warsaw, Poland, producing episodes of a Sherlock Holmes series for Polish television. Those two years seem to have had a profound effect on Andrea's views of justice and law. Near the end of her stay, she was detained by police and accused of bribery. She says she spent two nightmarish days in a Communist prison and was beaten, made to stand under a scalding shower and treated abusively until her husband Telexed $30,000 from London to the prosecutor in charge of the case. Even after she was allowed to leave, the Polish authorities kept her beloved dogs "hostage" for three months.

Andrea came away from this experience with an utterly cynical view not only of Polish justice, but of law in general. Her experiences in Rhode Island did nothing to disabuse her of these suspicious attitudes. "Rhode Island is the most corrupt state in the nation," she declared in the middle of the second trial. Though there was some debate about the general accuracy of her assessment among the lawyers, there was more embarrassment about the fact that she had made it publicly.

Throughout her involvement in the case, Andrea always took the cynical view, arguing that although Claus was clearly innocent, "innocence alone will not produce an acquittal in Rhode Island." She always advocated a multifaceted approach: "You can't rely alone on the good faith of prosecutors or judges," she would argue. She insisted on cultivating the right journalists, power brokers, and lawyers. "Everybody manipulates everybody" is her motto. Like a good chess player, she was always thinking four moves ahead. "What if we give the story to Barbara Walters? How will Ted Koppel react? What effect will it have on Arlene Violet? Do you really think the jury isn't hearing any of this? Can Judge Grande be as straight as she seems?" These were the kinds of questions she was always asking. Reynolds also ran her own press operation, flattering, cajoling, complaining and even threatening. She called one unfavorable journalist a "Commie pinko faggot"; smiling, hinted to another that, "I'm going to have to arrange for you to have a little accident"; and took favorable journalists along for dinner.

Andrea never had any doubt about Claus's innocence. "He couldn't possibly inject anyone against their will," she insists. "He almost faints at the sight of blood. He couldn't pull it off because his mind doesn't work that way. He would drop everything and vials would break. . . . He's just clumsy," a "klutz."

Nor does Andrea mince words about Sunny, who she believes was responsible for her own coma. "I think she bears a great deal of responsibility toward Cosima and even toward Claus, because she failed them." About Claus's stepchildren, she is even more critical: "spoiled brats," "inferior intellectually" and "leading a dissolute type of life . . . in the back rooms of Xenon and Studio 54."

Andrea was always at loggerheads with the lawyers, especially Tom. To her, the "legal team" was only a *part* of the entire enterprise of vindicating Claus. Tom might have been chief trial counsel, but Andrea was the commander-in-chief, pulling all the strings. Although she was excluded from the courtroom and the legal strategy sessions, she ran an independent operation, called whomever she wished, said whatever she wanted to and dealt with anyone she felt could help Claus's case.

In the end, it is impossible to evaluate her actual contribution to the case, for it is in the nature of the kind of actions she took that they are less visible and therefore less subject to appraisal. But

Andrea was anything but invisible. Her presence was seen and felt at every twist and turn.

With the decision made not to put Claus on the stand, the defense rested its case. The prosecution sought to introduce fourteen rebuttal witnesses, who are supposed to respond to new issues raised by the defense in its case. The defense had introduced nine witnesses, all experts.

In its case-in-chief, the state had introduced thirty-three witnesses, most of whom testified about the medical or forensic aspects of the case. Now the state wanted to put on several additional medical experts who would give their opinions that the comas were caused by insulin. Judge Grande ruled, essentially, that "enough is enough"—that the state knew that the defense would introduce experts to dispute the insulin theory and the state should have put on its entire medical case first, rather than try to split it up in order to have the last word. She did allow two prosecution witnesses to testify in rebuttal about some specifics of the defense's medical case. But the prosecutors, who had saved some of their best witnesses for rebuttal, had been outmaneuvered by the defense tactic of putting on a narrow medical case.

In her most hotly contested and widely criticized ruling of the trial, Judge Grande refused to allow family banker Morris Gurley to testify for the state in rebuttal. She had earlier disallowed his testimony about Claus's possible financial motive to murder his wife, but she had left open the possibility that he could testify in rebuttal. Since Claus had not taken the stand, there was nothing for Gurley, who knew nothing about the medical issues raised in the defense case, to rebut. The judge concluded in addition that "there is not a suggestion anywhere at all that financial gain impelled the defendant to take the actions the state says he took." Without foundation evidence, there was a risk that the jury might follow Chekhov's rules of drama rather than Wigmore's rules of evidence. As noted earlier, Chekhov says there are no coincidences in drama: a gun hung on the wall in the first act is to be used by the third; a chest pain in the first is to be followed by a coronary in the second; and a will showing a possible motive to kill is always followed by an attempt to kill. In contrast, Wigmore, the great codifier of American evidence law, says that real life is full of coincidences, so that judges must decide, on the basis of the evidence, whether the

jury should hear about a possible motive and be allowed to speculate on whether the defendant acted on it.

Judge Grande's decision to exclude Gurley's motive testimony
was greeted with a chorus of condemnation. The von Auersperg
children's new lawyer criticized her ruling as "astonishing—it
doesn't make sense as a matter of law or logic."* The prosecutor
went further, charging that Judge Grande "generally" decided issues
"in the defendant's favor."

Vocally criticizing a judge for ruling against your client is a
favorite tactic of lawyers. It is not designed so much to obtain a
reversal of the ruling—that occurs very rarely. Rather, it is usually
intended to try to "soften up" the judge and incline her to give you
a make-up call on the next important ruling. (Red Auerbach taught
me that tactic. When he was coaching the Celtics, he would always
scream at the officials after a bad call, and often obtain, for his
efforts, the benefit of the doubt on the next close call.)

Whether coincidental or not, the prosecution did receive the
benefit of the doubt on the next close judicial call—a call that
could have been the most important one at the trial: the judge's
instructions to the jury on the law.

But before a judge instructs the jury, the lawyers for the defense
and prosecution must summarize their cases. These summations or
closing arguments, as they are called, are the lawyers' last words,
their parting shots, to the jurors who will determine their client's
fate. Lawyers regard these arguments as their most important contribution to a case. But juror interviews suggest that most lawyers
exaggerate the importance of their arguments—and indeed their
own importance in general—to the outcome of the case.

---

* The jury did, of course, already know that Claus stood to benefit financially from
Sunny's death. The prosecutor had told them about the alleged financial motive in
his opening argument.

17

The Last Word

Under Rhode Island practice, the defense attorney summarizes his case first and the prosecutor gets the last word. This rule makes little sense and has no apparent justification, except to give an incalculable advantage to the prosecution. The natural progression would be for the prosecution, which presented its case first and has the burden of proof, to present its closing argument first; and for the defense, which presented its case second, to have the last word. The federal practice, which used to be the same as Rhode Island's, was changed several years ago. Now the prosecutor does sum up first and the defense second. But the prosecutor gets the opportunity for a final rebuttal. Of course, when the defense used to go first, it never got a rebuttal, and it gets no rebuttal in Rhode Island where it still goes first. The fixed principle seems to be that the prosecution always goes last; everything else is up for grabs.

The rationale for this rule is so downright silly that it is hard to argue it with a straight face. But prosecutors, judges and legislators make the argument without even flinching. It goes like this: Since the prosecution has the burden of proving its case beyond a reasonable doubt, it must counterbalance that heavy burden by getting the last word.

What this argument fails to acknowledge is that there is a very good reason why the prosecution has a heavy burden of proof. As the late Justice John Harlan put it in his classic statement in the case of In re *Winship*: "The requirement of proof beyond a reasonable doubt in a criminal case [is] bottomed on a fundamental value determination of our society that it is far worse to convict an innocent man than to let a guilty man go free."

Our system deliberately demands greater certainty for a conviction than for an acquittal. It is no answer to say that this policy needs to be balanced by giving a countervailing advantage to the prosecution that will *ease* its burden. Its burden should not be eased, certainly not through the back-door advantage it gets from arguing last.

The real reason for the rule is that many of those who administer the system do not really believe that the prosecution's burden should be as high as it is. They look for ways of easing it in practice, while maintaining its façade in theory. The "last word" gift to the prosecution helps to ease its burden, thus equalizing a contest that is not supposed to be equal. Of course, the contest turns out, in general, not to be even anyway. The enormous resources of the prosecution —not only financial, but the leverage it obtains by being able to coerce cooperation by plea bargaining—are rarely matched by the defense. And most judges favor the prosecution palpably, if for no other reason than that it is right most of the time because few defendants are innocent.

For whatever reason or reasons, the defense in Rhode Island gets to sum up its case first.

Thomas Puccio began his argument at the lectern speaking in his abrupt Brooklyn style:

> I'm asking you to keep your eye on the ball, and the ball here is insulin injection.
>   . . .
> Let me start with what I submit to you is the single most important issue in this case:
> The defendant stands accused of what could only be described as a monstrous, incredible allegation that he injected his wife on two occasions with insulin.
> The fact or lack of fact of insulin injection is at the heart of this case. You, ladies and gentlemen, have to find that there was an insulin injection to find the defendant guilty.

Puccio kept hammering home his theme that "this case rises or falls" on insulin. And he asked the jury to make it fall because all of his expert witnesses—"the cream of the crop, the top experts in the world"—had all concluded: "no insulin injection."

As for the prosecution's witnesses, Puccio reminded the jury that Dr. Gailitis himself had concluded that the first coma was not caused by insulin. He pounded the lectern with his pen as he made these points. Puccio also attacked Dr. Cahill. But his sarcasm was reserved for Dr. Bradley, who had testified he was 100 percent certain that the first coma was caused by insulin. Referring to him as "Mr. One Hundred Percent," Puccio told the jury that Bradley had reached that conclusion without ever considering the 216 blood insulin reading, which Bradley regarded as "icing on the cake."

> Mr. 100 percent. Ladies and gentlemen, he had no cake on which to put that icing . . . So he can sit up there until the cows come home and say I'm 100 percent sure and it doesn't mean a gosh-darn thing.

Puccio tried to blunt the testimony of Maria Schrallhammer by arguing that she never liked Claus and that she testified "with no love in her heart for von Bülow." He focused the jury's attention on the inconsistency between Maria's trial testimony and what she had told Richard Kuh. The "key to this," he told the jury, is the Kuh notes:

> Richard Kuhl had been hired by the children to investigate this matter after Mrs. von Bülow is in an irreversible coma. The first thing they do is bring in the maid so she could say what she saw, and in this critical interview, she doesn't say a word about an insulin bottle, she doesn't say a word about needles, she doesn't say a word about syringes. I submit to you, ladies and gentlemen, if she, in fact, saw those things back on Thanksgiving of 1980, that is the very first thing she would have done when she spoke to Mr. Kuh, she would have said, "This is what I saw."*

"One has only to thank the fact," Puccio concluded, "that the truth ultimately emerges . . . through Mr. Kuh's notes that describe the earlier interviews . . ."

Prosecutor Marc DeSisto stood close to the jury box and argued with more intensity than he had shown during the trial. He told the jury that the expert testimony was less important than the evidence of von Bülow's behavior: "You're more qualified than the experts because you can consider things that they can't." He urged the jury "to be courageous," and he conjured up a visual picture for them:

> He loads his needle and syringe with insulin. He goes to his wife. What's he thinking? And he finds the spot, and now he's pressing the

---

* Puccio's description of the Kuh notes was essentially the same as the one I had given on the courthouse steps back in January 1985—the description that Attorney General Arlene Violet had mendaciously characterized as "erroneous and false." Violet has never, to my knowledge, defended her misleading characterization.

plunger in, and what is he thinking as that insulin is released into her body?

Can you see it, he's pressing the plunger down and he's releasing all the tension.

He's going to be with Alexandra Isles. He doesn't have to find a job. Can you see it? Then he sits there and he patiently waits. Then he waits and she recovers.

He waits a whole year then he does the same thing all over again.

DeSisto concluded, as Puccio had, by recounting the testimony of Alexandra and Maria:

Alexandra Isles is the reason, the motive, the moving force behind each injection, each coma . . . You will recall the deadline set in April 1979 by both of them: "Let's be together by Christmastime." What a coincidence that the first coma happens at Christmastime.

He dramatically repeated Alexandra's testimony about what Claus had allegedly said to her:

I watched, I watched my wife, unconscious in a bad way. And finally when she was on the point of dying, I called the doctor.

He then asked the jury to follow him into the room that Sunny was lying in during the day of her first coma:

In your minds go to that room December 27, 1979, and sit there with the defendant and wait for his wife to die. Can you do it? She's unconscious and he's watching her. And now Maria Schrallhammer is coming in and out shaking her and she's unarousable.

Go there in your minds. He calls the doctor and lies to the doctor. "My wife had a lot of alcohol, but don't worry, she's been up."

In your deliberation room, think about that room, and ladies and gentlemen, stay there until you can hear Martha von Bülow rattle. Now watch as Maria Schrallhammer comes into the room and she holds her and asks the defendant, "Will you help me?" And he says no.

Both performances were full of drama and oratory. But the real last word is always had by the judge. In the charge to the jury, a judge can blunt the most eloquent lawyer's oratory. The jury knows that the lawyers are advocates who are supposed to be one-sided in the presentation. The robed judge is the epitome of impartiality and objectivity—at least in theory.

But in practice, many judges are result-oriented. They know which side they would like to see win and are not shy about planting a heavy thumb on the scales of justice. Word has it that there used to be an old judge in Washington, D.C., who had two sets of general instructions—about reasonable doubt, burden of proof, and so on—in his desk drawer. One was favorable to the defense, the other favorable to the prosecution. Both were acceptable as a matter of law, and so he could give either without fear of being reversed on appeal. If he thought the defendant was guilty, he would take out the pro-prosecution instructions. If he felt that the defendant might be innocent, he would give the pro-defense instructions. Since most jurors only hear one set of instructions in a lifetime, there was no way they could know how much they were being manipulated.

The judge's instructions are crucial not only because they are the last words the jury will hear before deliberating, but because jurors really tend to listen to the robed oracle delivering them. As the United States Supreme Court once observed: "[The judge's] lightest word or intimation is received with deference, and may prove controlling" because the judge fills a "position of special persuasiveness." Every nuance, every emphasis, every omission is latched onto by the jury as a sign of the judge's real feelings. Jurors always want to know how the judge feels, because he or she is so much more experienced at this sort of thing—and oh-so-objective. Otherwise they wouldn't have made him a judge!

Judge Grande was objective, but she was obviously stung by the criticisms directed toward her alleged favoritism to the defense. Whether consciously or unconsciously, she seemed to be seeking to balance the score with her instructions.

The most controversial portion of Judge Grande's charges—delivered in a soft, melodic tone—was her definition of proof beyond a reasonable doubt. The concept is one of the few that is not natural in the minds of most jurors, as it is rarely employed in everyday thinking and actions. A rational person acts on a preponderance of the evidence, even in the most important decisions of his or her life. If a doctor tells you that you need coronary artery bypass surgery, you think long and hard about it. But you weigh the likelihood of living a comfortable, healthy and lengthy life *with it* against the likelihood of living similarly *without it*. You might factor many other considerations into the equation as well—pain, distrust of doctors, imminence of death versus certainty, dislike of hospitals, etc. But in the end, if a rational person decides that the odds in favor or against the operation are 60–40, he or she should act on those percentages. After all, why *ever* go with the 40 percent chance when you get the 60 percent chance?

The decision in a criminal trial is supposed to be different. If the jurors decide, after considering all the evidence, that it is 60 percent likely that a defendant is guilty and 40 percent likely that he is not, they are supposed to acquit—to go with the 40 percent. This is even true if the percentages are 70 to 30. The law hates qualification and loves to deal with such amorphous concepts as "moral certainty." But that concept does not convert to 60–40 or even 70–30. Moral certainty is more like 90–10—a figure roughly reflecting Sir William Blackstone's edict that it is better for ten guilty to go free than one innocent to be punished. In criminal cases, the legal cost of one kind of error—convicting the innocent—is supposed to be much higher than the legal cost of another kind of error —acquitting the guilty.

But many judges either don't understand this principle or disregard it. Often they give the following instructions, which completely undercuts the difference between deciding on the guilt or innocence of a defendant and making other important decisions in life:

> Ladies and gentlemen of the jury, in deciding whether the state has proved the defendant's guilt beyond a reasonable doubt, you are not to demand that it be proved beyond all doubt, but rather that it be proved with *the kind of certainty that you act on in making your most important personal decisions*. [Emphasis added.]

Not a word about the different costs of different types of errors! Not a word about how it is better to acquit ten guilty than convict a single innocent! The message is clear: you should convict the defendant on the same odds at which you would choose surgery or get married or have children or change jobs.

Judge Grande's instruction was not quite this extreme, but it clearly inclined in the same direction. She told the jury this about reasonable doubt:

> Proof beyond a reasonable doubt does not mean that the state must prove this case beyond all doubt . . .
>
> Nor [must the state] prove the essential elements in this case beyond the shadow of a doubt; it does not mean that at all.

. . . Simply stated, this defendant is entitled to a doubt based on reason, no defendant is ever entitled to the benefit of any or all doubt.

The oath that you took requires you to return a verdict of guilty if you are convinced beyond a reasonable doubt. And, members of the jury, equally, your oath requires you to return a verdict of not guilty if you are not convinced beyond a reasonable doubt.

Judge Grande emphasized the word "convinced" and cautioned the jurors that reasonable doubt "isn't a speculative doubt, a feeling in your bones. [It] is more than a doubt based on guesswork or possibilities."

Judge Grande's emphasis on what reasonable doubt is *not* certainly may have conveyed the impression that a juror would be wrong to acquit if he ended up with a feeling in his gut—a feeling that he couldn't explain but that seemed right to him—that the defendant may be innocent. Indeed, she instructed the jurors that they had a "duty to vote guilty" if their doubts were based on "a feeling," rather than on the evidence. It sounded almost as if the jury needed to have as strong a reason to acquit as to convict. After listening to that part of the charge, it was difficult to remember which side had the heavy burden of proof.

Judge Grande then went on to tell the jury that "*probability* of guilt, however strong, will never sustain or justify a verdict of guilt." That instruction is equally absurd and reflects a misunderstanding of probabilities. Probabilities are all we ever have to go on in life, and certainly in law. As Justice Harlan correctly put it in the *Winship* case: "All the factfinder can acquire is a belief of what *probably* happened." In a case like von Bülow's no one will ever know anything for certain. What should be required is a very high probability of guilt. How high or how strong is precisely the question the law should answer and the judge should instruct on, but Judge Grande did not.

The next controversial aspect of her instruction was on the elusive and confusing subject of circumstantial evidence. Courts are constantly telling juries that "circumstantial evidence is every bit as good as direct evidence." Some judges add, "even better." That misunderstands the difference between circumstantial evidence and direct evidence. Indeed, the misunderstanding is inherent in the words themselves. There is no such thing as circumstantial *evidence*, only a circumstantial *case*. All evidence is by its nature direct: for example, Maria testified that she "*saw* insulin in Claus's black bag."

That is eyewitness evidence and it is as direct as anything can be: she says she saw it with her own eyes and read the label. The only issues are: Is she telling the truth? Is she remembering accurately?

Another example of direct evidence is the testimony of Alex that he found Dalmane with Claus's name on it and a needle encrusted with some substance in the black bag.

What is circumstantial is the *conclusion* the prosecutor was asking the jury to draw from all the direct evidence in the case: to infer that *because* insulin was seen in the black bag in November, and *because* a prescription with Claus's name on it and an insulin-encrusted needle were found in the same bag in January, *therefore*, the bag containing the attempted-murder weapon must have belonged to Claus,who must have injected his wife with the needle.

That reasoning process—inferring conclusions from direct evidence—comprises the circumstantial nature of the case. The case would have been direct had Maria testified that she had seen Claus fill a needle with insulin and then inject Sunny while she was sleeping. In that kind of unlikely scenario, the only real issues would be the accuracy of Maria's eyewitness testimony. The jury would not be asked to make many circumstantial leaps of logic.*

In the von Bülow case, the jury first had to decide whether it believed the eyewitness accounts of Maria and Alex about the insulin and Dalmane in the black bag. If it decided to believe that testimony, it had to take the next step and decide whether these—and other—circumstances gave rise to a compelling inference that the attempted-murder weapon belonged to Claus, who had used it on his wife.

When seen this way, it becomes clear that it is illogical to tell a

---

* Rhode Island has a rule that recognizes the difference between cases based on exclusively direct testimony and those requiring circumstantial inferences. It does not permit the jury to base a conviction on what it calls a "pyramiding of inferences," or a "piling of one inference upon another." What this means is that after a jury is asked to draw *one* inference from direct evidence, it may not then be asked to draw a *second* inference from the first inference, unless it is the *only* logical inference that can reasonably be drawn. As the Rhode Island Supreme Court put it in its leading case: "An inference resting on an inference drawn from established facts must be rejected . . . where the facts from which it is drawn are susceptible of another reasonable inference."

Thus, under Rhode Island law, a circumstantial case is not regarded as "every bit as good" as a direct case, and for understandable reasons. In a direct case, all the jury has to do is assess the credibility of the eyewitness; the inferences flow naturally from what was allegedly observed. In a circumstantial case, the jury must do two things: it must first *assess* the credibility of the eyewitness, because if his direct testimony is false there is no foundation upon which to build inferences; it must then draw inferences from the direct evidence.

jury that "circumstantial evidence is every bit as good as direct evidence." That is like saying a mathematical equation is every bit as good as the numbers that go into it, or a scientific theory is every bit as good as the facts it is based on.

The correct way of putting it would be that a circumstantial case can *never be better than* the direct evidence on which it is based. All things being equal, a circumstantial case can never be as good as or better than the *same* case based exclusively on direct evidence. Had Maria and Alex seen Claus put insulin in the bag, remove it and inject his wife, that would be a stronger case than the same Maria and Alex seeing only the insulin and the needle and *inferring* that Claus had injected his wife with it.

Of course, in real life all things are not equal. Some circumstantial cases *are* stronger than some cases based on direct evidence. Thus if seven people of unimpeachable reputation—prior to the Marriott-Magaldi situation I would have said "seven priests"—had each independently sworn they had seen one particular event, and the seven events led logically to only one conclusion, that would make a stronger case than if one pathological liar—someone like David Marriott—had sworn he had witnessed the conclusion itself. This truism doesn't make circumstantial evidence every bit as good as, or better than, direct evidence. It only demonstrates the obvious: that a strong circumstantial case can be better than a weak case based on questionable direct evidence. It is also true, of course, that a strong direct case is far better than a weak circumstantial case.

Now, all this by way of introduction to the devastating instruction Judge Grande gave to the jury on circumstantial evidence. Notwithstanding the tough Rhode Island standards for cases based on circumstantial inferences, Judge Grande instructed the jury as follows:

Circumstantial evidence is every bit as good as direct evidence. . . . The probative force of circumstantial evidence is equal to the probative force of direct evidence and there is no valid distinction to be drawn between [them].

She then offered the jury an example of circumstantial evidence:

Let's take a hypothetical case in which a jury must decide whether the handle of a frying pan was hot. The facts are these:

The father takes the stand and testified that he put a frying pan on the stove and he thought he turned the stove off. He saw his three-

year-old child reach up and touch the handle of the pan; he heard
the child cry out and dropped the pan.

The father ran into the kitchen, looked at his child's hand. The
hand was red. The father testified he took the child to a doctor. The
doctor testifies that he examined the child and he made a diagnosis
that the child's hand was burned.

Members of the jury, if that jury were satisfied that the testimony
of the father was true and that the testimony of the doctor was true,
that jury may draw the reasonable and entirely logical inference that
the handle of the pan was hot, even though no one testified directly
to that point . . .

That example was heavily loaded in the prosecution's favor, for
two reasons: first, there could be no real dispute about the correctness of the father's observations or about his credibility; second, the
inference to be drawn from the direct observations was inescapable.
In the actual von Bülow case, both the truth of the observations
and the inferences to be drawn from them were subject to substantial challenge.

Puccio was furious with Judge Grande's instructions. For the
first time in the trial, he seemed to lose his temper, accusing the
judge of giving a one-sided charge. The "emphasis" she placed on
certain "buzzwords"—such as reasonable doubt and circumstantial
evidence—"had a devastating cumulative effect." Tom asked her to
reconsider and to give a "more balanced charge." Grande responded
that she had "always been reasonable." Tom snapped back, "Yeah,
except on reasonable doubt."

Notwithstanding Puccio's protests and some emergency research
we hastily put together in Cambridge, the judge refused to change
her instructions.

The case was now in the hands of Claus von Bülow's twelve
peers, none of whom had very much in common with him or his
alleged victim. A social worker, a stitcher, a maintenance administrator, a factory supervisor, a retired letter carrier, a Head Start
counselor, a bank teller, a health administrator, a lab technician,
a housewife, an accounting student and a city finance director—
these were the "peers" who would sit in judgment over a man who
certainly did not regard such working-class people as his equals.

18

The Jury Decides

The second case against Claus von Bülow went to the jury at 11:30 A.M. on Friday, June 7, 1985. Following Judge Grande's charges on reasonable doubt and circumstantial evidence, it was anyone's guess what the jurors would be thinking. They had been told two very different stories, neither responsive to the other. The defense had not even tried to erase the prosecution's detailed portrayal of Claus as an unhusbandly cad who was willing to sit around watching his wife die. And the prosecution had not been able to rebut the powerful medical and forensic case put on by the defense. It was almost as if the jurors had spent six weeks listening to two different cases.

Prior to Judge Grande's instruction, most observers seemed to believe that the defense case had succeeded in raising a reasonable doubt about the prosecution's medical and forensic case, but had not raised enough doubt about its soap-opera case. Now, following the charge on reasonable doubt, it was unclear which story the jury would focus on.

The key to the jury's secret deliberations lay in three small windows into their minds: first, the kinds of questions they might send out to the judge while they were deliberating; second, the length of their deliberations; and third, the kinds of looks they gave the defendant—especially as they were about to render a verdict.

Trial lawyers invoke all sorts of mythologies about deciphering jury behavior. One reason for this creative enterprise is that while the jury is out deliberating the fate of their clients—which may take hours, days or even weeks—the trial lawyer has little to do but sit around and wait. And trial lawyers, most of whom seem to have the kind of personality unsuited to waiting, have to come up with some activity to keep them busy. Jury speculation and mythology is a favorite. Among the current myths are the following:

- A jury that asks lots of questions is good for the defense, because they are clearly troubled about something. (More, of course, may depend on the *nature of* the questions than on their number.)
- A jury that stays out for a long time is good for the defense, since that suggests disagreement, and disagreement creates the possibility of a hung jury.
- Jurors who can't look the defendant straight in the eye as they are about to decide his fate are probably going to convict him.

These myths are questionable at best and reflect hope more than empirical science. Most defense attorneys and their clients have little objective basis for holding out much hope because the vast majority of defendants are convicted by the jurors who sit in judgment on them. The percentage of convictions, however, is lower in retrials following an appellate reversal.* This difference reflects several phenomena at work. The defendant, at a retrial, has the advantage of knowing far more about the case against him and thus being better able to prepare for it. The cases selected for reversal by the appellate court are, most often, the closer cases with some valid basis for a claim of innocence. And retrials take place farther away in time from the events in question than first trials, resulting in faded—or at least more questionable—memories, fewer witnesses and a general reduction in the strength of the case.

Though I am aware of no statistical studies, I am certain that even in the majority of cases where the jurors ask questions, deliberate at length, and look the defendant squarely in the eye, they still render verdicts of guilty—though probably in a somewhat lower proportion than in other cases. Mythology takes on a life of its own in the frustrating business of being a criminal lawyer where even the best lose most of the time.

During their second day of deliberations, the jury asked to rehear the testimony of Maria and Alex concerning the sighting of

---

* About three fourths of all criminal trials end up in jury convictions. According to the New York *Times,* "Experts estimate that about half of retried cases end in an acquittal."

the black bag after Thanksgiving. They also wanted to hear what Dr. Rubenstein, our expert on the unreliability of the insulin finding on the needle discovered in the black bag during the January search and seizure, had said. We were elated by these requests. They showed that the jury was focusing on whether insulin had actually been seen in the black bag and whether there was any insulin on the needle that was found in the bag. We hoped a rereading of Maria's and Alex's testimony—especially their cross-examination —would reinforce doubts about the truthfulness of their accounts, and would highlight the inconsistencies between their trial testimony and their more contemporaneous interviews with Kuh.

After this testimony was read to them, in the flat delivery of the court reporter, the jury resumed its deliberations.

On the Saturday morning of jury deliberations—the second day —a front-page story in the Boston *Globe* reported that a Rhode Island grand jury had secretly indicted Father Magaldi for perjury. The indictment was "secret" so as not to influence the von Bülow jury's deliberations. But it was leaked to the press—by someone in the Attorney General's office, according to an unimpeachable source —precisely in order to influence their deliberations. It was thought that the indictment of one of von Bülow's witnesses—even one who had never testified—might cast a negative light on the defense. The Attorney General's office self-righteously denied further comment, but none was necessary. The point had been made by leaking the indictment. Although the jury was sequestered, it is well known that few sequestrations are entirely leak-proof. A story as volatile as the indictment of one of Providence's respected and most popular parish priests had a high likelihood of seeping into the jury room. This was especially so, because, according to one reporter, "several of the members [of the jury] were acquainted with Father Magaldi" —a fact known to the prosecution.

It is no wonder that Rhode Island Superior Court Judge Thomas Calderone, Jr., angrily declared, upon hearing of the leak, that "Any law enforcement officer who leaked that should be dismissed. If he worked for me, I'd throw him out. It's deplorable."

But as far as I know, nothing was ever done to determine the source of the leak. Rhode Island justice does not seem to extend to members of the Attorney General's staff.

Whether the jury learned of Father Magaldi's indictment during the deliberations will never be known. Nor will it ever be known who leaked the information. The jury continued to deliberate throughout Saturday without coming to a verdict.

I was hoping that the jury would not be sitting on Sunday, June 9, because another important decision would be rendered on that day. It was the sixth game of the National Basketball Association finals. My beloved but beleaguered Celtics were facing the Los Angeles Lakers. The Lakers, led by the inspired playing of Kareem Abdul-Jabbar and Magic Johnson on the court and the taunting of Jack Nicholson off the court, were leading the Celtics three games to two. If they took this one, the series was over and the world championship moved from Boston to L.A. If the Celts managed to win this one—despite an injured Larry Bird, a hobbled Cedrick Maxwell and an exhausted Kevin McHale—they would face the Lakers in a seventh and decisive game on Tuesday.

During the regular season I get to about half of the home games (and a smattering of the away games when I can manage to be in the appropriate city on "business" at the right time). Our season tickets are just a few rows in front of Celtics president Arnold "Red" Auerbach's seats, and he takes attendance of his friends, (God forbid any friend of Red Auerbach should ever walk out of a game even seconds before it's over—regardless of how lopsided the score. He will get a scowl from the "President's Box" that will make him remember the worst rebuke he ever got from his father.)

During halftime, Red—a frustrated lawyer—often comes down to ask me about my cases and to offer advice about how to win them. He was especially interested in "that guy von Bülow." I generally counter with equally sage advice about how to improve the Celtics' fast break or rebounding game. We both really believe that we know what we're talking about, and Red is probably right.

I almost never miss a playoff game, and I certainly didn't want to miss this classic matchup. But I knew that I would have to be in Providence as soon as the jury rendered its verdict. Judge Grande, obviously not a true-green Celtics fan, required the jurors to deliberate over Sunday. (My suggestion was that the jurors should be provided a VCR and be able to watch the game on a five-minute delay—to assure that any news report about the trial would be edited out.)

The game was to begin at 3:30 P.M. The deliberations were scheduled to start at 2:00 P.M., so that jurors could attend morning church. (Claus and Andrea Reynolds barely missed running into several of the Catholic jurors who attended a later service at the same church.)

After consulting with several knowledgeable observers in Providence who were sympathetic to my plight, I concluded that a verdict early on Sunday afternoon was very unlikely. I calculated the distance from Boston Garden to the Providence courthouse as about fifty minutes, donned my Celtic-green rooting shirt, packed a suit in the backseat of my car, brought a small TV to the game and took my chances. Every five minutes I would tune in to the Providence stations to hear if a verdict was imminent. I took pains to tell Red, before the game, that if he saw me racing out during the third quarter, it was not for a lack of faith in the green bouncing back, but rather because a verdict was coming down.

But there was only one verdict that afternoon. The Lakers trounced the home-court favorites by a score of 111 to 100. Amid sad good-byes to the fans in our section—"winter friends," we called them, because we never saw each other except during the season— I went home to wait out the other verdict.

Within minutes of my return home, Claus called. "The word around the courthouse is that the verdict will be in tomorrow morning," he told me with an air of certainty. "And I really want you to be there," he insisted. "Not so much as my parachute, though you certainly are that, but to be part of whatever verdict is rendered. You have been through this with me longer and more supportively than anyone outside my family and closest friends. Neither Cosima nor Andrea will be in the courtroom tomorrow. I want you there."

I said I would be there and made plans to drive down early in the morning with my son Jamin, who had assisted me in various aspects of the case, from researching newspaper accounts of the Gilbert Jackson murder, to witnessing meetings with David Marriott, to collating and delivering copies of the appellate brief.

During the drive down, we found ourselves taking part in precisely the kind of mythology and speculation that trial lawyers nervously engage in to pass the time before a verdict. "It's too soon," I worried, noting that the jury had deliberated only about ten hours.

"But remember the first trial," Jamin reminded me. "That jury took six days, and look what they did."

"I don't like the questions," I grumbled. "Why did they want to hear Maria again? That's the soap-opera part of the case. If they focus on that, it's bad for Claus."

"I still think he should have taken the witness stand," Jamin complained. He had always advocated that course in our family disputes.

"That's why you're going to law school for three years," I twitted him. "To learn something about how trials work. There was no way Claus could have taken the witness stand once the decision was made to go entirely with a medical defense. Maybe *that* was the wrong decision, but once it was made the die was cast."

"But when lawyers cast the die wrong, it's their clients who die," Jamin quipped. "That's why I'm not going to practice criminal law." Jamin, who had just been admitted to Yale Law School, was looking forward to a career in government service.

We arrived at the Providence courthouse just as the jury was filing in for their morning instructions preceding their deliberations. I looked at each juror as he or she sauntered past the defendant. Claus put on a half-smile. But not one of the jurors looked at Claus. Most of them had their eyes down in the direction of the wooden floor. Some looked in the direction of the judge. This was not a jury that was trying to comfort the defendant.

As soon as the jurors were seated, Judge Grande told them to go back to the jury room to continue working. She advised one juror that her husband had called and another that his personal matter had been dealt with. And then they were off again, to determine whether Claus von Bülow would spend the rest of his days on this earth as a free man, deemed innocent of any crime, or as a guilty man sentenced to spend the remainder of his life behind bars—or worse!

Claus and his lawyers went back to the small room assigned to us. It was a stuffy office with no amenities and few comforts, which usually served as the chambers for one of the judges. In Rhode Island there was little judicial grandeur behind the pomp of the courtroom.

While we waited, Claus and I kibitzed with each other. Despite his stern exterior, Claus von Bülow is something of a clown. (The image is a difficult one to assimilate at first.) He loves silly jokes, especially puns. He also delights in telling jokes on himself. Throughout the case, he was always the first one to tell me the perverse Claus joke then making the rounds. ("What do you call fear of insulin? Claustrophobia." "What do you give a wife who has everything for Christmas? An injection of insulin.")

In a futile effort to keep his mind off the jury's deliberations, I took the courthouse menu and started a silly word game with Claus. Every item had to be given a legal-sounding name. So the beef patty was named the "Warren Burger" (after the Chief Justice). The hot dog became a "Felix Frankfurter" (after the late Justice). The roast beef was a "Brandeis Beef" (after the famous "Brandeis brief" developed by its namesake). The soft drink had to be "Lord Coke" (even though the famous British barrister pronounced "Coke" as "Cook"). Judge Learned Hand gave his name to the ham sandwich ("Learned Ham"), and Lord Bacon became part of the club sandwich. (Several judges I knew qualified for the turkey part, but we decided that in the spirit of good humor we would only dub the food with positive appellations.)

As we were finishing our silly list, the bailiff announced that the jury had arrived at a verdict. Pursuant to a previously made agreement with the media, the lawyers and the judge, there would be a fifteen-minute delay in reading the verdict so that the press and the lawyers could all scurry back from wherever they were spending the waiting time and be in the courtroom for the dramatic "opening of the envelope."

These were going to be the hardest fifteen minutes. Claus asked me to come with him into a small room off the side of the lawyers' room to "talk for a minute."

"I want to thank you *before* we learn the verdict," he said in a very solemn tone. "You know that none of this would be possible without you and your team. Nobody thought I would win the appeal and a new trial. Only you had faith."

He paused and then he said: "I had to say this now, because if I lose I won't be in much of a mood to thank anyone. And I would feel terrible not thanking you, because if it weren't for you and your team, I wouldn't be here today with a second chance."

I tried to correct him by insisting that it was his own innocence that was the single most important factor in persuading the judges to give him a second chance, but he cut me off. "Now look, Alan," he said quite pedantically, "I've read *The Best Defense* and I know that innocence has very little to do with results in the American legal system. It was your persistence, your doggedness, your energy, your team."

It was no time to try to explain to Claus that he had misunderstood the thrust of my book. That although some innocent defendants do end up in prison—and certainly some guilty ones do not—innocence weighs very heavily, even in the appellate process where it's not supposed to. I thanked Claus for his confidence in me and told him that I thought the signs looked good for an acquittal. "The only thing I can promise you is that there won't be a hung jury. They weren't out long enough for that."

As I was leaving the room, Claus called after me in a soft voice: "Alan, just one more thing. If we lose, are you ready to make a bail application?"

It was a serious question. Tom Puccio overheard it and quickly said: "If the jury says guilty, then it's all in your hands, Alan."

I reassured Claus that none of us thought it would come to that, but that I was ready to make a bail application and confident that it would be granted. What I did not tell Claus—the *only* thing I didn't tell him during the entire course of our more than three-year legal odyssey—was that I had actually prepared a written bail application, just in case. It would be time enough to tell him if and when the jury uttered the dreaded word "guilty." This was one time to be somewhat reassuring.

Claus emerged from the lawyers' room, lit a cigarette and wandered toward another room where the prosecutors and state police were awaiting the verdict. They seemed nearly as tense as Claus. Although their fates—existences—were not in the hands of the jurors, many months of their lives had been devoted to attempting to prove Claus guilty. The professional career of Officer Reise had been intertwined with Claus's life over the past five years. Although attorneys DeSisto and Gemma had come into the case more recently, their involvement was also intense. Careers, reputations and deep feelings would be affected by the words pronounced in the next few minutes. It was entirely fitting that Claus von Bülow and his prosecutors would be spending those last minutes in the same room, sharing a cigarette, exchanging niceties, even laughing at one another's nervous attempts at tension-breaking humor.

Another announcement. It was time.

Everyone filed into the courtroom in an orderly procession: Claus first, followed by his lawyers and then the prosecutors. After we had taken our seats, the press was let in along with the few members of the general public who had been lucky enough to get seats to this always-sold-out soap. Then came the judge. And finally, the jurors.

This time it was for keeps. Claus, surrounded by his lawyers, was all alone. Everyone else but him would leave the courtroom with their status unchanged. It was like waiting for the doctor to come back after conducting a biopsy. Your family may be with you, but you feel alone, knowing that when they wheel you into the operating room, they take only you.

This time everyone's eyes were riveted on the jurors as they entered. Within minutes they too would go home to the anonymity of their private lives. Tomorrow they would be ordinary citizens powerless to affect much of what mattered to them. But today they had more power over Claus von Bülow than the President of the United States. As they filed into the courtroom past the defense table, everyone in the room noticed the same thing: not a single juror looked at Claus. Everyone must have been thinking the same thoughts, but no one uttered a word. There seemed to be widespread communication by silence.

Then, as the jurors entered the jury box, I noticed one of them sneaking a glance over in the direction of the defense table. After some hesitation, she looked at Claus. He was looking down. It was too late to influence anybody or anything. Now he was turning inward, praying to whomever he believed might still answer his prayers. The juror quickly looked away, as if she had been caught violating a private moment.

The solemnity of the occasion was broken by the bailiff shouting, with his gruff Providence accent, "Hey, Charlie, quiet 'em down." It was also broken by a woman reporter leaning over to Claus and whispering, "What is your last word before they speak?" Claus gave her a steely cold look of disapproval and raised the middle finger of his left hand, but then—with a half-smile—began to scratch the bridge of his nose with his raised finger, as if to add an element of ambiguity to an unambiguous gesture.

Then the clerk asked the foreman of the jury, "On the charge that the defendant committed on December 27, 1979, the crime of assault with intent to murder, how do you find, guilty or not guilty?"

Without pausing even for dramatic effect, the foreman responded, "Not guilty."

Upon hearing those magic words, Claus allowed his rigid composure to drop just a bit. There was some murmuring from the audience. Claus turned slightly in their direction, pursed his lips, placed a finger near them and sternly let out with a "Shh." I immediately thought of a patrician opera lover, seeking to quiet the members of the claque that was beginning to applaud its favorite diva before the aria was quite over. His action seemed so out of place, yet so quintessentially Claus von Bülow.

The aria was not entirely over. There was still the second verse:

Count II, the stronger count, the one on which the medical evidence was more solidly based. The clerk again inquired. This time there was a slight pause and then another "Not guilty."

I leaned over to touch Claus and whisper, "Congratulations. Now the world knows you are an innocent man." He heaved a sigh of such relief that it seemed to release five years of pent-up tension. He put his head down on the table for an instant, as if to hide a tear, and then lifted it, not even bothering to brush the tear away. It was the first time in all those years that he had been a truly free person. Andrea Reynolds, who entered the courtroom for the first time after the jury announced it had reached a verdict, embraced Claus.

Hardly anyone paid attention as the judge recited the legally required formulas of freedom: dismissing the jury, entering a formal order of acquittal, returning the bail, thanking everyone.

Claus could now leave the courtroom, the courthouse, Rhode Island, the United States, and go anywhere he pleased. I could throw away the thousands upon thousands of briefs, memos, notes and other papers that cluttered my office and my mind. To a defendant, acquittal means freedom. To a defense attorney, it means not having to save all the documents. Since there is no appeal from an acquittal, the case of Claus von Bülow was finally over.*

Claus von Bülow first called his daughter, Cosima. He then met with the press to express "gratitude to my lawyers." Above all, "I'm grateful to my attorneys. It's their work." Later, he and Andrea dropped in on a farewell party the exhausted jurors were giving themselves.

The prosecutors complained bitterly, but off the record, about Judge Grande's handling of the case, suggesting that she was motivated by "ambition for higher office."

As Judge Grande bid her final farewell to the out-of-town lawyers, she said, "You're always welcome here"; then she added with a smile, "But only if Jack Sheehan is with you." The Rhode Island Shuffle never stops.

---

* In a preposterous publicity grab, the office of the Manhattan District Attorney—the office Richard Kuh once headed—announced that if Sunny von Bülow were to die in New York, it would be a "brand-new ball game," and that office would consider trying von Bülow for murder. Any first-year law student knows that New York would have no power to do so, since all the alleged criminal acts took place in Rhode Island. If A shoots B in Rhode Island and then B is taken to a New York hospital, where he eventually dies, it is clear that no crime has been committed in New York by the transfer of the body into that state.

Part
IV

THE AFTERMATH: RESIDUES AND REVENGE

19

Jury versus Jury

The day after the jury rendered its verdict heard round the world, one of the jurors—a middle-aged factory supervisor named Rose Carlos—gave the public a rare glimpse into the secret deliberations of the von Bülow jury. "One of the deciding factors," she told an interviewer, "was the evidence of the maid and others about the discovery of the black bag." She explained that the prosecutors had tried to get the jury to believe that Maria and Alex found insulin and syringes in the bag and didn't tell anyone about it! "This is her son and he did nothing. I don't buy it. . . . Just when the maid, when she claims she found insulin, she went to [Mrs. von Bülow's] son . . . This is his mother and [he] did nothing? I don't buy it. I personally don't buy it. No way. He just glanced at this thing . . . ?"

Another juror agreed that there was "so much doubt." The prosecution's story "just did not hang together." It was "disjointed." And an alternate juror also said that she had doubts about Maria's account of finding insulin in the black bag.

When my team heard and read the jury interviews, we felt vindicated. The material we had won on appeal—the Kuh notes—really had made a difference. Maria Schrallhammer's testimony had been a decisive factor at both trials. At the first trial, without the benefit of her original interview, the jury had believed her entirely consistent story. At the second trial they apparently disbelieved her far more self-contradictory account, especially her claim that she found insulin, showed it to Alex and then neither one ever mentioned it again until after the insulin theory began to emerge. That was one of the deciding factors at the second trial. And the jurors' response to it was "No way."

I wondered what Richard Kuh was thinking now about his representation that his files contained not a single "scrap of paper" which "might even arguably be viewed as exculpatory." Kuh's scraps of paper might have made the critical difference between a verdict of guilty and not guilty.

The man who was the beneficiary of the not-guilty verdict certainly believed that the Kuh notes had made a difference. In an interview on the day of the verdict, Claus von Bülow was asked, "Do you think Maria made up the fact that she saw the insulin bottle [in the black bag]?" This was his response:

I will answer that question by referring you to the Kuh notes. . . . The Kuh notes were an absolutely vital element in discrediting the earlier alleged sighting, the November, December sightings (when Miss Schrallhammer said she saw insulin, needles and syringes and other drugs in the black bag). And that's why Kuh resisted so strongly to handing them over. . . . I think one person's perception of preparation for trial is another person's coaching. But that is why the original notes are so important.

The second jury verdict also vindicated, in my view, the appellate process of review. All too often we hear the claim from the highest officers of our government that appellate courts throw out convictions on mere technicalities. That characterization was repeatedly placed upon the Rhode Island Supreme Court's reversal of Claus von Bülow's conviction. The Washington *Post*, the Philadelphia *Inquirer*, the New York *Times* and *People* magazine, among others, described the von Bülow reversal as based "on technical grounds," technicalities or "procedural niceties."

The word "technicality" implies form without substance, rule without relevance, result without purpose. It suggests that the courts are reversing the conviction of an undoubtedly guilty defendant in order to assure compliance with some abstract principle that bears no relation to the fairness of the particular trial or the possibility that an innocent person may have been convicted.

Sometimes that may be true. When a conviction is reversed—and relatively few are—on the ground that indisputable evidence of guilt was obtained in violation of the Fourth Amendment, the purpose underlying that reversal is not to cast doubt on the guilt of the defendant. In that kind of case, the purpose of the reversal is to send a message to law enforcement officials about *their* conduct that unless corrected may affect *other* citizens who may be innocent.

But in a large number of appellate reversals—I would venture to suggest a majority—the judges are, either expressly or implicitly, reflecting some real concern about the guilt of the defendant and the correctness of the verdict. The Rhode Island Supreme Court's reversal of Claus von Bülow's conviction plainly reflected such a concern. As the majority opinion itself had recognized, the "selective use of the Kuh notes" cannot be said "to have promoted the interests of society or defendant in reaching a fair or accurate resolution of the question of guilt or innocence." Our access to those notes at the second trial certainly helped to present a fuller and fairer story.

Although the Rhode Island Supreme Court also reversed the conviction on the ground that the state police had failed to obtain a warrant for their scientific examination of certain pills found in the black bag, I am confident that the court must have been influenced by more fundamental evidentiary doubts surrounding the mysterious black bag: its questionable sightings, its sloppy seizure, its doubtful handling—points we had hammered home during the appeal.

Throughout the appellate process, we had emphasized that if given a new trial, we would be able to prove Claus von Bülow's innocence. In the end, we succeeded in raising a reasonable doubt about his guilt. That is all a defendant can ever do under our system. Indeed, the jurors who were interviewed seemed to have more than merely a reasonable doubt about the prosecution's case; they simply didn't buy it. Judge Grande, who had spoken to the jurors after their verdict, commented: "This is a jury who clearly hasn't had any trouble coming to a decision." The jury foreman, while declining comment on the merits of the case, said he had known there would be a quick verdict.

In the end, the second von Bülow trial was not even close; the defense won a decisive and unequivocal victory. The paradox is that the first trial was also not close; the prosecution won a decisive and unequivocal victory back then. The interesting question is why two trials of the same man for the same crime should have produced two such dramatically and decisively different outcomes.

Critics of the second verdict point to the evidence that was admitted at the first trial, but excluded from the second: the banker's testimony about Claus's financial motive; Claus's "cover-his-ass letter" to Dr. Gailitis; evidence that Claus had injected his wife with vitamins back in 1969—as well as the speculative medical testimony about scratches and a possible struggle. At least as important, however, was the evidence suppressed at the first trial but admitted at the second: the failure of Maria and Alex to mention syringes and insulin to attorney Kuh at the initial interview; the evidence of a plan to buy off Claus; Alex's insistence on not losing Clarendon Court under any circumstances; Dr. Gailitis's suppressed medical opinion that the coma he witnessed was not caused by insulin. Also important was the medical and forensic evidence gathered after the first trial for the new-trial motion and introduced at the second trial: expert testimony that the needle was never injected into Sunny; that Sunny's insulin-level readings were not reliable; and that several of the world's leading authorities were of the medical opinion that neither of Sunny's comas had been caused by insulin. It is fair to conclude that the dramatic difference in the outcomes of the two trials was more a function of what the second jury heard and saw than what was kept from it. Indeed, Judge Grande, who heard *all* the evidence—even that which she ultimately kept from the jury—has apparently been telling her judicial colleagues that the case was not even close: "He simply didn't do it. It wasn't even a close case." To put it another way, the second jury found Claus von Bülow "not guilty by reason of innocence."

Justice is as much a process as it is a result. The appellate phase of the process worked in this case. I believe that, on balance, the second trial told a more complete story and was fairer than the first. Whether it produced a more accurate result will continue to be debated, especially in light of Claus von Bülow's decision not to present his account to the jury. Under our system, Claus need not ever tell *his* story. Thus far he has answered only selected questions.* Perhaps someday he will decide to tell his complete account. When he does so, it will be because he chose to. It will not be under compulsion, under oath or subject to cross-examination.

I will pay close attention to Claus's account if and when he tells it, because although I believe he is innocent, I also suspect we have

---

* Von Bülow did answer questions put to him by the Rhode Island police prior to his indictment. The state succeeding in keeping the contents of that interview from the jury, on the ground that it was self-serving hearsay.

never been told the whole story. Under our system, the legal story is almost never the whole story. Some of the juiciest parts end up on the cutting-room floor. And that is the right way. When government judges people, it must employ rules of relevance, of privacy and of probity. The result is a film edited and cut drastically from the vast footage of real life. Only Claus von Bülow has seen all the footage concerning him. And the law imposes on him no obligation to let the rest of us in on what really happened on those two days in Newport. Like so many other legal mysteries, the law will never resolve all of the doubts in the minds of those who still wonder "Who done it?" or whether anything criminal was done at all. As we argued in our appeal, "the adjudication of guilt in our system" is neither a "multiple-choice test" nor "a true-or-false contest between prosecution and defense." It is an imperfect mechanism designed to determine whether a defendant shall be convicted of the crimes charged against him.

Every legal system has to decide—on the basis of probabilities, not certainties—what to do with persons accused of crime. In some countries, it is enough if there is a suspicion of wrongdoing. In others the defendant's guilt can be established by a preponderance of the evidence. In the United States the defendant cannot be convicted unless the state proves his guilt beyond a reasonable doubt.

This rule means that American law requires some *factually* guilty defendants to be set free even if the proof establishes that it is more likely than not that they committed the crime.

Although our legal system proudly proclaims its commitment to this principle of super-certainty, many Americans have difficulty understanding why we go so far in resolving doubts in favor of those accused of crimes. What about the victims? Wouldn't it be better for a few innocent defendants to go to jail so that some innocent *victims* might be saved from suffering?

But history teaches that countries that trample the rights of those accused of crime tend also to ignore the rights of persons victimized by crime; and that countries that respect the rights of the accused also promote the rights of victims. The manner in which a government treats *all* of its citizens—whether victims of injustice or victims of crime—is what distinguishes democratic nations from repressive ones. And the principles of reasonable doubt and due process of law are among the hallmarks of a true democracy.

Resolving doubts in favor of the accused may seem a high price to pay for democracy. But would we really want to live in a country where any person could be imprisoned on the mere whim or suspicion of those in power?*

---

* The Attorney General of the United States, Edwin Meese, seems to think so. He has recently explained that "you don't have many suspects who are innocent of a crime. That's contradictory. If a person is innocent of a crime, then he is not a suspect."

20

Suitable for Framing

From the very beginning, the cloud of a possible frame-up has hung over the von Bülow case. During the first trial, Sheehan suggested to the press that "Kuh—or his overeager investigator—may have planted the needle with the insulin on it." Kuh denied the charge, calling it "outrageous." The investigator "declined comment." In his closing argument at the first trial, prosecutor Famiglietti rhetorically invited the jurors to "rush back" with a verdict of acquittal if they believed the defendant was "framed and set up" or the contents of the black bag "planted." The first jury obviously rejected any possibility of a frame-up.

Shortly after I entered the case I began to suspect that evidence might have been tampered with in an effort to enhance the likelihood of conviction. The more I learned about the case, the more my suspicions deepened that we might be dealing with a frame-up of an unusual kind.

I surmised that various members of the von Bülow household honestly, but erroneously, believed that Claus had tried to kill Sunny. They also believed that he was far too clever to be caught, and that he would get away with the second attempt as he had with the first. Sunny's stepfather, Russell Aitken—a big-game hunter who Claus believed might be capable of a frame-up—summarized to Dominick Dunne, a reporter for *Vanity Fair*, the mixture of contempt and fear that Sunny's family felt for Claus after the second coma when he described Claus as "an extremely dangerous man because he's a Cambridge-educated con man with legal training. He is totally amoral, greedy as a wolverine, cold-blooded as a snake. And I apologize to the snake."

I came to believe it was possible that in order to prevent what was believed would be a gross injustice, someone may have tampered

with the evidence—physical evidence and/or memory evidence.
Items may have been repositioned; events may have been reconstructed after the fact; memories may have been enhanced. In a
case like this, the slightest changes could make the difference
between a scenario suggesting guilt and one suggesting innocence.
For example, if it was the medicine vial containing Inderal rather
than the vial containing Dalmane that was found in the black bag,
then the bag was more likely used by Sunny than Claus. If Maria
saw a bottle of liquid Tagamet rather than insulin—they re-
semble each other closely—then there may never have been insulin
in the bag, even if Maria was not deliberately lying.

The most difficult question is whether the reconstructions, if
they did occur, were spontaneous, unconscious and individual, on
the one hand; or deliberate, premeditated and conspiratorial, on
the other. The most dramatic piece of evidence bearing on this
issue is the needle encrusted with solution: Was it deliberately
dipped and planted? Or was it found the way Alex and the investigator testified? There is certainly some evidence supporting
the "plant" theory: the testimony of the locksmith that the investigator who went into Claus's closet to look for the black bag
emerged saying "It's not there"; the forensic evidence that the
needle was probably dipped, and almost certainly never injected
into Sunny; the strange sequence of memory reflected in the Kuh
notes.

If Claus von Bülow was, in fact, framed by someone who believed
he was guilty, this would constitute one of the most remarkable
frame-ups in the annals of crime. I had never heard of such a case.

Nevertheless, the benevolent frame-up theory—tampering with
evidence to help convict a man believed to be guilty—eventually became my working hypothesis, my conceptual framework, for winning
the case. Whether or not we could ever prove a frame-up, the possibility that it had occurred provided a coherent theory against
which to test our new evidence. It led me to predict what the
Kuh notes would show even before I saw them, and it led me to
have confidence that if Claus were granted a new trial—a second
chance—we would win.

A clever frame-up can rarely be established conclusively. Since
the object of a frame-up is generally to plant convincing evidence
of guilt, the discovery of such evidence under questionable circumstances is often a "knife that cuts both ways," (or, as my son Elon

paraphrased Dostoyevsky's metaphor, "a needle with two points").
It could support either a theory of guilt or a theory of frame-up.
An intriguing vignette following the von Bülow acquittal demonstrates this paradox. Shortly after the verdict, Dominick Dunne
reported in *Vanity Fair* magazine that while the jury was out deliberating, Alex and Ala invited him to stay at Clarendon Court and
inspect it for the article he was writing. The stepchildren led him to
the "attempted-murder scene"—the bedroom where Sunny suffered
both her comas. This is what the writer claims he observed:

> On von Bülow's side of the bed is an old silver-framed photograph
> of him in a striking, almost noble pose. I opened a handsome box on
> his bed table. It was filled with cartridge shells. *Under the shells was
> a used syringe.* [Emphasis added].

If this is true, then what the writer observed was perhaps the
most important piece of evidence since the discovery of the black
bag. Remember that Judge Grande had excluded all references
to Claus injecting himself and Sunny with vitamins back in 1969,
in Majorca. She ruled that this episode—some ten years before the
first coma—was too "remote in time" from the crimes charged. If
the prosecutors had known there was "a used syringe" in Claus's
cartridge box, they would almost certainly have been able to introduce that fact *and* the Majorca episode. Moreover, they would
have had the used syringe tested for residues.

What is the likelihood, however, that this highly relevant piece
of evidence could have escaped the probing investigation of the
police, the prosecutors, Maria, Alex and the private investigator—
all of whom examined the "crime scene" with care after the second
coma? The finding of this used syringe leads to one of two possible
conclusions: first, that the Rhode Island police and prosecutors
were unbelievably negligent in conducting their investigations; or
second, that the syringe was *placed* in Claus's box sometime after
the authorities completed their investigations. Since that time, however, Claus has not been permitted to stay in Clarendon Court. So
if the used syringe was placed there, Claus could not have done
it. That leaves two possibilities: either it was inadvertently left or
hidden there by a user of syringes other than Claus; or it was
planted there precisely in order to have the writer—who was led
into the bedroom by Alex and Ala—"discover it." We will never

know for certain which, if any, of these scenarios is true. But here is an example of evidence that could support either a theory of guilt or a theory of frame-up—or even a theory of trying to plant evidence against a man believed to be guilty.

The case for a frame-up cannot be proved beyond a reasonable doubt. But that does not mean it didn't happen. "Frame-up" is a matter of degree, ranging from individual falsification of testimony to tampering with physical evidence to a full-blown conspiracy to convict an innocent man.* Even if there was no frame-up, that does not, of course, mean Claus von Bülow was guilty or that the second jury did not render a just verdict. Paradoxically, even if there was a frame-up, that would not necessarily mean that Claus was innocent. A frame-up—of any degree—always distorts the *process* of justice. It does not always distort the *ends* of justice.

Whether the ends of justice were served in the case of Claus von Bülow is a question that will be debated for many years. Since no one but Claus knows the answer to that question, speculation has run rampant as to what actually happened. Among the theories I have been offered by the cognoscenti—in addition to the two obvious possibilities: total innocence or total guilt—are the following:

The Frame-up Theories

• Claus is innocent, but his stepchildren really believed that he was guilty and that he would get away with it because he is so clever; so they tampered with the evidence in a sincere but misguided effort to see that justice was done. They framed an innocent man whom they mistakely believed to be guilty.
• A variant on the above is that Claus is, in fact, guilty; but the stepchildren tampered with the evidence because they believed that he would otherwise get away with it—they framed a guilty man.

The "Two Comas, Two Causes" Theories

• Claus is innocent of the first coma, which was caused by a combination of Sunny's reactive hypoglycemia and overindulgence in sweets, alcohol and pills; but when Claus learned that Sunny was afflicted with reactive hypoglycemia he then decided to inject her with insulin. Under this theory, the state made the mistake of trying him

---

* Ironically, Alex also claims that he was the victim of an attempted frame-up—by David Marriott. A New York Court of Appeals judge once characterized some police as being tempted to "tamper with the truth."

for the first coma and staking its credibility on the highly speculative medical evidence relating to the first coma.*

• Claus did engage in unhusbandly conduct sitting around watching Sunny almost die during her first coma from a self-administered drug overdose (as Alexandra testified), but was not at all involved in her second coma.

The Drug-Use Theories: "High Society"

• Claus did, in fact, inject his wife with a combination of drugs; but he did it with her acquiescence as part of their routine joint drug indulgence, or as part of some exotic drug-sex adventure.

• Sunny was a secret drug user (as Capote swore) who was, in fact, obtaining drugs from an outside source, but not necessarily from David Marriott. Marriott could have found out about this from his drug friends and concocted the part about his own involvement.

The Alexandra-Suicide Theory

• Claus and/or Alexandra Isles deliberately or unconsciously tried to drive Sunny to suicide by flaunting their affair; Alexandra's delivery of love letters and presents to the von Bülow apartment just prior to Sunny's aspirin overdose and final coma are cited as evidence of Alexandra's complicity.†

The Deliberate Coma Theory

• Claus did not try to kill his wife but rather to put her into a coma so that he could control her wealth without having to marry Alexandra. It would require unbelievable medical sophistication to produce such a precise result.

The possibilities and variations are almost limitless, some of them involving Maria, the stepchildren and other equally bizarre combinations. There is even a theory concerning a mystery man

---

* Apparently the state had originally decided to charge von Bülow only with causing the second coma, but Dr. Cahill's near-certainty that insulin had also caused the first coma persuaded Famiglietti to charge both crimes.

† We had learned— although this story was never introduced at the trial—that several hours before the aspirin overdose, Alexandra Isles had delivered to 960 Fifth Avenue, in an open unmarked shopping basket, a collection of the love letters and presents Claus had sent her over the past two years. The head doorman in the building confirmed bringing this package, which was not marked specifically for delivery either to Claus or Sunny, up to the von Bülow apartment at a time when Sunny was at home, but Claus was not. Just before Sunny's final trip to Newport, Alexandra sent her Christmas presents for Claus over to the apartment. There was a stipulation at trial that Sunny never learned of this second delivery. These calculated and peevish actions by the scorned mistress may fall under the general heading "you do some crazy things" when you're in love.

named Paul Molitor, who lived in the carriage house at Clarendon
Court, and who apparently committed suicide shortly after the first
trial. Dominick Dunne reported:

> . . . a young man named Paul Molitor, was hired by Claus von Bülow
> in 1979 from the China Trade Museum in Massachusetts to work for
> the Newport Preservation Society, of which von Bülow was then an
> officer. He beat out 120 other applicants for the job. Shortly after his
> arrival in Newport, von Bülow invited him to move into the carriage
> house on the grounds of Clarendon Court. Extremely personable, he
> soon became a popular extra man at Newport dinner parties. He was
> in residence at the time of Sunny von Bülow's second coma, and his
> friends recall that he was extremely fearful of having to testify at the
> first trial. He was not called to the stand, but one night six months
> later he jumped off the Newport Bridge. A persistent rumor in the
> resort colony is that he was pushed. He was wearing a dinner jacket.
> Some claim his feet were bound.

The truth may lie in none of the above scenarios, but in some
mundane series of coincidences that reflect the muted grey of in-
difference rather than the clear white of total innocence or the deep
black of unmitigated guilt. The blunt instrument of the law is rarely
refined enough to discern subtle shades of intent, motivation or
character.

In Chekhov's theater, in Conan Doyle's stories and in modern
television, there is always an unambiguous resolution: guilty or
innocent, true or false, murder or suicide. But in the real-life drama
that is law, doubts—reasonable and otherwise—often remain.
Perhaps that is why the surrealistic and somewhat nihilistic approach embodied in the classic film *Rashomon* may be among the
most realistic presentations of the law's dilemma in seeking to resolve problems of life and death.

In this book I have tried to present the various stories that com-
prise the legal portion of the vast matrix. In presenting that
important part, I am reminded of the famous quip of Justice
Oliver Wendell Holmes, Jr., to a youthful critic: "This is a court of
law, young man, not a court of justice."

The court of criminal law has spoken with finality in the case
of Claus von Bülow. I believe that it has spoken honestly. Because
of the human fallibility of all the participants in any legal process,
the court of justice rarely speaks, however, with the certainty of a
heavenly tribunal.

21

Money Talks,
but Who Listens?

Inexorably tied into the question of whether Claus von Bülow received justice is the role that money played in his case—and in the American justice system in general.

The case against Claus von Bülow may well have been the most expensive prosecution in history against a single individual charged with a crime of violence. Various estimates have been given of the cost, but they have all been based on speculation. I know how much the defense lawyers were paid, and I have a pretty good idea— based on information disclosed during the pretrial hearings—of how much the private prosecutors were paid by the Aitken and von Auersperg families. It is not difficult to calculate what the state of Rhode Island must have spent between 1981 and 1985 on salaries, witnesses, juror costs and other expenses directly attributable to the trials and appeal of Claus von Bülow.

On the basis of conservative extrapolation from facts I know, it is fair to estimate that the cost of the case was somewhere between $3.2 million and $3.8 million altogether; a rough price tag of $3.5 million would not be far off base. Slightly more was spent by the defense than by the prosecution, but that is because the prosecution has access to more free services—or more precisely, services on which it is difficult to place a price tag. Moreover, state salaries are lower than private fees and so the same service will cost a defendant considerably more than it will cost the state. After these differences are accounted for, the person-hours and services utilized by the defense and prosecution were approximately the same.

Nor were the lawyers' hourly fees out of line in this case. Again, I know what most of the defense attorneys received, and their hourly fees were on the middle or middle-low side for this kind of case. Lawyers' fees for white-collar and corporate cases range between $200 and $350 an hour for the most experienced and highly regarded attorneys. (The fees in drug cases are often considerably higher.) The fees in this case generally ran toward the lower end of that range. And because so much of the work was done by students, who received $7–10 an hour rather than the $50–$75 an hour paid to young lawyers right out of school, the totals were kept down.

Throughout the case, two questions were raised. The first was how Claus von Bülow came up with that kind of money; the second, which I was asked by Ted Koppel on *Nightline* and numerous other commentators, was whether one has to be a millionaire to get justice in the United States. Put another way, could a poor defendant obtain the kind of second chance von Bülow got in this case?

As to the first question, people often forget that although it was Sunny who brought the enormous wealth into the von Bülow marriage, Claus was a wealthy man in his own right by the time he married at age thirty-nine. Nor did he have to spend any of his own money during the marriage, since Sunny's wealth supported the entire family. And Claus was apparently a real tightwad when it came to family expenditures. He repeatedly introduced economy moves to cut down on the penchant for lavish spending by other family members. I observed Claus's penny-pinching during the case; while doling out checks for enormous sums for lawyers, experts and court transcripts, he would always look for ways to cut corners on unnecessary extravagances. And he would show great self-satisfaction when he had saved a few dollars.

Back in July 1981, after his indictment, Claus sold many of his personal possessions—paintings, sculptures and the like—to help raise money for his defense. He bargained hard with his lawyers to keep legal costs down. He also borrowed money from some friends, both to help raise the million-dollar bail and to finance the appeal and the new trial.

Robert Lenzner, a writer who interviewed J. Paul Getty, Jr., has quoted the billionaire as acknowledging that he had loaned Claus one million dollars for his bail and defense:

> The fact is that a friend needed help and I was able to give it . . . It's no heroic thing . . . I am certainly not going to ask for it back. I have always told him I wanted it to be applied to the legal bills, otherwise he'd be broke.

Getty regarded Claus as a "close friend," and categorically believes in his innocence:

> Of course he was innocent . . . the children of [Sunny's] first marriage [Ala Kneissl and Alexander von Auersperg] and that mother—evil, really evil. They've never liked him and didn't want him to get any-thing. They staged the whole thing . . . Do you leave little black bags around? Who leaves little black bags loaded with evidence, incrimi-nating evidence, around?"

One reason why Getty may have been particularly sympathetic to Claus's plight was that his own wife, Talitha, had died of an apparent drug overdose and he, Getty, had reportedly been under some suspicion of negligent homicide following the tragedy. Even-tually, he was cleared of all suspicion.

In the end, no one—except Claus himself—can know for certain the precise sources of all the funds he expended—well in excess of the million-dollar Getty loan—on the enormously expensive defense he mounted. But he was certainly *forced* to raise it, because his very life was at stake and the resources on the other side were unlimited. While Claus von Bülow may have been able to raise somewhat more than a million and a half dollars in an effort to prove his innocence, the Aitkens and von Auerspergs had at their disposal hundreds of millions of dollars. And they were determined to prove that Claus had attempted to murder their beloved Sunny.

In addition to financing the original investigation—searches, lab tests, legal memoranda, witness interviews, investigative reports—the family took primary responsibility for preparing the medical witnesses. They hired, with no expense to the prosecution, an eminent law professor and author of the standard textbook *Law, Medicine and Forensic Science*, William Curran. Curran helped select, interview and rehearse most of the state's medical witnesses. The family lawyers also prescreened and prepared many of the state's nonmedical witnesses.

Nor was the family's money limited to directly funding much of the state's case. It was also used as leverage to prevent Claus from obtaining support for his case. Several potential witnesses told me that they had been threatened with social ostracism if they in any way supported—or testified for—Claus. As if to show they meant business, the Aitkens cut Cosima—the only child of Sunny and Claus—completely out of Mrs. Aitken's will specifically be-cause the sixteen-year-old girl stuck with her father during his legal ordeal (while still maintaining a deep love for her comatose mother). This act of disloyalty by young Cosima cost her approximately $30 million—and earned her half-sister, and -brother, Ala and Alex, an extra $15 million each. Mrs. Aitken died after the first trial, leaving Cosima disinherited. To her enormous credit, Cosima refused to be bought and remained loyal to her father throughout.

There can be little doubt that no family in recent history has ever used more private money and influence to assist a state in bringing public charges against a defendant. Claus von Bülow had to do battle not only against a state prosecutor's office—a formidable enough opponent—but against the combined forces of a state and a family wealthy enough to *be* a small state. Moreover, a family— being private, and hence not bound by the constitutional constraints imposed on governments—could do things that no prosecutor could ever get away with: conduct searches without warrants, suppress exculpatory evidence, subtly threaten witnesses, hire a public relations agent, and engage in other acts which have not yet been—and because they were private, may never be—disclosed.

This case was unique, therefore, in its triangular nature: there were three sides—private prosecutor, state prosecutor, and defense —and two of them combined resources against the third.

In a case like this, the answer to the second question, whether a defendant must be a millionaire to obtain justice, seems clear: it *would* take a wealthy person to marshal sufficient resources to fight back against the combined resources of a family like Aitken– von Auersperg *and* a state. If the proverbial "butler" had been charged with injecting Sunny, there would be no way for him to have fought back effectively. Under our constitution, the state would have been required to provide the indigent butler with counsel. (If he did not meet the standards of indigency, he would first have been required to spend his meager funds on as much of a lawyer as he could afford. One notorious Boston judge used to tell defendants who had a hundred dollars, "Okay, go out and get yourself a hundred-dollar lawyer.")

The *manner* in which counsel is provided to indigent defendants varies enormously from state to state. Some states have excellent public defender systems, staffed by young, aggressive lawyers with first-rate legal backgrounds. Although they are generally paid rather poorly—in contrast with private lawyers—they earn about as much as their counterparts in the prosecutor's office (though the political stepping-stone often provided by prosecutors' offices can rarely be matched by public defenders.)

In the handful of states that really take seriously equal access to justice, the public defenders even have decent investigative facilities staffed by retired police and FBI personnel. Their budgets are, of course, limited and each office must allocate its resources fairly among the thousands of indigent defendants who require its services.

If our hypothetical butler-defendant had been indicted in one of these states, his legal team might have been able to put up a good uphill fight against the combined resources of a wealthy family and the state prosecutor's office. But even then, there would be no way for the butler to secure the expert testimony that the defense was able to pay for in the von Bülow case. Public defender budgets simply do not provide for flying world-class experts in from around the globe to dispute the world-class experts employed by the state and family in the von Bülow case. Moreover, even those experts who did not charge for their time would be far more reluctant to contribute their talents to an unpublicized case against an obscure defendant than they were to the most highly publicized case of the decade.

States and cities that do not have public defender systems often simply assign lawyers in private practice to defend indigent persons accused of crimes. The remuneration for representing an indigent defendant is often a minuscule fraction of what the lawyer could get in a "paying" case. The hourly rates are very low and, more important, there are often fixed maximum limits for an entire case. In a long, complicated case like von Bülow's, these fixed maximums would result in an appointed lawyer being compensated at the rate of pennies per hour. Not surprisingly, many lawyers run for the nearest exit when an appointing judge looks in their direction for a long trial. Again, if the case is a notorious one—a reputation-builder—lawyers may clamor for the opportunity to become involved. But if the case is a reputation-killer or merely an obscure one with no promise of reward, the desirability of spending a lot of uncompensated time diminishes to the vanishing point.

Moreover, even if an able lawyer were willing to become involved in a von Bülow–type "butler" case, the possibilities for securing necessary investigative and expert backing would be non-existent. Recently the United States Supreme Court ruled that if a criminal defendant has a bona fide claim to an insanity defense, the state must provide for some minimal degree of psychiatric evaluation to help him establish his claim. But that is still a far cry from the kind of massive medical defense John Hinckley's parents could afford to provide for him. Moreover, many defendants require investigators, ballistics experts, laboratory evaluation, accountants and other ancillary services that the state does not provide for the poor. For example, in the first von Bülow trial— though not in the second—the defense hired a social research firm that specializes in doing surveys of potential jurors to assist in the selection of a jury likely not to be unduly favorable to the prosecution—which many juries are. Some defense lawyers regard this kind of assistance as essential to counteract the advantages prosecutors typically enjoy in jury selection. An indigent defendant— indeed, anyone but a wealthy defendant—cannot afford such legal luxury.

The remarkable thing about American justice is how many indigent defendants do manage to receive adequate representation. When they do, it is often *despite*, certainly not because of, the system used by the state to provide representation. It is a credit to those lawyers who do not consider the checkbook the most important volume for a lawyer to read before going into court.

It is remarkable that whenever a wealthy defendant wins a case, there is a constant clamor about how unfair the system is. The system *is* unfair—not because the wealthy can sometimes obtain justice, but rather because too often the poor and middle class cannot. A wealthy person's acquittal should not be the occasion for demanding *fewer* resources for those who can afford them, but rather *greater* resources for those who cannot.

When U.S. Attorney General Edwin Meese asked the federal government to pay his lawyers' bills of $700,000, incurred in defending him against charges of impropriety in accepting loans from people who were later appointed to federal posts, the disgrace was not that Meese's lawyers billed at a rate of $250 per hour. They deserved and earned every penny of that for the excellent work they did. The scandal was that the same Attorney General Meese —at the very time he was demanding that the government pay $250 an hour for his lawyers—was insisting that the same government be limited to paying $75 an hour, with fixed maximums, for the defense of indigents, even those charged with far more serious violations.

In an angry column following Judge Needham's decision to grant von Bülow bail pending his appeal, Jeremiah Murphy of the Boston *Globe* railed against the double standard of justice for rich and poor. But his criticism was off the mark. It was not wrong for von Bülow to be out of prison while his case was reviewed and retried. It would have been wrong for him to remain confined during the three years required for his vindication. And it is equally wrong that some innocent people who can't afford to post bail are, in fact, kept in jail before their cases are considered by the appellate courts.

The American system of criminal justice, which surely is among the fairest in the world, does provide a double standard for rich and poor. Reform efforts should be directed, however, not at reducing the justice available for the rich, but at raising the standard of justice for all.

Several lawyers I know have the same cynical cartoon hanging in their offices. It shows a lawyer sitting behind his desk, asking a new client the pressing question: "Well, now, just how much justice can you afford?" Or as another cynical friend of mine put it: "Can you buy reasonable doubt for an unreasonable fee?" We are a long way from a society in which these questions are not asked. But few other countries—even those that boast equal opportunities for the poor—provide a higher standard of justice, on the whole, than we do.

22

The Ongoing Story

A criminal trial, like the emergency ward of a hospital or the bridge at San Luis Rey, artificially brings together many different kinds of people who would never have met except for an accident of fate and whose paths will never again cross. When the von Bülow trial ended, the participants scattered to diverse corners of the world. The day after the verdict, Maria "retired" from her "job" as Ala's maid and returned to Germany. Ala began work on a film about victims of homicide; Alex went back to his job with E. F. Hutton. Their natural father, Prince Alfred von Auersperg, now also lies in an irreversible coma, suffered in an automobile accident while he was driving in Europe with Alex.

Yet complex criminal cases rarely end in the "bang" of a decisive verdict, but rather with the "whimper" of ancillary lawsuits, recriminations and quiet settlements. This is especially so when vast sums of money are involved, as they are in the von Bülow case.

Within days of his acquittal Claus von Bülow and Andrea Reynolds left for an extended European vacation. Dominick Dunne reported in *Vanity Fair* that Claus was prepared to take his vacation regardless of the outcome of the case: "At Mortimer's restaurant, a French visitor said that if Claus had been found guilty, there was a plan to spirit him out of the country on the private jet of a vastly rich Texan."* Andrea's estranged husband, Sheldon Reynolds, declared that "if Claus has to marry Andrea, he will

---

* Dunne's article is replete with unattributed negative quotations from "von Bülow's closest friends," "swellest friends," "another woman," "a French visitor" —and even "some claim." The evanescent nature of his sources makes many of these allegations impossible to check.

wish he had been convicted." But neither Claus nor Andrea were thinking about marriage as they boarded the plane for a secluded spot in Italy. The most pressing concern on Claus's relaxed mind seemed to be who might play him in a movie based on his case: "Woody Allen," was his first sardonic reply when a reporter asked him the question; then he proposed Robert Duvall.*

But Claus's tranquility was soon disturbed by the filing of a $56 million lawsuit against him by his stepchildren, Ala and Alex. The suit claims that despite the jury's acquittal, the stepchildren should be entitled to prove that Claus twice tried to murder their mother in order to defraud her estate. Because the standard of proof in a civil case is lower than it is in a criminal case, they believe that they can still convince a jury, by a "preponderance of the evidence" rather than "beyond a reasonable doubt," that Claus "did it."

If there ever is a civil trial, it promises to be a rerun of the second criminal trial, with a very high likelihood of the same verdict. Indeed, the family's case promises to be considerably weaker than the state's weak second case. Several witnesses will probably be unavailable and memories will be even dimmer. Moreover, it seems absolutely clear that the jury at the second trial would not have found that Claus injected his wife *under any standard*.

But in the meantime, the new lawsuit certainly has some harassment value and will continue to focus public attention on the von Bülow–von Auersperg–Aitken–Kneissel dispute (which Claus once characterized as "the Second War of Austrian Succession"). Among the counts is one charging Claus, in effect, with being a racketeer within the meaning of the RICO (Racketeering Influence in Corrupt Organizations) statute. The suit claims that the comatose Sunny von Bülow was "an enterprise . . . engaged in interstate commerce." For a family that says it eschews publicity, this latest ploy seems somewhat out of character.

Another ancillary legal proceeding is the criminal case against Father Philip Magaldi. Two days after von Bülow's acquittal, Attorney General Violet officially announced that Father Magaldi

---

* In addition to proposals for movie and TV versions of the von Bülow case, E. Howard Hunt—the convicted Watergate conspirator—is writing a musical, entitled *Beautiful People*, based on the case. There were also several ballads written about the case during the trial and played on the local radio stations.

had been indicted for perjury and conspiracy to obstract justice.* The indictment charged that "the entire contents" of the Magaldi affidavit was "falsely fabricated and created by Philip Magaldi and David Marriott." David Marriott was named as a co-conspirator, but he was not indicted because he had been given immunity in exchange for testifying against the priest. The irony was now complete: the witness who we had believed was a liar telling the truth about delivering drugs to Clarendon Court, was now being used by the state, which also believed he was a liar who was now telling the truth about Father Magaldi. The state did, of course, have tape recordings—illegally obtained in violation of Massachusetts law—to back up its case against Father Magaldi. But how the state could still rely on Marriott's sworn testimony raised eyebrows among lawyers. And why the state decided to give Marriott, an admitted perjurer and obvious extortionist, immunity from all prosecution was unclear.†

What was also unclear was the relationship between Marriott and Magaldi. If, in fact, Father Magaldi had falsified certain information contained in his affidavit, it seemed likely that he had been pressured—blackmailed—into doing so by Marriott. But what did Marriott have on the priest that could serve as a powerful enough threat to warrant taking the risk of being charged with perjury? Speculation centered on the tape recording in which Marriott had gotten the priest to admit that when they had first met, Father Magaldi was using the name "Paul Marino." The indictment charges that they first met "in a Boston bus station," and Marriott says he did not know that "Marino" was a priest until sometime later. Was the priest leading a secret life? Did he have a sexual relationship with Marriott? Father Magaldi was denying all of this, insisting that he had not lied and that Marriott had set him up. Five thousand Rhode Island parishioners petitioned former nun

---

* Violet refused to be interviewed after the von Bülow acquittal, claiming that she has always treated the von Bülow case as a routine criminal matter, no different from any other. Violet had even sworn under oath that she treated the von Bülow case "like any other case. . . . I don't give any undue weight to this one. . . ." What she conveniently forgot was the major media event she convened to announce that she was not dropping the case—hardly a routine way of treating a typical case.

† The new lawyer for the von Auersperg–Kneissl family immediately announced that the indictment against Father Magaldi is "proof" that von Bülow was engaged in a "smear campaign" against his clients. Indictments, of course, do not prove anything. They simply charge something. Moreover, the indictment does not charge that von Bülow knew that the priest's affidavit was false and the tapes establish that he did not.

Arlene Violet to show mercy for the priest. They described Father Magaldi as a "sincere, honest, trustworthy and reliable" priest and warned her that the signers "feel in good conscience we could never vote for you again" if the case is pursued. But Violet's office said that the case would go forward "without consideration as to whether or not to do so is unpopular or may lose her votes."

After the second trial, Attorney General Violet fired Henry Gemma, the co-prosecutor, because he refused to admit that his visit to the Florida condominium of a man under indictment gave the appearance of impropriety. Violet declared, "I am not going to have as chief prosecutor . . . someone who is impervious to the fact that the public has the right to hope and believe that their prosecutors are not socializing or professionally hanging around with persons who are under indictment and whose indictments they can control." Shortly after Gemma was fired, Marc DeSisto, the other von Bülow prosecutor, resigned to enter private practice. A few months later, a local magazine charged Violet with violating her own ethical standards by having held a political fund-raiser in 1984 at the home of a man who had been convicted in 1969 of bringing a seventeen-year-old girl across state lines for prostitution. Violet said she did not remember whether she actually attended the event, but the convicted felon said that she had spent about a half-hour at his home. Violet also disputed the magazine's comparison between her actions and Gemma's on the ground that "as a candidate, I would not have had access to any information about the guy." The story made headlines in Providence.

Yet another proceeding that was taking place at about the time of the second von Bülow trial was the investigation into charges of organized crime associations leveled against the chief justice of the Rhode Island Supreme Court. The investigation, conducted by former U.S. Supreme Court Justice Arthur Goldberg (for whom I had worked as a law clerk), was said by many "to raise questions . . . about the overall quality of justice in the state." In the end, Chief Justice Joseph A. Bevilacqua was censured and agreed to remove himself from the bench for four months. Justice Goldberg characterized the public censure as "the most drastic sanction imposed upon any judge" who has been the target of a disciplinary inquiry.* The overall quality of justice in Rhode Island is still ques-

---

* In light of the criticisms leveled at Chief Justice Bevilacqua, it seems fair to note that he was *not* the source of information about the pending appeal.

tioned by many. Despite the favorable outcome of the von Bülow case, this writer is among those who entertain serious questions.

As this book nears completion, on a bright sunny day on Martha's Vineyard, the last loose threads of the von Bülow tapestry remain unconnected. As the fifth anniversary of Sunny's final coma approached, Claus resumed his visits to her hospital suite. He also announced that he planned to move to Europe and make his home there, though he would return to this country periodically to defend against the civil suit and see that Cosima receives justice.

Whatever the outcome of the civil suit, Claus von Bülow will forever be deemed not guilty in the eyes of the law. His legal innocence has been recovered. Sunny von Bülow's health will never be recovered. She will remain in a coma until she dies. The case of Rhode Island versus Claus von Bülow will continue to fascinate, confound, anger and even entertain the millions of people who read, watched and listened as it pursued its circuitous and intriguing legal path from guilty to not guilty.

Epilogue

As the page proofs of this book were being sent to the printer for final revision, printing and binding, the publisher received a series of legal communications on behalf of Alexander, Ala, Richard Kuh, William Wright and Sunny's committee. It seemed to us like a highly coordinated effort by Alexander and Ala to halt publication. A few months earlier David Marriott told us that he had somehow secured an early draft of the manuscript and threatened to "spread it around town" unless we changed it.

The lawyers representing Alex and Ala would not disclose how they had obtained the embargoed manuscript, but they did acknowledge that their office had reproduced it, sent a copy to Kuh and showed at least parts of it to others named in the book. Attorney Michael Armstrong—the lead counsel for Alexander and Ala—told us, at the end of a day-long meeting, that their goal was to "derail" publication if at all possible.

Armstrong did agree to play for us tapes that Marriott surreptitiously made of his conversations with me and a few snippets of taped conversations between Marriott and Father Magaldi. I agreed to listen with an open mind. I told Armstrong that I was happy to hear or see any documentation that might make the book more accurate.

Hearing the tapes of Marriott's conversations with me, I appreciated by comparison the scintillating nature of Claus' repartee with Marriott about wine and castles. I was even more boring than Claus, droning on about how "my interest is only in making sure that the truth comes out" and that there be "no false testimony at any time." The Marriott-Magaldi tapes, however, told a rather different tale. They seemed to confirm that Marriott had made up the story of delivering drugs to Alexander. Marriott certainly said as much, although the context was not always clear.*

One conclusion did emerge with absolute clarity. Nothing David Marriott ever said—about drug deliveries, about Claus von Bülow, about anything—should now be credited. Every Marriott accusation that cannot be independently corroborated has to be discounted and ignored. To the extent that we and others had ever believed him, we had been conned by this consummate con artist.

Nor had Marriott's days as a con man ended when he began working with the other side. Near the end of our tape session, one of the lawyers for Alex and Ala produced a photocopy of a "new" document he was confident we had never seen. He was right. The handwritten page purported to be a notarized affidavit written and placed "on file" by Marriott on August 15, 1983—only ten days after he signed the first affidavit about alleged drug deliveries. This document was addressed "to whom it may concern," and it attests that "this whole story of me and my involvement of bringing drugs to Clarendon Court is not true."

The new document plainly appears to be a recently concocted fraud, written well after the date it bears. The best proof of its fraudulent nature lies in its claim that "I [Marriott] have tapes of conversations between Claus, Andrea Reynolds and Father Magaldi which show that this whole thing is a set up." But all of the Marriott tapes I know about *postdate* August 15, 1983. If that is the case, he was lying either *in* that affidavit, or he wrote it *after* he made his tapes (which, by the way, do not show involvement of Claus or Andrea in the drug story).

So David Marriott continues to try to con anybody and everybody who will listen to him and purchase his tainted wares. When he conned us, there was no public record of his machinations. And his account was corroborated by a priest who was held in the highest regard. But now everything has changed. Any lawyer who currently vouches for Marriott's credibility—whether it be the State of Rhode Island in the Magaldi case or anyone else—now does so against a rather conclusive record of continuing fraud, forgery and perjury.

---

* The tapes themselves make it clear that at least some of them were recorded in Massachusetts, where it is a felony to "secretly record" conversations. Massachusetts also makes it a crime to disclose surreptitiously recorded conversations. Thus we cannot publish the transcripts of these conversations. The Rhode Island authorities apparently intend to disclose the tapes of David Marriott and Father Magaldi at the latter's trial. This may raise interesting legal issues.

Alexander and Ala were not able to derail this book.* They have, however, mounted an aggressive public relations campaign to present their side of the case, in which they vilify their step-father. I welcome them and others who disagree with what I have to say to compete with it in the marketplace of ideas. The best way for truth to emerge is for all those who claim knowledge of relevant facts to submit them to the crucible of public opinion. American readers are fully capable of making up their own minds about controversial cases and ideas. Let the debate over the von Bülow case continue, as it has over other notorious trials through-out history.

* As a result of some information provided me in the legal communications, I was able to make this a more complete book, and I am pleased to express my appreciation for being given this information.

Chronology

December 27, 1979
Martha ("Sunny") von Bülow became unconscious over the Christmas holidays at her Newport, Rhode Island, mansion, Clarendon Court. She quickly recovered.

December 21, 1980
Martha von Bülow lapsed into a coma during a visit to her mansion and was hospitalized, then transferred to Columbia Presbyterian Hospital in New York City, where she remains comatose.

July 6, 1981
Claus von Bülow was indicted by a Newport County grand jury on two counts of assault with intent to murder, alleging he injected insulin into his wife in December 1979 and December 1980.

July 13, 1981
Claus von Bülow pleaded not guilty before a Superior Court judge in Providence and was released on $100,000 surety bond.

February 1, 1982
The first trial began in Newport.

March 16, 1982
After hearing thirty-one days of testimony and deliberating for thirty-seven hours, the jury found Claus von Bülow guilty of two counts of assault with intent to murder.

May 7, 1982
Von Bülow was sentenced to thirty years in prison but was granted $1 million bail, pending appeal.

March 15, 1983

The defense filed a 100-page brief with the state Supreme Court, seeking reversal of von Bülow's convictions.

June 16, 1983

Prosecutors filed their 101-page brief, seeking affirmance of the convictions.

April 27, 1984

The state Supreme Court reversed von Bülow's convictions.

July 23, 1984

Rhode Island Attorney General Dennis J. Roberts II petitioned the U.S. Supreme Court to review the case.

October 1, 1984

The U.S. Supreme Court refused to hear the case.

January 5, 1985

The state announced plans to retry von Bülow.

April 25, 1985

The second trial began in Providence.

June 10, 1985

Claus von Bülow was acquitted on both counts of assault with intent to murder.

A Note on Sources

The facts contained in this book are derived primarily from court documents: transcripts, affidavits, briefs, et cetera. Most of the quotations are copied verbatim from these or other documents. Some, as indicated by the context, are reconstructions of interviews or conversations during or following some of which I took notes. Some dialogue that is reconstructed in the book as a single conversation for ease of understanding represents composites of several conversations.

Index

About the Author

ALAN M. DERSHOWITZ was born in Brooklyn and graduated from Yeshiva University High School and Brooklyn College. At Yale Law School he was first in his class and editor-in-chief of the *Yale Law Journal*. After clerking for Judge David Bazelon and Justice Arthur Goldberg, he was appointed to the Harvard Law faculty, where he became a full professor at age twenty-eight, the youngest in the school's history. Since that time, he has taught criminal law, psychiatry and law, constitutional litigation and human rights. *Newsweek* has described him as "the nation's most peripatetic civil-liberties lawyer and one of its most distinguished defenders of individual rights." In 1983 the Anti-Defamation League of B'nai B'rith presented him with its William O. Douglas First Amendment Award for his "compassionate eloquent leadership and persistent advocacy in the struggle for civil and human rights." He has received numerous other awards and fellowships for his work in defending liberty.

In addition to Claus von Bülow, Professor Dershowitz's clients have included Patricia Hearst, Senator Mike Gravel, Harry Reems, Anatoly Scharansky, F. Lee Bailey, William Kunstler and several death-row inmates. His syndicated column currently appears in more than forty newspapers, and his articles are published in periodicals as diverse as the *Yale Law Journal*, *TV Guide*, the *American Bar Association Journal*, *Penthouse* and the New York *Times*. He appears frequently on national television as an advocate of civil liberties. He plays basketball, regularly attends Boston Celtics games, and occasionally comments on the Boston sports scene.